Travelers' Tales Books

Country and Regional Guides
America, Australia, Brazil, Central America, China, Cuba, France, Greece,
India, Ireland, Italy, Japan, Mexico, Nepal, Spain, Thailand, Tibet,
Turkey; Alaska, American Southwest, Grand Canyon, Hawai'i,
Hong Kong, Paris, Provence, San Francisco, Tuscany

Women's Travel
Her Fork in the Road, A Woman's Europe, A Woman's Path, A Woman's
Passion for Travel, A Woman's World, Women in the Wild,
A Mother's World, Safety and Security for Women
Who Travel, Gutsy Women, Gutsy Mamas

Body & Soul
The Spiritual Gifts of Travel, The Road Within,
Love & Romance, Food, The Fearless Diner, The Adventure
of Food, The Ultimate Journey, Pilgrimage

Special Interest
The Best Travelers' Tales 2004, Not So Funny When It Happened,
The Gift of Rivers, Shitting Pretty, Testosterone Planet,
Danger!, The Fearless Shopper, The Penny Pincher's
Passport to Luxury Travel, The Gift of Birds, Family Travel,
A Dog's World, There's No Toilet Paper on the Road
Less Traveled, The Gift of Travel, 365 Travel,
Adventures in Wine, Sand in My Bra and Other Misadventures,
Hyenas Laughed at Me and Now I Know Why

Footsteps
Kite Strings of the Southern Cross, The Sword of Heaven,
Storm, Take Me With You, Last Trout in Venice, The Way of
the Wanderer, One Year Off, The Fire Never Dies

Classics
The Royal Road to Romance,
Unbeaten Tracks in Japan, The Rivers Ran East,
Coast to Coast, Trader Horn

WOMEN IN THE WILD

TRUE STORIES OF ADVENTURE AND CONNECTION

To one of my tuily adventurous fiends....
Wishing you all the best in yr next big adventure.
may you find excitement, passion, laughter &
love ....
Spk to you soon on the net...

Love

your suburban friends...Gail, Steve, Osa & mini-bump (dot
2 dogs
+ padut
fine course slippy & cash)

TRAVELERS' TALES

WOMEN IN THE WILD

TRUE STORIES OF ADVENTURE AND CONNECTION

Edited by

LUCY MCCAULEY

Series Editors
JAMES O'REILLY AND LARRY HABEGGER

TRAVELERS' TALES
SAN FRANCISCO

Credits and copyright notices for the individual articles in this collection are given starting on page 287.

We have made every effort to trace the ownership of all copyrighted material and to secure permission from copyright holders. In the event of any question arising as to the ownership of any material, we will be pleased to make the necessary correction in future printings. Contact Travelers' Tales, Inc., 330 Townsend Street, Suite 208, San Francisco, California 94107. www.travelerstales.com

Art Direction: Michele Wetherbee
Interior design: Kathryn Heflin and Susan Bailey
Cover photograph: © Richard Price/Taxi. Woman hiking, Antelope Canyon, Arizona.
Page layout: Cynthia Lamb, using the fonts Bembo and Boulevard

Distributed by: Publishers Group West, 1700 Fourth Street, Berkeley, California 94710.

Library of Congress Cataloguing-in-Publication Data

Women in the wild : true stories of adventure and connection / collected and edited by Lucy McCauley. — 1st ed.
     p. cm.
   Includes index.
   ISBN 1-932361-06-5 (pbk.)
   1. Women travelers. 2. Women adventurers. 3. Travelers' writings.
4. Voyages and travels. I. McCauley, Lucy.
   G465.W655 2004
   910.4'082—dc22

2004004309

First Edition
Printed in the United States
10 9 8 7 6 5 4 3 2 1

At a certain point you say to the woods, to the sea,
to the mountains, the world, Now I am ready.
Now I will stop and be wholly attentive.
You empty yourself and wait, listening.

—ANNIE DILLARD,
Teaching a Stone to Talk

Table of Contents

Part Two
SOME THINGS TO DO

Part Three
GOING YOUR OWN WAY

Part Four
IN THE SHADOWS

Part Five
THE LAST WORD

Women in the Wild: An Introduction

I live about as far from the wild as you can get, in the city, above a busy four-lane avenue. Every amenity of modern life surrounds me: designer coffee shops, convenience stores, a fax/mail place that I call my "office." It's all here. Everything, that is, but *green*.

I crave green—green fields, green woods, green mountains, the aqua-green sea. And it is travel that has brought me opportunities to satisfy those cravings. In Morocco, I climbed tourmaline switch-backs into the High Atlas Mountains. In Panama, I scuba dived among manta rays in an emerald sea. In California, I walked through silent forests, the moist scent of greenery buoying my spirit.

But I have many friends who aren't satisfied by greenery alone. They crave the golden dust of Southwestern deserts, the rocky brown of the Tibetan plateau, or the blinding white of Antarctica. We all agree, though, that it has been in these places, outside of our familiar contexts, where we have felt the truest sense of freedom—exploring the "wild" in our own natures and foraging the external wilderness in ways that we somehow never manage to at home.

When I first began to bring together this collection, I suspected it would be dangerous. And I was right. As the months rolled by and I read the manuscripts that filled my mailbox, I found myself at various points deciding—and each time adamantly—to hike into the desert and camp alone, to hang glide over Big Sur, and to find Jane Goodall and convince her to let me follow her and her chimps around Gombe. That's the thing about these stories: they take ideas that would normally seem impossible, crazy, outlandish, and usher them into the realm of the possible.

I think most women instinctively recognize in nature a direct connection to their feminine power. Travel into the wilderness takes us away from modern life, and its ceaseless routines, into our own wildness. There we can affirm our self-sufficiency and creative force as we make pilgrimages back to our own instincts.

The women in this volume do that in myriad ways. They offer stories of high adventure in the wild—rafting a river in Borneo, diving in Mexican cenotes, climbing Mt. Everest. They share with us their journeys into the natural world: a lone hiker trekking the Appalachian Trail, a wildlife worker who is attacked by a hyena in Israel, a traveler who pulls off a gutsy rescue of endangered animals in Vietnam. They give us stories of women exploring the wildness of their own natures—the affinity a mother-to-be feels with skunks, bears, and mice, a woman who confronts her hunter's instincts while fishing for mackerel in Ireland, another who navigates through the wildish aspects of her sexuality after witnessing a Sicilian tuna slaughter.

These tales transform possibility into reality. They remind us that there is a seasonal longing in our natures—as regular as the tides and the phases of the moon, as mysterious as the cycles that all women share with Mother Earth—to foray into the wild, both within and without. Reading these stories, and feeling the stirrings of my own restlessness, brought to mind something a friend once told me: that envy is a wake-up call, a message to stop ignoring the soul's deepest longings.

As the couriers of that message, let these stories act as an invocation, calling us all to our own ventures into the wild.

—Lucy McCauley

PART ONE

ESSENCE OF THE WILD

ANN JONES

Looking for Lovedu

*Three women travel across Africa
to the land "where women rule."*

I SET OUT FROM LONDON IN A BRIGHT BLUE ARMY SURPLUS
1980 Series III Land Rover bound for Capetown. With me was
my friend Muggleton, a British photographer and ace mechanic,
who coaxed our disintegrating vehicle some 6,000 miles from
London to Nairobi. In five months, we crossed the Sahara on our
own, dodged roadblocks in Nigeria, ferried across a river in central Africa on a home-made bamboo raft, slogged through the bot-
tomless mud and revolutionary politics of eastern Zaire—while
our Land Rover got smashed, scraped, dented, bashed, fractured,
crumpled, crimped, and very nearly sunk. Muggleton loved to do
manly battle with hostile soldiers, corrupt police, rough roads, wild
animals, greedy bandits, and Mother Nature—that was his idea of
travel—but at last, after two bad bouts of malaria, he bailed out of •
the expedition, sold off the remains of the Land Rover (which
only he could fix), and went home.

Hakuna matata, I told myself. No problem. Muggleton's defec-
tion left me in Nairobi with a second chance to focus on the real
purpose of my expedition. All along, as Muggleton propelled us
into macho adventures, I had imagined myself on a quest: a mysti-
cal mission in search of a peaceable land ruled by a great queen.

3

I first got wind of the queen on a visit to the Natural History Museum in New York City. There in a display of African household articles, I'd read this caption: "Except for a few tribes like the Lovedu, where women rule, they seem unimportant in political life." The words "where women rule" stopped me in my tracks. Did some mad feminist lurk in the back rooms of the museum, writing subversive signs? Or could it be true?

A search of the library turned up *She,* written in 1886 by the popular British novelist H. Rider Haggard, a minor classic reputedly based on legends of a powerful Bantu queen. Haggard called her "She-Who-Must-Be-Obeyed." More important, I found a scholarly study published in 1943 by two South African anthropologists who had actually visited the Lovedu tribe and met the Queen—Modjadji. They reported that she lived in seclusion with her wives.

Yes, wives. What distinguished the Lovedu from other Bantu tribes was that women as well as men held property. And what is a wife but a piece of property? Wives came as payments to Modjadji, like cattle or corn: as tributes, taxes, bribes. At her *kraal,* the wives did for the Queen, their husband, what ordinary Lovedu wives did for theirs: they hoed her fields, brewed her beer, cooked her food, and kept her in domestic comfort. And she used them in trade and diplomacy like any other commodity. In this way, the anthropologists said, Queen Modjadji built alliances and knit her realm into a family.

It was a family without a husband or father, for the royal lineage of the Lovedu is a succession of single mothers. It was founded perhaps three or four centuries ago by Dzugudini who—unmarried, expecting—fled her father's kingdom in Zimbabwe with sacred charms to set herself up in the mountains of the Transvaal as a Rain Maker.

Under the rule of Queen Modjadji, Lovedu society placed the highest value on traditionally "feminine" ideals: cooperation, appeasement, compromise, tolerance, generosity, peace. Invading Europeans who took over the Transvaal in the 1890s saw Queen Modjadji III as a powerful, unscrupulous madam, little better than a bordello keeper, who pacified intruders with beer and girls, and dealt diplomacy by poison. Accustomed to shooting Africans, they branded her pacifist tactics "immoral" and stole her lands, reducing her realm from 600 square miles to 150.

Africans, on the other hand, so revered the Modjadji queens that even Shaka, the great Zulu warrior-chief, paid homage. And in the 1930s, the visiting anthropologists reported that Modjadji III still ruled "without official husband to cramp her authority." She was still thought to be immortal and possessed of magical powers to transform clouds into rain. The Modjadji dynasty, the most powerful queens in southern Africa, made rain, not war.

Here were rulers after my own heart. I tried to learn more about them, but I kept running up against experts whose scholarly objectivity wasn't up to the job of contemplating powerful black queens. A couple of anthropologists told me the Lovedu queens were fair-skinned, probably descended from white European traders. A curator at the British Museum assured a colleague who inquired on my behalf that the Lovedu queens were actually men in drag. What could I do but go and see for myself?

In Nairobi I met Debo Kingsland, an Australian-born, British-based filmmaker, temporarily between jobs. Yes, she said, she'd love to meet the queen. Somehow we persuaded UTC, the United Touring Company, the biggest tour operator in Africa, to lend us a Land Cruiser for our search; and in November, a little more than a year after I originally set out from London, Debo and I hit the road in earnest in search of the Great Queen.

We'd invited another friend to come along. Joanne Luhongo, a Kiswahili-speaking Luhya woman, a young widow with two small daughters, had never traveled outside Kenya before. On the morning of our departure from Nairobi, she showed up at dawn carrying a small duffle bag, a cooking pot, and a big bottle of the ashy water that Kenyan women use to tenderize tough green vegetables. Four-year-old Sweetie and two-year-old Charleen clung to her skirts. We would drop off the girls in western Kenya at Joanne's home place, with her mother, Mama Beritah. A strong woman of great dignity, Mama Beritah is the daughter of one of the ten wives of a powerful Luhya chief, and her mother as well was the proud daughter of a chief. It seemed only fitting that we should pay our respects to this royal lineage as we set out in search of the Queen of the Lovedu.

With Joanne and the girls ensconced in the back of the Land Cruiser, we crossed the Rift Valley, passing by soda lakes ringed with pink flamingos. Then the western hills rose around us, patched with garden plots of cabbages and beans and greens, tall rows of maize, and stands of exotic eucalyptus trees raised for firewood. At Mago village, a radiant Mama Beritah waited for us in her front yard, her head wrapped in a beautiful red scarf. *"Mirembe,"* she said, clasping our hands. *"Mirembe, mirembe.* Peace, peace." Brothers Mahagwa and Gichuru were there too, to say *"safari njema"*—good journey. Mama Beritah ordered platters of *matoke* (stewed bananas) brought to us. She prayed over us. And quietly she embraced Joanne's weeping children as we drove away.

We came out of the hills above Kisumu and descended the escarpment to the broad plain that stretches away to Lake Victoria. The Kenyan patchwork of tiny gardens dissolved into the bush of Tanzania—dry flaxen grass studded with leafless shrubs and thorny acacias—broken only here and there by clusters of crumbling mud-and-wattle thatched houses. Herds of dusty cattle—white, dun, and black—plied the roadside tended by Masai children.

> No matter where I go in the world, travelling renews my faith in humankind, as well as in myself. It's a journey of remembrance back to my original self, the one who is wholly connected to all beings and nature.
>
> ◆
>
> —Barbara Sansone,
> "Under the Mango Tree"

For days we drove the rough roads eastward across the Serengeti, from the rolling bush-covered western hills to the flat grassy eastern sector, while all around us the wildebeest tramped on their annual migration. They came in long lines, not massed in one herd but strung out like streamers converging, strand upon strand, braiding themselves into a single thickening rope of wildebeest.

One day, after we passed through the shadow of Mount Kilimanjaro and turned south along the shoulder of the Usambara Mountains, we followed a dirt track into the hills and began to set up camp, miles from nowhere. Just then a woman walked out of the bush. Wrapped in faded cloth of red and yellow, she was a little stick of a woman—so slight that the machete she carried appeared to be enormous. "You are welcome to camp," she told us in Kiswahili. She, Hadijah, had seen campers before, she told us proudly, and she would inform her neighbors that we did not intend to stay and steal their land. We were surrounded, it seemed, by an invisible community of squatters who survived by raising maize and chopping wood for charcoal—as Hadijah had been doing.

Hadijah is a widow, she told us, and must get money for her three surviving children—she had eight—who stay with her mother miles away in the village where the school is. Most of the time, Hadijah lives alone on this mountainside in a mud hut no bigger than a garden shed. She sleeps on the dirt floor and spends her days chopping firewood. She's strong and lithe and swings the machete with an easy grace, but this is back-breaking work.

In the morning a man dressed up in trousers and velveteen sport coat materialized near our tents. He was the husband of Hadijah's friend and neighbor Amina, and as the headman of the area he had come to greet us officially with many rhetorical flourishes of Kiswahili. We walked down the hillside with him to the squatters' homes. There the women were working outside Amina's hut, pounding maize kernels in a wooden mortar with wooden pestles the size of fence posts. Rhythmically they raised the heavy poles and brought them down again and again while half a dozen men lounged on the big sacks of maize meal the women had already prepared.

This is the standard arrangement in Africa, where women do something like 80 percent of the work and produce something like

90 percent of the food. (The statistics vary from study to study, but you get the idea.) It's not that men do nothing. They supervise. They make decisions. They accumulate the fruits of women's labor. They hold the capital: goats, cattle, machines. These men, notified of our presence by Hadijah, had gathered to look us over and express opinions. When they saw me give a Polaroid photo to Hadijah and Amina, the men let it be known that they collectively were prepared to pose for such a portrait. One raised his machete in salute. Another unwrapped one carefully saved cigarette and put it in the corner of his mouth, at a rakish angle. A third dragged his goat into camera range. A fourth displayed his portable radio. They stood up proudly—the menfolk. They had the goods.

As we drove on toward Lovedu land, we tried to imagine what it might mean to be a queen in Africa. All around us, all along the way, we saw women doing nothing but work. Debo, who had been filming women at work, had footage of women hoeing, planting crops, weeding, harvesting, gathering wild edibles, shucking maize, pounding maize, grinding maize at the mill, carrying maize meal home, chopping wood, gathering firewood, carrying firewood home on their heads or on their backs, building fires, cooking, serving food, washing dishes, scouring pots, making clothes, buying clothes, washing clothes (after first carrying the laundry to the river, or carrying the river water home), selling clothes and just about anything else in the marketplace or beside the road, building houses, painting houses, gathering thatching, preparing mud plaster, polishing floors with cattle dung (to keep out insects), scrubbing floors, weaving palm fibers, making mats, making baskets, making hats, dying fabrics, sewing, knitting, embroidering, making pots, minding children, doctoring children, teaching children, feeding children, washing children, dressing children, plaiting hair, milking cows, feeding chickens, butchering chickens, shopping, making brooms, sweeping houses, sweeping yards, cleaning churches, cleaning wells, planting trees, and keeping accounts. So far she had no footage at all of women being queens. What would a queen do?

When we filled out exit and entry permits at border crossings, I noticed that Joanne always checked the box for "single." One day I asked her why she didn't check "widow."

"No, no," she said emphatically, as if alarmed at the thought. "A widow must have permission to travel from the father-in-law."

Among the Kisii, the tribe of Joanne's late husband, a woman belongs to her husband's family. When he dies, she may be claimed in marriage by his brothers—together with all her property. Joanne has avoided that fate, probably because she owns nothing but her own independent spirit. But it's hard to imagine an African Queen when the average African woman has no right to her own property, or even to herself.

We inched our way—almost 900 kilometers—down the skinny passage that is Malawi, passing the barren windswept hills of the high Nyika plateau, the rolling surf of the great inland sea of Lake Malawi, the steaming lushness of the Shire River

—————⏾—————

I came upon a group of women kneeling, arms outstretched over a vast stone sunken tank, busily scrubbing clothes. I thought of the big bag of washing accumulated since a laundromat in Vigo washed it for 1,000 pesetas. Could I bring it here, I wondered, and plucked up the courage to ask. *"¡Claro, mujer!"* Of course, woman!

Later I nervously approached the tank with our bag of dirty clothes. The women chatted as they soaked and scrubbed, keeping a weather eye on my method and progress. A pair of David's socks I began on were snatched from me. "No, no—outside like *this* and now inside like *this*..."

By the time I had emptied the bag and despite all the help, my energy was at a low ebb. "She's used to a washing machine, the poor one!"

Later when I went to gather the clothes, smelling of tallow soap, sun, and fresh air, I felt full of pride.

◆

—Anna Kenning,
"Romantic Journey"

valley where the lake drains away into the forest. We camped on the beaches of the great lake where mango trees dropped their ripe fruits beside our tents. Thousands of kilometers still lay between us and the Rain Queen, but as we drew closer the skies darkened and fierce winds whipped sheets of rain across the road. The windshield wipers whooshed back and forth whispering, "Rain…Queen…Rain…Queen…Rain…Queen."

We crossed Mozambique through the Tete Corridor, passed into Zimbabwe, and pressed on—on good roads now—to South Africa and the Transvaal. Exploration not being what it used to be, we learned that to visit the Lovedu we must ring up the Tribal Council to make an appointment. Phone calls sputtered along uncertain wires, and soon word came back: Her Majesty Mokope, Modjadji V, reigning (and raining) Queen of the Lovedu, would grant us an audience.

On the morning of the day appointed, we drove through the Drakensburg mountains as fog rose from the valleys. Spectral plantations of eucalyptus covered the hillsides, cloaked in mist. We turned a corner into the valley of GaModjadji—into the realm of the Rain Queen—and the factory forests were replaced by a human landscape of huts and maize fields and people walking in the road. A long, winding gravel track carried us up a mountainside to the tribal headquarters of the Lovedu. There waiting for us were two men smartly dressed in western sports shirts and trousers: Nerwick Molokwane, a teacher who would serve as translator, and Victor Mathekga, a member of the royal family and the Queen's Council.

Our guides led us through an iron gate marked "Modjadji Head Kraal" to a small *rondavel* surrounded by a dozen slumbering yellow dogs. We removed our shoes and followed our guides into the hut. There a barefoot Queen Modjadji V was seated on her throne—a red leatherette LA-Z-BOY Recliner with the label still attached. She was dressed for the occasion in a navy blue polo shirt and a wrap of leopard-patterned cotton. She wore gold earrings and a bright red print scarf about her head. On her face she wore a look of queenly implacability.

"Fierce!" Debo hissed.

That look intimidated me no end and filled me with chagrin that the meeting I'd looked forward to for more than a year, the meeting I'd trekked all the way across Africa to bring about, should occasion so little response in the object of my quest. What had I expected? A smile? A handshake? A warm embrace?

Bowing awkwardly before the Queen, we presented our gifts—gold earrings, cloths of regal purple, a waterproof flashlight—then shuffled backwards to seat ourselves in fat vinyl chairs opposite the throne, while our guides crept across the floor to kneel on grass mats.

"You may ask your questions now," Nerwick said, after he had expressed our greetings and thanks to the Queen.

"Do we find the Queen in good health?"

"Yes."

"Is the Queen responsible for the current rains?"

"Yes."

The Queen seemed a woman of few words—though she kept Nerwick and Victor chuckling at remarks they did not translate into English.

"Did the Queen take action to end the recent drought?"

"Yes."

Nerwick elaborated. Every October the Queen carries out three ceremonies, one at each of three sacred shrines. The Queen pours out bowls of beer, and important men, including Nerwick and Victor, drink it from the ground. She beats the sacred drums. Everyone dances. The rain falls.

"Is it true that the Queen has many wives?" I asked.

"Plus or minus twenty-five," Victor said. They are given to her by the *indunas,* or headmen, who govern the villages. They live in huts within the royal compound, together with their children, and they serve the Queen. Certain men of the royal family see to it that the Queen's wives bear plenty of children.

"It is my duty," Victor said proudly. He explained that the Queen herself gave birth to two daughters (one of whom died) and a son—although of course she has no husband.

"Does the Queen enjoy good relations with the new government of South Africa?" Debo asked.

"Yes." The new government brings electricity to her villages. But she enjoyed good relations with the old government of South Africa too. Compromise, appeasement, reconciliation, tolerance, peace. The great ideals of Lovedu culture.

High on her hillside in GaModjadji, what should Modjadji V care who rules the country? She is not an educated woman, she told us. She grew up in one of the small huts of the compound and succeeded her mother Makoma, Modjadji IV, who reigned from 1960 to 1980. All the land of GaModjadji is hers, and so is responsibility for the welfare of the people who live upon it— perhaps 50,000 of them. Her job is to keep the peace and bring the rain. She and her predecessors have done so for 400 years. When you think about it, that's no small achievement.

"Is there anything the people of the western world need to learn from you, Your Majesty, and the women of your culture?" we asked as our audience drew to a close.

What the Queen said made Nerwick laugh. "Yes," he said. "Her Majesty says she could teach you to dance."

Debo and I drove south into Lesotho, hired a couple of Basotho horses, and rode to a village high in the Maluti mountains. Joanne had flown home to her children, but we planned to drive on to the Cape to complete the journey from one end of Africa to the other. Then, to return the Land Cruiser to UTC in Harare, we would drive back through Namibia and Botswana and Zimbabwe.

But that night in the mountain village in Lesotho we sat quietly in the doorway of a stone hut and watched the full moon rise. I was deep in thought about Modjadji and the curious persistence of her "feminine" domain where aggressive individualism is barbarous and harmony is the highest ideal. Soon the moon was covered by fast moving clouds. Then lightning came, stabbing the mountainside across the deep valley. And then rain. It poured on the thatch of our hut. It poured on the cows huddled in the stone *kraal* just below our doorway. It poured on the horses, tethered out there in the dark. It poured as though it would wash the whole world clean.

"That Modjadji," Debo said. "Does she never rest?"

Ann Jones is best known for what she calls her "heavy duty feminist books" such as Women Who Kill *and* Next Time, She'll Be Dead. *She is also the author of* Looking for Lovedu: Days and Nights in Africa, *a book-length version of this story, and* Guide to America's Outdoors: Middle Atlantic.

✳

Before the Germans came along to "set 'em straight," Nauru, an island in the South Pacific, was a matriarchy. There was a queen, a female god, the works. The Germans got rid of most of it, largely by locking the twelve local chiefs in a shed until they "saw reason." But, here and there, bits of the matriarchy resurface.

Meet the traditional Nauran national sport: Itsibweb. I met it on a muddy field, on a warm, rainy day. I still get nightmares.

The Itsibweb players assembled on the pitch. There were two teams, around ten players a side. All women, most barefoot or wearing flip-flops. They ranged in age from about twenty to about sixty. Their faces were smeared with brightly coloured war paint and they all seemed pretty cheerful, in spite of the fact that one of the teams was passing around a cannonball-sized rock loosely covered by a leaf.

The game began with the teams facing each other. Three women from the rockless team stood in front of their colleagues and made a defensive wall with their bodies.

A woman from the armed team ran towards them, bouncing the rock in her hand then swatting it as hard as she could at the human wall. One of the women tried to catch it and failed. A cheer went up. She went down. One point for the rock thrower.

They continued to throw rocks at each other until one team called it quits because many of its players were bleeding.

It was impressive.

—Cleo Paskal, "Saturday Night in Nauru"

To Jump or Not to Jump?

In Iceland, under the gaze of elves,
the author tests her spirit.

IN ANTICIPATION OF OUR ARRIVAL, SUNNEVA, OUR ICELANDIC guide, had consulted the American-Indian medicine cards to ascertain a symbol for us and our trip. The symbol she got was the Raven.

"If Raven appears in your spread, you are about to experience a change in consciousness...."

Well, we were into our second day and our tour bus was coming to a stop. We would have a picnic lunch, Sunneva told us, but first, she and Hildur would walk to a special spring from which they would carry its naturally carbonated water back to us. Just minutes before she had informed us about Bardur and Helga, the two Icelandic nature energies, one male, one female, who imbued different things on Earth with primarily male or female energy.

Icelanders were like that. They could talk about the most sophisticated technology for the conversion of hot seawater locked under their rocks into electric power that lights up all of Reykjavik and then they could say in the same breath, "See that mountain over there? That's were the elves live."

While Sunneva and Hildur would be gone to get the water, we were to look for lava rocks and go exploring the steep triangular lava mountain on one side of the bus. The group fanned out towards it, except for me. I chose to explore what was at the other side of the bus, away from everyone else.

The area I had chosen featured an expanse of moss and grass which tilted gently toward a wide, dark and flat-topped mountain. The terrain gave me several options. The first one was to walk on the soft moss and grass and to experience that feeling. It was exceedingly comfortable just to move about at a slight incline and to do nothing but look at the ground, where often the patches of moss turned out to be tricky little bogs which made my Reeboked feet sink into accumulations of shallow water. Then, all at once, a rushing stream struck a course straight across my territory. Like a thick brush of paint, it slashed from right to left across my moss canvas. The existence of this stream now split my area in two—the one in front of the stream and the one behind the stream, and it became instantly clear that if I wanted to continue my exploration, I would have to cross the stream. A choice had to be made.

"If you have chosen Raven, magic is in the air. Do not try to figure it out: you cannot. It is the power of the unknown."

Not having practiced jumping across streams in New York City and being short legged to boot, the thought occurred, of course, that I could return to the group and that I need never let on that the reason for my reappearance was because I did not have the courage to jump.

But, no, I did not want to turn back. The territory ahead beckoned. A natural obstacle had to be overcome and I wished to try myself out. No one was watching anyway, except the elves.

"Realize that you will fear Raven only if you need to learn about your inner fears of self-created demons."

And so my eyes began to measure the width of the stream from bank to bank, scanning for a spot where the distance across was narrowest. Having made a choice, I jumped over the cold, gushing stream and landed safely on the other side. And now the climb towards the mountain began in earnest. I gazed up and measured my vis-a-vis—its wide, dark mass and slate grey ridge were like a crown of a kingdom I was not at all familiar with. Were elves looking at me now, musing at this lone human standing like a speck in the grass? Was I seen by beings I could not see? Were there forms of life and streams of energies dancing all about? I could not fathom.

And as I stood there wondering about what there might be dancing all around me, my physical perception of myself became very small and the desire to simply meld into what was there took over. In a somnambulant instant, I lay down, letting Mother Earth, the moss and the grass be my cradle. I gazed into the sky and also across the way where I could still see my friends in the distance. Two of them had gone straight up the peaked mountain. I could see them resting half-way. The others were walking along a rock-strewn hillock gathering lava stones. I could see all this very clearly because Iceland has no trees. This lack makes for a different experience as far as mountains are concerned. It shows you the total gestalt of the mountain, from the ground to the top, its massiveness, its immovability, its *thereness*, and the recollection of what Erdla, an Icelandic geometaphysican, said—that there are different colors which emanate from various mountains, depending on their geology and specific energies.

——— ☽ ———

*P*each coloured low dunes rose and fell slowly, time left the hour glass and I was left alone. As if by reflex, I did a ritual I had learned from my very Buddhist grandmother, Bima, when I was a little girl growing up in Malaysia. She taught me to feel the spirit of a place with my bare feet, to "read" deeply, instinctively for the meaning of that place. I would take my sandals off and stand with her, very still. This meditation gave me another geography of the world, another map by which to navigate my life. "Your soul remembers this," she said. I took into my being a knowing that is inchoate, palpable and as unique to each place as the soft mathematics of a genetic helix.

◆

—Rohini Talalla,
"Dune: A Day in the Namib-Nauklauft Reserve"

"Raven's color is the color of the void—the black hole in space that holds all the energy of the creative source."

I have climbed mountains in Switzerland above the timberline. But there the idea was to get to the top, to achieve the feat, to reach the pinnacle, and to enjoy the view—human beings putting themselves on top of mountains.

Not so in Iceland. There was no desire to put myself on top of anything. Rather, the need was to let the mountain speak and to open myself up. It was to meld into something much grander than the individual self and to hopefully get a clue on how the self fits into that grander scheme.

And as I lay there by myself, with the unclimbed mountain behind me and the two mountains across the way where my tour mates looked for lava stones, I heard a most beautiful sound. Of course, I thought it was a bird. It trilled first into my left ear and then into my right. It changed back and forth from left to right. But was it a bird? Why could I not see it, particularly since it was so close? Obviously, it would not be sitting in a tree, were I would expect it to be if I were back home. Perhaps then it was in the grass? But why did I not see it fly when the sound changed position? Or was it a nature spirit telling me something? Something about things which are not logical in our terms. I felt it say, Welcome to our realm. We greet you in our way. It will make you wonder. That is what we want. To instill wonder. So that when you get back to your realm, you will remember. Our sound will stay with you at the right moment when you need it. Remember the wonder when you connect with your fellow beings in your city. It will translate itself into a kind of love. It will always get you beyond the obvious. Beyond the physical. It will soften the blows....

Yes, *"If you have chosen Raven, magic is in the air."*

Hannelore Hahn is the chair of the Foreign Languages Department and director of the International Studies and Study Abroad Programs at the College of St. Elizabeth in New Jersey. She is also the executive director of The International Women's Writing Guild, which she founded in 1976.

Her memoir, On the Way to Feed the Swans, *about her childhood in Nazi Germany and trying to become an American at age eleven, was included in the 1983 American Book Awards.*

★

Listen!
let's just decide to stay
no one'll notice—
really!

the air's good
your butts need exercise
there's berries to be picked
our backs bent over
like stones in sun

We make good meals
Not a lot of flies
We'll write books together
great philosophy
poetry

I'll buy a green convertible
we'll go tooling in the country
I don't like building
someone else will do it
I don't like working
someone else will earn the money

MONEY!
We!
We don't need money!

We have beautiful breasts
and souls
good sneakers
Roz has a fine hat
and socks we've got

We have everything!

—Natalie Goldberg, "Eight Nude Women on Sunday in the
Mountains," *Chicken and In Love*

MARGO CHISHOLM AND RAY BRUCE

Climbing Mt. Everest

At mid-life, she faced her greatest challenge ever.

CLOUDS HAD CLOSED IN AS WE LEFT CAMP I, SURROUNDING US with white. The air was filled with swirling snow, and my sense of space became altered, tilted, ungrounded as we moved toward Camp II. In the whiteout I could only determine the way by the footsteps of others in front of me. The resulting vertigo and my memories of being lost on Vinson increased the uneasiness in my stomach. My feet became lead weights and the muscles seemed to be missing from my legs. Though not roped, five of us followed closely behind one another so we wouldn't lose our way in the soft blanket that effectively closed out the rest of the

> "*R*ob," in this story, refers to Rob Hall, a highly regarded New Zealand mountain guide who was among the first to lead commercial trips up Mt. Everest and who reached the summit five times. He perished, along with seven others, in a storm on Everest in May 1996. "Gary" is Gary Ball, Rob's long-time climbing partner who died of altitude sickness on Dhaulagiri in October 1993.
>
> ◆
>
> —LMc

world. I was moving very slowly, but despite my protestations, Rob insisted that I lead....

After the first hour, the route eased into a low-angle, easy meander with crampons up the left side of the Western Cwm. When I had walked it in 1992, I had moved well and was strengthened by the awe I felt at being in this incredible valley surrounded by the walls of some of the highest mountains in the world. On this day the mountains were concealed by the smothering whiteness, and the route seemed endless. The four-and-a-half hours it took to reach Camp II were some of the most difficult physical times I've ever had in the mountains.

The mildly increased angle of ascent just below Camp II required my stopping every few minutes. "Hold it," I mumbled yet another time and stopped, leaning on my ski poles for support. "I'm sorry, Rob," I said, shaking my head in embarrassment and fighting back tears.

"No problem, Margo. We're making good time and there's no rush. Camp isn't going anywhere." He had taken back the lead and now stepped down to me, the end of a climbing rope in his hands. "Let's help you out a little." He tied me into the rope and then attached it, only a few feet away, to his own harness. When he turned and continued up the hill, the rope pulled me forward. Short-roping he called it. I was being hauled up the mountain. And right then, I was too tired even to care. I felt as if I'd been transported to another world, where my body weighed three times as much as I was used to, where time was warped, each moment seeming to drag on for an hour. I wanted only to go to bed. How could I possibly make it to the summit if I felt like this below Camp II? I was mentally and physically exhausted.

Still totally spent at dinnertime, I wanted to stay in my sleeping bag but knew I needed food and drink. I was done in and spoke to no one. I couldn't find the place inside that believed I could climb this mountain. Head aching, stomach lurching, I was devoid of hope of getting any higher and just wanted to go to Base Camp. "You don't have to go down tonight, Margo. Just eat and sleep. We'll decide tomorrow." The words held little comfort for me, and I could not imagine feeling any differently in the morning.

After twelve hours of nearly comatose sleep, I awoke feeling like my own body had been returned to me, able once again to touch the place of hope where my dream of climbing this mountain lived. I dressed and walked out of my tent into the growing heat of a sunny day in the Western Cwm. The sun's rays bouncing off the ice of the valley floor and walls created nature's own reflector oven. The tents would soon become too hot to stay in.

It was a day of rest and acclimatization, one of several before we moved any higher on the mountain. During the afternoon Jan and I sat on our air mattresses in the sun, once again testing our altitude-impaired brains with crossword puzzles. Jan, officially the expedition doctor, was also on the climbing permit. Although her initial plan was to remain at Camp II, she was exceptionally strong and had climbed very quickly through the icefall. The idea of going higher on the mountain, perhaps even to the summit, was clearly in her mind as we tossed crossword clues back and forth to one another, laughing at the sluggish manner in which our minds worked at over 21,000 feet, and talked about what it would be like even closer to the summit.

"You seem much better, Margo. I felt so badly for you last night." Jan had a warm and caring heart, and we were fast becoming friends on this climb, able to talk about life and love and things that were important to us back home. She and Rob adored each other. They were two people who clearly were meant to be together, and it was a joy to be around them. She continued with her encouragement. "It's so awful to have to climb when you feel shitty. You managed very well."

"Thanks. I appreciate that. I felt hopeless last night. Exhausted and ashamed Rob had to short-rope me. I don't know how I would have gotten to camp any other way." The memory of the previous afternoon was still fresh, and it was easy to touch the feeling of exhaustion and shame.

"You'd been sick, Margo. Anyway, it doesn't matter what yesterday looked like. You got here. And this is today. A different

day. And look how you've bounced back! I admire your gump-
tion. So what's a ten-letter word for 'personification'?" I looked
at her blankly, and we laughed again at how slowly our minds
were working.

As I had anticipated, the women on this climb, particularly Jan
and Helen, were making an enormous difference for me. I could
share my fears and doubts with them as well as my hopes and
dreams. I didn't have to keep my feelings hidden away as if they
were somehow wrong. By bringing my fears into the light, they
dissipated; the dreams seemed possible.

I hit an emotional wall the day before we were to climb to
Camp III. It looked a lot like the Lhotse Face, which rose 27,923
feet and stood like a bridesmaid dramatically at the head of the
Cwm next to Mount Everest, providing a natural access to
Sagarmatha's summit. Days before succumbing to my illness last
year, I'd climbed a few pitches up the fixed ropes secured by ice
screws and pickets. I had found the climbing intimidating, and my
memory of its difficulty had been magnified by not going back up.
Unresolved feelings of intimidation had grown into fear during
the last ten months.

Sitting in my tent at Camp II, feeling my body struggle to adjust to the 21,500-foot altitude, my fear showed its many faces,
each one a different question colored with self-doubt. Would I get
sick again before I had a chance to go higher? Should I go down
to Base Camp with Veikka today? Would I be able to handle the
constant cold and exhaustion climbing at Camp III and above? Was
I too slow to make the sustained effort needed for summit day? I
talked about some of my fears with Gary as we sat in the community tent that evening.

He looked up from the cup of cocoa he was holding in his
hands for warmth, "Maggot, sometimes you just have to pick your
commitment level and go for it. His brown eyes looked deeply
into mine, speaking the strength of his own commitment to climbing and to life.

It sounded so easy when he said it. I didn't know what mine

was. That didn't seem to be my way. I could only put one foot in front of the other until I couldn't do it anymore. What if Gary's way was the right one, the one that would get me up the mountain? Slowly, my truth emerged from the cloud created by my fear. Radical trust. My spiritual guides and my own heart were what I could rely on. Not my mind's ability to figure out what was right or wrong, not by following someone else's way. I'd tried that last year and failed. I'd know what I was supposed to do when I was supposed to do it—not before. Being on Mount Everest for a second time and preparing to climb the Lhotse Face was already a miracle, an incredible victory in itself. My task was to show up and find out what the Universe had in store for me.

The next morning I walked strongly up the Cwm to the foot of the Lhotse Face, following Rob's long-legged stride. The plan for the day was for us to make the two-hour hike to the bottom of the Lhotse Face, then spend a couple of hours climbing the fixed lines that protected climbers from falls down the ice of the Face. Rob and I started two hours behind the others. I'd been up all night with severe menstrual cramps and had asked for a couple of hours of extra time for the medication I'd taken to begin working. Was it a sign of God's perverse sense of humor that

----)----

I was the last person on the rope. My friend Jini was just ahead of me. All at once, the rope connecting us jerked tight and I was pulled off balance.... The seven of us were in a snow slide—perhaps in falling we had fractured the fresh, unstable powder. I realized the snow and climbers were sliding down the mountain together, then all of a sudden I stopped moving. Like an anchor, the snow had caught me fast. All the others on the rope were arrested in sequence, like dolls on a long rubber band. It took me a moment to realize I could still breathe. My face was up, covered with only a light layer of snow.

◆

—Barbara J. Euser, "Coma on Mount Communism"

I once again started my period on a day requiring sustained effort on a mountain?

Within an hour of leaving camp, the pain was gone, and I felt strong and healthy in the startling beauty of this magical valley. I was in my "Go Mode," walking and breathing rhythmically, my mantra singing in my head: God's love, God's strength, God's will, I can. I could and I was.

When we reached the beginning of the fixed lines, Rob and I took a water break. We were standing above 22,000 feet, looking down the length of the Western Cwm, across the Khumbu Glacier to 23,442-foot-high Pumori, its summit rising only slightly above us....

"Rob, this is truly magnificent." My words were inadequate.

"That it is, Margo, that it is."

He, too, studied the view as if to memorize it. He had been there several times before, both as a climber and a guide and had already stood on the top of Everest three times. His reverence for it had not faded with familiarity. It was that depth of feeling, as much a part of him as his strength and leadership ability, which had drawn me to him.

Rob broke my reverie as he placed a hand on my shoulder and nodded at the bottom of the fixed ropes. "Let's head up, pal."

"You got it." I smiled, reminded once again of Skip [a guide and friend from previous climbs]. The two men were alike in many ways, included their guiding styles: supportive rather than autocratic teachers who placed importance on the process of the expedition as well as on reaching the summit. I attached my ascender onto the first rope, dug the points of my crampons into the ice and began to climb the Lhotse Face.

Less than two hours later, we met the rest of the team as they were heading down.

"Maggot, you're moving well today," Gary called to me from the top of the section of line I was ascending. I tilted my head back to look up at him and waved my thanks for his encouragement. There was a fairly flat section of ice at the top of this length of fixed line, and once there I unclipped my ascender and moved aside to greet the others waiting there. "We only turned around a wee while ago," Gary said. "You've made good time coming up here."

In four hours of climbing, I'd made up one and a half of the two-hour time deficit I'd started with. My "Go Mode" had stayed with me while I climbed the ropes, a first time I'd felt it on terrain this steep. I felt strong and knew I could have made it to Camp III if it had been on the agenda. It wasn't, and Rob decided that we would return with the others.

I looked out once again over the Western Cwm. From the shelf where we stopped I could see all the way to the top of the Icefall. "Gary, how high do you think we are? Looks like we're even with or above Pumori."

"We're certainly above seven thousand meters, Maggot. Maybe closer to seventy-one hundred. Higher than last year, yes?" Gary remembered that my first goal was to get higher on the mountain than I had last year. Rob and I had moved up the 35-degree pitch for close to an hour and a half, much longer than last year. Clearly it was a new personal high altitude for me. I felt proud: I knew I could get to the summit.

I turned to head down, then stopped. "Hey, Rob. Just in case I don't get back up here, I'd better take a picture. Do you mind?"

"Glad to, my friend." He took off his gloves and reached out for my camera. "But you'll be back."

"I believe that." I felt the same conviction his voice had projected across the Cwm. "But I'd hate to have something happen and not have a photo."

"Smile," he commanded. And I did. The next time I was here, it would be on my way to Camp III. I'd faced my fears and walked through them once again. I had no doubts about being able to reach Camp III when the time came.

The climb down was uneventful, bright sunshine heating our bodies, allowing us to move in lightweight Capilene layers. From time to time, I'd realize that I was climbing down the Lhotse Face on Mount Everest into the Western Cwm. Sometimes I'd allow myself a glimpse between Nuptse and the west shoulder of

Everest to Pumori standing proudly across the valley. As I walked down the Cwm, my crampons creaked with each step in the ice and snow. I laughed, filled with the awe of my being there and thought to myself, "Ho hum. Just another uneventful climb back to Camp II on Mount Everest."

We left on our planned descent to Base Camp early the next morning to avoid moving through the Icefall in the heat of the day. Continual freezing, melting, and refreezing made the ice unstable, increasing the chances of injury and death as the sun softened the ice. The light was miraculously clear, crystallizing the beauty and magic of the Western Cwm in my memory. I walked by myself, accompanied only by the squeaking of my crampons on the snow, moving quickly to get the circulation going in my cold toes, feeling strong and confident....

> *W*hen life gets tangled there's something so reassuring about climbing a mountain. The challenge is unambiguous. Ice and snow and rock. Self-discipline. Concentration. Focus. As you push higher you work yourself into a trance. Can I reach that ledge? Are my fingers strong enough to hold on to this crack? Will this ice screw hold? Eventually the weight of the world—the stalled career, the broken marriage, the shattered confidence— slides away.
>
> ◆
>
> —Stacy Allison with Peter Carlin, *Beyond the Limits: A Woman's Triumph on Everest*

Two hours later,...I struggled through the icy maze. My strength decreased with each step as I descended. My chest was gripped in an unseen vise, and my lungs began to complain. I fought to hold in coughs that threatened to pitch me off the unstable ladders and left searing pain in their wake.

I had felt so great when I left Camp II. What happened? It seemed that my body was once again betraying me when I needed it most....

I walked slowly to the dining tent to bolster myself with a cup of hot chocolate before Jan examined me. Her diagnosis: Bronchitis. Again.

Three days later I sat in the sun in front of my tent, tired, unwell, discouraged. I had been awake coughing for most of the night, and that morning I felt beaten. I couldn't imagine going back up the Icefall for any reason. Thoughts of being done, of just not wanting to continue putting out the effort anymore filled my mind. And yet during the night, even in the midst of the coughing, I had a clear, positive image of getting to Camp III. My body was mired in a bog of physical and emotional exhaustion, but my spirit didn't seem to recognize those limits.

Base Camp was filled with climbing energy as people prepared to head back.

It was a year to the day since we'd come down from the many nights at Camp II last year. I was ill then, too. There appeared to be many similarities between this year and last, yet I knew that was only how it looked on the surface. Guy stopped by my tent to check on me.

"How're ya going, Maggot? Any better? He crouched down next to me.

I let my book drop into my lap. "I'm getting there." I hoped the words would make it true.

"I thought it might help you to know that last night Gary and Rob and I were talking about the trip and climbers we've been with. We all commented about how much courage and dignity you show under tough conditions. We really like having your determination and positive attitude around."

"Thanks." I had tears in my eyes and didn't have to hide them as he wrapped me in a heart-soothing bear hug. I wished I could see myself through his eyes. All I could do was take care of myself the best I knew how and keep listening to my heart and my body.

I looked up at the jumble of ice leading to Camp I and reminded myself, "This is my climb and my choice. There will be no disgrace or failure in not going back up...." The truth was that I'd already reached a summit higher than I could have imagined just by showing up. I had not idea what would happen next. One day at a time I could accept what was presented to me and allow my heart to enjoy the beauty, camaraderie, and fun of being there in that place at that time.

Margo Chisholm is a practicing therapist who also publishes a weekly internet newsletter called "Celebrating the Journey." Ray Bruce is co-founder of The Writing Center in San Diego and is an editor for Self-Help Psychology *magazine. This story was excerpted from* To the Summit: A Woman's Journey into the Mountains to Find Her Soul, *an account of Chisholm's quest to scale the highest peaks of the Earth's seven continents.*

✳

9 October
Nepal

Dear Martha, Walt, Sarah, and Lewis,

Well my dears, I made it—17,600 feet to the Base camp of Mt. Everest. I can hardly believe this 52-year-old lady has made it this far. The others have had serious doubts as well about whether I'd make it, except maybe Bill who really heard me when I said I was slow but stubborn. We climbed first across a sand beach with a lake at the end and then onto a glacier topped with a thin layer of scree over rocks and shale. It was slogging time. The day was shining as we climbed around huge ice formations.

....So why does one do it—tax yourself to the extreme of physical endurance? I guess there are no real words to describe why one does such a thing or its personal impact. Although this trip is the most physically exhausting experience I've ever had there is a sense of peace from having attained a goal, from the affiliation with other human beings and from the knowledge that one's own daily cares and brief existence are minuscule in the scheme of time. It makes the time between life and death more precious.

I love you all. Be happy,
Mom

—Brenda Townes, "Wish You Were Here"

BRENDA PETERSON

Bread upon the Waters

A nomad finds that "home"
is the sea and the gulls.

"Seagulls memorize your face," the old man called out to me as he strode past on his daily walk. I stood on the seawall feeding the flock of gray-and-white gulls who also make this Puget Sound beach their home. "They know their neighbors." He tipped his rather rakish tweed motoring cap and kept walking fast. "Can't let the heartbeat stop," he explained.

I meet this man many days on the beach. We rarely talk; we perform our simple chores: I feed the seagulls and say prayers, he keeps his legs and his heart moving. But between us there is an understanding that these tasks are as important as anything else in our lives; maybe they even keep us alive. Certainly our relationship with each other and with this windswept Northwest beach is more than a habit. It is a bond, an unspoken treaty we've made with the territory we call home.

For ten years I have migrated from beach shack to cabin, moving along the shore like the native tribes that once encircled all of Puget Sound. But unlike the first people who loved this wild, serpentine body of cold water, my encampments have changed with the whim of my landlords rather than with the seasons. Somehow mixed up in my blood of Seminole, Swede, and French-Canadian

Indian is my belief that I may never own land even if one day I might be able to afford it. Ownership implies possession; as much as I revere this inland sea, she will never belong to me. Why not, then, belong to her?

Belong. As a child the word mesmerized me. Because my father's forestry work moved us every other year—from southern piney woods to soaring Montana spruce to High Sierra fir—the land-scape seemed in motion. To belong in one place was to take deep root like other set-tled folk, or like the trees themselves. After I have lived a long life on this beach, I hope that someone might someday say, "She belonged here," as much as the purple starfish that cling to rock crevices covered in algae fur.

> *O*ne learns first of all in beach living the art of shedding; how little one can get along with, not how much.
>
> ◆
>
> —Anne Morrow Lindbergh,
> *Gift from the Sea*

The Hopi Indians of Arizona believe that our daily rituals and prayers literally keep this world spinning on its axis. For me, feed-ing the seagulls is one of those everyday prayers. When I walk out of my front door and cross the street to the seawall, they caw wel-come, their wings almost touching me as they sail low over my shoulders, then hover overhead, midair. Sometimes if it's been rain-ing, their feathers flick water droplets onto my face like sprinklings of holy water. The brave fliers swoop over the sea and back to catch the bread in their beaks inches above my hand. Then the ca-cophonic choir—gulls crying and crows *kak-kak*-ing as my special sidearm pitch sends tortillas whizzing through the air, a few of them skipping across the waves like flour frisbees.

I am not the only neighbor who feeds these gulls. For the past three years, two afternoons a week a green taxi pulled alongside the beach. From inside, an ancient woman, her back bent like the taut arch of a crossbow, leaned out of the car window and called in a clear, tremulous soprano. The seagulls recognized the sun-wrinkled, almost blind face she raised to them. She smiled and said to the taxi driver, "They *know* I'm here."

It was always the same driver, the same ritual—a shopping bag full of day-old bread donated by a local baker. "She told me she used to live by the sea," the driver explained to me once. "She don't remember much else about her life—not her children, not her husband." Carefully the driver tore each bread slice into four squares the way the woman requested. "Now she can't hardly see these birds. But she hears them and she smells the sea. Calls this taking her medicine."

Strong medicine, the healing salt and mineral sea this old woman took into her body and soul twice a week. She lived in the nursing home at the top of our hill, and every time I saw the familiar ambulance go by I prayed it was not for Our Lady of the Gulls.

This fall, when wild hurricanes shook the South and drought seized the Northwest, the old woman stopped coming to our beach. I waited for her all autumn, but the green taxi with its delighted passenger never came again. I took to adding two weekly afternoon feedings to my own morning schedule. These beach meetings are more mournful, in memory of the old woman who didn't remember her name, whose name I never knew, who remembered only the gulls.

Not long afterward my landlady called with the dreaded refrain: "House sold, must move on." I walked down to the beach and opened my arms to the gulls. With each bread slice I said a prayer that Puget Sound would keep me near her. One afternoon I got the sudden notion to drive down the sound. There I found a cozy white cottage for rent, a little beach house that belongs to an old man who's lived on this promontory since the 1940s. A stroke had sent him to a nursing home, and the rent from his cottage will pay for his care.

Before I moved one stick of furniture into the house, I stood on the beach and fed the gulls in thanksgiving. They floated above my head: I felt surrounded by little angels. Then I realized that these were the very same gulls from two miles down the beach near my old home—there was that bit of fishline wrapped around a familiar webbed foot, that wounded wing, and the distinct markings of a young gray gull, one of my favorite high fliers.

Who knows whether the old man was right? The seagulls may have memorized my face and followed me—but I had also, quite without realizing it, memorized them. And I knew then that I was no newcomer here, not a nomad blown by changeable autumn winds. It is not to any house, but to this beach I have bonded. I belong along-side this rocky inlet with its salt tides, its pine-tiered, green islands, its gulls who remember us even when we've forgotten ourselves.

Brenda Peterson has worked for The New Yorker, *lived on a farm near Denver, where she was a fiction editor for* Rocky Mountain Magazine, *and taught at Arizona State University in Tempe. Now an editor and environmental writer who lives in Seattle, she is the author of several books, including* Duck and Cover, Singing to the Sound, Build Me an Ark, Spirited Waters, *and* Living by Water.

★

My name has prompted people to ask my favorite bird, but I follow a bird-watching Zen, and I watch for moments rather than feathers. Though people see owls and nightjars, they must usually exert some considerable effort looking for them. My favorite moments are the ones I don't look for, the ones I hear so closely, whose voices touch my imagination. If I found myself face to face with an owl or a nightjar I think I should shut my eyes. I would like my whole life filled with memories of darting shapes and clear, night voices.

—Bird Cupps, "*Kituo* (Stopping Place)"

ANNIE DILLARD

* * *

The Deer at Providencia

A traveler faces the fact of suffering.

THERE WERE FOUR OF US NORTH AMERICANS IN THE JUNGLE, IN
the Ecuadorian jungle on the banks of the Napo River in the
Amazon watershed. The other three North Americans were met-
ropolitan men. We stayed in tents in one riverside village, and visited others. At the village called Providencia we saw a sight which
moved us, and which shocked the men.

The first thing we saw when we climbed the riverbank to the
village of Providencia was the deer. It was roped to a tree on the
grass clearing near the thatch shelter where we would eat lunch.

The deer was small, about the size of a whitetail fawn, but apparently full-grown. It had a rope around its neck and three feet
caught in the rope. Someone said that the dogs had caught it that
morning and the villagers were going to cook and eat it that night.

This clearing lay at the edge of the little thatched-hut village.
We could see the villagers going about their business, scattering
feed corn for hens about their houses, and wandering down paths
to the river to bathe. The village headman was our host; he stood
beside us as we watched the deer struggle. Several village boys were
interested in the deer; they formed part of the circle we made

around it in the clearing. So also did four businessmen from Quito who were attempting to guide us around the jungle. Few of the very different people standing in this circle had a common language. We watched the deer, and no one said much.

The deer lay on its side at the rope's very end, so the rope lacked slack to let it rest its head in the dust. It was "pretty," delicate of bone like all deer, and thin-skinned for the tropics. Its skin looked virtually hairless, in fact, and almost translucent, like a membrane. Its neck was no thicker than my wrist; it was rubbed open on the rope, and gashed. Trying to paw itself free of the rope, the deer had scratched its own neck with its hooves. The raw underside of its neck showed red stripes and some bruises bleeding inside the muscles. Now three of its feet were hooked in the rope under its jaw. It could not stand, of course, on one leg, so it could not move to slacken the rope and ease the pull on its throat and enable it to rest its head.

Repeatedly the deer paused, motionless, its eyes veiled, with only its rib cage in motion, and its breaths the only sound. Then, after I would think, "It has given up; now it will die," it would heave. The rope twanged; the tree leaves clattered; the deer's free foot beat the ground. We stepped back and held our breaths. It thrashed, kicking, but only one leg moved; the other three legs tightened inside the rope's loop. Its hip jerked; its spine shook. Its eyes rolled; its tongue, thick with spittle, pushed in and out. Then it would rest again. We watched this for fifteen minutes.

Once three young native boys charged in, released its trapped legs, and jumped back to the circle of people. But instantly the deer scratched up its neck with its hooves and snared its forelegs in the rope again. It was easy to imagine a third and then a fourth leg soon stuck, like Brer Rabbit and the Tar Baby.

We watched the deer from the circle, and then we drifted on to lunch. Our palm-roofed shelter stood on a grassy promontory from which we could see the deer tied to the tree, pigs and hens walking under village houses, and black-and-white cattle standing in the river. There was even a breeze.

Lunch, which was the second and better lunch we had that day, was hot and fried. There was a big fish called *doncella*, a kind of catfish, dipped whole in corn flour and beaten egg, then deep fried. With our fingers we pulled soft fragments of it from its sides to our plates, and ate; it was delicate fish-flesh, fresh and mild. Someone found the roe, and I ate of that too—it was fat and stronger, like egg yolk, naturally enough, and warm.

There was also a stew of meat in shreds with rice and pale brown gravy. I had asked what kind of deer it was tied to the tree; Pepe had answered in Spanish, "*Gama.*" Now they told us this was *gama* too, stewed. I suspect the word means merely game or venison. At any rate, I heard that the village dogs had cornered another deer just yesterday, and it was this deer which we were now eating in full sight of the whole article. It was good. I was surprised at its tenderness. But it is a fact that high levels of lactic acid, which builds up in muscle tissues during exertion, tenderizes.

After the fish and meat we ate bananas fried in chunks and served on a tray; they were sweet and full of flavor. I felt terrific. My shirt was wet and cool from swimming; I had had a night's sleep, two decent walks, three meals, and a swim—everything tasted good. From time to time each one of us, separately, would look beyond our shaded roof to the sunny spot where the deer was still convulsing in the dust. Our meal completed, we walked around the deer and back to the boats.

That night I learned that while we were watching the deer, the others were watching me.

We four North Americans grew close in the jungle in a way that was not the usual artificial intimacy of travelers. We liked each other. We stayed up all that night talking, murmuring, as though we rocked on hammocks slung above time. The others were from big cities; New York, Washington, Boston. They all said that I had

no expression on my face when I was watching the deer—or at
any rate, not the expression they expected.

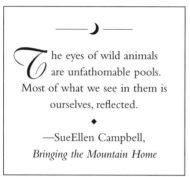

*he eyes of wild animals
are unfathomable pools.
Most of what we see in them is
ourselves, reflected.*

♦

—SueEllen Campbell,
Bringing the Mountain Home

They had looked to see
how I, the only woman, and
the youngest, was taking the
sight of the deer's struggles. I
looked detached, apparently,
or hard, or calm, or focused,
still. I don't know. I was
thinking. I remember feeling
very old and energetic. I
could say like Thoreau that I
have traveled widely in
Roanoke, Virginia. I have
thought a great deal about carnivorousness; I eat meat. These
things are not issues; they are mysteries.

Gentlemen of the city, what surprises you? That there is suffering here, or that I know it?

We lay in the tent and talked. "If it had been my wife," one
man said with special vigor, amazed, "she wouldn't have cared
what was going on; she would have dropped *everything* right at
that moment and gone in the village from here to there to there,
she would not have *stopped* until that animal was out of its suffering one way or another. She couldn't *bear* to see a creature in
agony like that."

I nodded.

Now I am home. When I wake I comb my hair before the mirror above my dresser. Every morning for the past two years I have
seen in that mirror, beside my sleep-softened face, the blackened
face of a burnt man. It is a wire-service photograph clipped from
a newspaper and taped to my mirror. The caption reads: "Alan
McDonald in Miami hospital bed." All you can see in the photograph is a smudged triangle of face from his eyelids to his lower

lip; the rest is bandages. You cannot see the expression in his eyes; the bandages shade them.

The story, headed MAN BURNED FOR SECOND TIME, begins:

> "Why does God hate me?" Alan McDonald asked from his hospital bed.

> "When the gunpowder went off, I couldn't believe it," he said. "I just couldn't believe it. I said, "'No, God couldn't do this to me again.'"

He was in a burn ward in Miami, in serious condition. I do not even know if he lived. I wrote him a letter at the time, cringing.

He had been burned before, thirteen years previously, by flaming gasoline. For years he had been having his body restored and his face remade in dozens of operations. He had been a boy, and then a burnt boy. He had already been stunned by what could happen, by how life could veer.

Once I read that people who survive bad burns tend to go crazy; they have a very high suicide rate. Medicine cannot ease their pain; drugs just leak away, soaking the sheets, because there is no skin to hold them in. The people just lie there and weep. Later they kill themselves. They had not known, before they were burned, that the world included such suffering, that life could permit them personally such pain.

This time a bowl of gunpowder had exploded on McDonald.

> "I didn't realize what had happened at first," he recounted. "And then I heard that sound from thirteen years ago. I was burning. I rolled to put the fire out and I thought, "Oh God, not again."

> "If my friend hadn't been there, I would have jumped into a canal with a rock around my neck."

> His wife concludes the piece, "Man, it just isn't fair."

I read the whole clipping again every morning. This is the Big Time here, every minute of it. Will someone please explain to Alan

McDonald in his dignity, to the deer at Providencia in his dignity, what is going on? And mail me the carbon.

When we walked by the deer at Providencia for the last time, I said to Pepe, with a pitying glance at the deer, *"Pobrecito"*—"poor little thing." But I was trying out Spanish. I knew at the time it was a ridiculous thing to say.

Annie Dillard is the author of numerous books, including Pilgrim at Tinker Creek, An American Childhood, *and* Teaching a Stone to Talk: Expeditions and Encounters, *from which this story was excerpted.*

★

"You have to mix death into everything," a painter once told me. "Then you have to mix life into that," he said as his cigarette ashes dropped onto the palette. "If they are not there, I try to mix them in. Otherwise the painting won't be human."

—Gretel Ehrlich, *Islands, the Universe, Home*

TERRY STROTHER

* ⁕ *

Rocks in My Head

Amid fears about her health, a traveler
finds comfort in nature's bounty.

BY FAR THE HARDEST PART WAS DECIDING TO GO ON THE TRIP.
Once it was decided that Tad and I were going around the world
no matter what, the obstacles were easier to handle. So my mind
was made up, the destinations worked out, before the melanoma
was discovered. Just a black spot on the bottom of my foot that
seemed to change slightly. "It's really a chance in a million that this
is anything," the doctor had said, giving the impression that he was
humoring me by removing it at all. I've never felt quite the same
about statistics since. But everything went well, my foot healed
more quickly than expected, and I was on my way—with one
hitch. There was also a small spot on my lung that was "probably
nothing, but could be related." I needed to get a follow-up X-ray
in Hong Kong. A shadow was cast...

On Maui there is a plant called the sensitive plant that when
touched shyly folds up its leaves and then, ever so slowly, relaxes
open again. Walking through a field of these plants was an eerie
sensation. Passion fruit and strawberry guava grew all around the
place where we pitched our tent, on a cliff overlooking the ocean;
a fecund motherly earth, rich and ripe. How far away that was
from the city. As a child, I allowed myself to recieve what the wild

39

spaces around me had to offer. After a decade in New York City, I was not sure I knew how to do that anymore. I felt like I was sitting on the edge of the Grand Canyon with a paper bag over my head.

Tad and I hiked in silence to deep freshwater pools and treaded water over what seemed to go to the center of the earth. Though the sun was bright, the trails through the bamboo forest were pitch black. The sound of the wind through the bamboo was an eerie creaking and groaning of voices. Like an ancient language I could almost understand. Next to the Waimoku falls, I found a small cave in which I sat huddled, water pouring over the opening, dozens of rich mosses covering everything inside this earthy womb. Was it minutes? Hours? Time lost all frame of reference and I found myself simply wanting to retreat into the primordial energy of the earth itself, becoming swallowed up by her elements.

Before we had left on our journey, I overheard an old friend advising my travel companion, "The thing to remember about Terry is you just have to hang on for the ride." At the time, I was puzzled. What could he mean? And yet, in the weeks that followed there were times I would catch Tad looking at me as though that was exactly what he was doing. His solid but unobtrusive presence was what was required for us to stay connected.

I had longed for this trip, but my mind wouldn't cooperate. Though appreciative of the natural beauty that surrounded me, something about it rubbed me raw. I tried to meditate, remembering a buddhist monk we had met one afternoon who said, "You must heal your mind; whatever happens to your body, you shouldn't be sick twice." But I was more endarkened than enlightened by my efforts.

In the end it was the animals that enticed me out of this state of muddled reverie. The turning point came in New Zealand, when we were camping on Otago, a short crooked thumb of land jutting out into the Pacific Ocean. On the end of this rocky peninsula was an albatross colony and a farm of rugged land where there were penguins, seals, and spotted shags. We rang up the farmer who gave us permission to hike out and camp near the beach which was home to a colony of small yellow-eyed penguins. Just before dawn, we'd crawl out to the edge of a cliff. Lying propped up on the frost-covered ground, shoulder to shoulder under the blanket, we'd listen as the penguins called to one another from their beds. A haunting high-pitched keening sound calling and fading from different parts of the beach. Then, as if they were calling forth the sun itself, the world would begin to lighten and in this dim light we could barely make out small groups of two or three penguins very slowly, carefully, making their way down the hill leading out to the sea. Occasionally they would stop and look back, waiting up for one another. As it became lighter you could see that they were gesticulating animatedly with their flippers: conversing, telling jokes, performing daring antics. Obviously social by nature, they waited for any stragglers and in twos, threes or fives waddled out into the lapping water, flopped down and wizzed out, leaping through the waves like tiny porpoises. I was filled with delight down to my toes. What silly, funny little people they were. In the evening they returned to trudge their way up the steep hill—heads bent, conversations much less animated—to keen the sun away again.

The days were spent singing in caves and sitting on the rocks next to the big lazy seals, watching the pups tumble-play in the waves and loving that I could—I wouldn't, but I could—touch them as they slept on the sun-baked rocks. There was a track that led around a point to more caves and blow holes and little islands and beautiful vistas. It led to another bay with a small beach. Cows were hanging out on the beach, lazing in the sun, apparently just taking the day off. There is a special way that the wind and the sea sculpts the shoreline of Otago. The seals all along the shoreline are wonderfully playful and alive, tumbling over each other like children or puppies. Yipping and barking and squeaking at one another through the crashing surf over the rocks and in caves, they would stop to stare at me with their huge, round, wet eyes, and then go back to play. So different seeing animals on their own terms, in their own homes.

As the shadow gradually lifted, there was no closing my eyes to the sheer beauty and grandeur of this place, with its diverse land-scape and physical geography, so abundantly accessible by foot. The power of the mountains and waterfalls was evident, as was the sacredness of the land and of the slow, wild Tasman Sea. Sometimes it was too much to take in, like the feeling of being overwelmed by a work of art: shocking, simple, beautiful. I had felt the same way at an exhibit of Van Gogh's last works. The tremendous fiords, the bays, the sea caves and blow holes, the rocky coasts of the west and the wonderfully alive rainforests leading down to the water was a feast for the senses.

Then, one day, after a three-hour hike back through a rainforest to the small camper van we had splurged on (which was parked rather precariously in an area prone to avalanches), I realized I had taken the keys out of my pocket and laid them on the low tide beach next to me as I meditated. Without a word of recrimination from Tad, though we were at least a full day's hike from anyone who could help us out, back we went. The whole way back I prayed the keys would not be swallowed up by the sea. In the richness of the rainforest twilight, the tree roots and shadows were indistinguishable (please let them be there), tripping, slowing up (please let them be there), the quiet of the day replaced with layer upon layer of sound.

When we finally arrived at the spot, darkness had enveloped the sea and the gentle waves lapped up within an inch of where the keys lay. Something gave inside me. I sat in the wet sand and wept at this gift, this small sign of benevolence from the physical world itself. And somehow I got that I mattered, was matter, was of this world. To the extent that I had been able to see how incredible and beautiful the world is, I was now able to feel a part of it.

It didn't seem so much that I had learned anything new, but that someone had gently reminded me of some things that I had forgotten. That I am not a spectator. That I truly love this earth and am happiest traipsing, tramping, swimming, skipping, or just lying quietly against her, feeling our hearts beat together. That I am nourished by this as surely as I am by the food I eat because we are part of the same continuum, this earth and I: matter.

Life is so easy sometimes. So...I let it be easy. I felt intensely happy and lighthearted out under the moon, gathering rocks and seashells. And what rocks! Undoubtedly the most varied and lovely rocks I'd ever seen, and they were everywhere: lakes, streams, creeks, ocean, waterfalls. A bit obsessive when it comes to rocks, I began filling up my pockets, backpack, the glove compartment, any nook or cranny. I tried to control myself but... More than one postal worker shook his head in disbelief as I mailed home boxes of the most beautiful matter.

In Hong Kong, a follow-up X-ray revealed the spot on my lung to be a small calcification, a tiny rock, one might say, embedded in my lung; a speck of matter. We might have enjoyed this vic-

> *Y*ou were scared
>   and your mama was
>   chased away
> by the waves....
> But don't worry,
> 'cause I have found your
>   mama at last.
> She's a leaf mama to you.
> Mama is up in the trees
> looking like a ghost.
> Don't be scared anymore.
> I have found your mother
> and brought you an eagle.
>
> ◆
>
> —Emma Strother, age 4, "Big
> Spots" (written for Terry
> Strother when her mother died)

tory more except that we were a bit distracted, searching out a compatible rabies vaccine to finish off the series begun in Java after an encounter with a monkey; but that's another story.

Tad hung in there, and is still along for the ride. Instead of using building blocks, our daughter builds her paths and towers and ponds and corrals and zoos and mountains and cities with the most amazing variety of rocks. Our travel is mostly to Central Park these days. There Emma can be a mountain climber, exploring the "big rock" next to the lake or lying down in a soft bed of pine needles in the forest, pretending to be a fawn in the thicket. Sometimes, in these quiet moments, I whisper to her a poem that I fashioned out of a more traditional prayer to God:

The light of the sun surrounds me
The love of the earth enfolds me
The power of the sea protects me
The presence of the moon watches over me
Wherever I am, these things are with me.

We've been known, at times, to put off bedtime in favor of a bike ride through the park, looking for racoons and enjoying the night sky in the only dark place around. And sometimes, when I'm tucking Emma in bed and telling stories of the earth and sea, of animals or the phases of the moon, I like starting with, "When I went around the world...." It has a certain ring to it, a destiny. It also speaks of a certain freedom I never imagined possible. And though her Papa and I traversed the same itinerary together, there is nevertheless a certain pathway across land and sea circumventing the globe that feels uniquely mine.

Terry Strother lives with her husband and daughter in New York City. She struggles to balance a life of adventure and motherhood while teaching yoga part-time and continuing her efforts to write and travel.

★

When I am troubled I run away to nature, much as a wounded animal might. Sometimes I just sit, or stand, or lie; maybe I am at the beach, or in the woods, or my fingers are entwined in the fur of some obliging dog. I think it is hard for people who care for me to let me be alone, as they see it, when I am hurting. They do not see that I am letting nature heal me.
—Archer T. Gilliam, "Healing"

LYNNE COX

✦ ✦ ✦

The Pelican

A swimmer answers a bird's SOS.

MALIBU BEACH, BEFORE DAWN. MY FRIEND LOUISE COMAR AND I tightened our goggles and slid our feet into the surfline. For the past six months I had been coaching Louise. Today we would swim fifteen miles, from Malibu pier to the Santa Monica pier—the longest distance Louise had ever swum and the ultimate test to determine whether she would be able to reach her goal that summer: to swim across the Catalina Channel, from Catalina Island to the California mainland, about twenty-seven miles.

Swimming was a hobby for Louise. By profession, she was a deputy district attorney in Los Angeles. She was dedicated, intense, driven, and relentless in the courtroom—all attributes that easily carried over to the sport of long-distance swimming.

But swimming in ocean was completely different from the pool, and I felt very responsible for her during our training sessions, especially today. Many dangerous obstacles would not be apparent to a new open-water swimmer.

"When you go around the pier," I coached her, "swim on the outside of me and stay at least one hundred meters out so you don't get tangled in fishing lines."

She nodded. Her eyes were focused like lazers on the water,

45

mentally rehearsing her swim as if she were about to present a case to a jury. She was wound up tight. Way too tight. If I didn't calm her down and reassure her, she would quickly burn herself out through nervous energy.

"Louise, let's put this workout into perspective," I said. "The longest you've ever swum is ten miles. We're adding five, and that's a big stretch. If you can complete even eleven or twelve miles today, you've done a great job. Just remember, whatever distance you do today will bring you closer to your goal," I said.

Louise took a deep breath. "I understand," she said. "But I want to swim the distance."

I told her that was fine, but that she had to pace herself. "Long-distance swimming is about going the distance, but it's also about enjoying the journey."

We decided to unwind a little by watching the sunrise. Rosy light spread across the cool blue Pacific, washing over the old wooden pier and highlighting a flock of pelicans that silently glided toward us in single file and perfect formation, riding on the air current created by the breaking waves.

We dove beneath the waves, swam around Malibu pier, and paralled the coast. As we swam south just outside the surfline, we watched the earth awaken. Sunlight poured slowly over Malibu canyon's undulating walls, saturating the soft green grasses, silver shrubs, and wild mustard in warm morning light. A breeze stirred the hillsides and carried the fragrances of sage, rosemary, and creosote mingled with rose. We drew in deep wonderful breaths and the breeze-beveled water sparkeled like a zillion diamonds. Light streamed below the surface, illuminating silvery bubbles rolling rythmically off Louise's finger tips and out of her mouth. She was feeling great. She even smiled. She was precisely on pace.

Then out of the corner of my eye, I noticed something in the water. It was a young pelican, a fledgling. It was paddling directly toward me.

"I think something's wrong with that pelican," I said to Louise. "They don't usually swim with people."

The pelican moved closer. It seemed as if it were asking for my help. I swam around the bird. Surprisingly, it didn't move away. I moved closer to take a better look. I saw a fishing line tangled around its beak, breast, and wings.

If I could guide the bird to a rock, I thought, it could climb out and I could untangle it. With Louise swimming just ahead of me, I spotted a rock rising from the water. The pelican paddled right along beside me until we reached it. But when the bird tried to leap onto the narrow shelf, it flailed; its legs and feet were also tangled in fishing line. I tried to get out of the water, but the rock was covered with barnacles.

I continued swimming down the coast, searching for another rock on which to land, and the pelican followed. Louise, swimming just ahead, looked back. "What are you doing?" she shouted. She sounded annoyed.

"I'm trying to find a place to free the pelican from the fishing line," I said. I thought of going ashore with the bird, but wasn't sure I should leave Louise swimming alone. And I knew she didn't want to stop. I was torn between ensuring Louise's safety and saving the pelican's life.

About a mile ahead was Las Tunas Beach. I knew Louise could swim safely there; the surf that day was less than a foot, and there were no underwater obstacles. I gave her a choice to continue swimming to Las Tunas or come ashore right then with me.

"I want to keep going," she said. "I'll be fine."

But I could tell she wasn't happy about going alone. I felt like I was letting her down, but I couldn't just let the pelican die. I turned to shore at Big Rock Beach and guided the bird in with me. The swells began lifting us four and five feet up then dropping us down again. Sensing the danger of the waves, the pelican suddenly veered away from the surfline.

If I were going to help this bird, I'd have to pull it to shore. I looked at its pouch and neck. They were covered with lice and large, black ticks; the pelican had been unable to preen itself because of the fishing line. An enormous wave rose above us and the bird started to panic. I grabbed its giant, soft beak and started swimming with one arm and kicking as fast as I could. The wave caught us and tossed us over the falls, whitewater crashing around us. I tried to hold on and keep the bird's head above water, but the wave tore it from my grip.

Desperately, I scanned the water. Finally the young pelican emerged in the surf, tumbling, completely bound and helpless, sliding in the backwash toward an oncoming wave. Sprinting toward it, I grabbed its beak and rode with it on the whitewater into the beach.

Onshore, I let the stunned pelican stand there a few moments to get over the shock of tossing in the waves. I saw it had a deep gash in its leg from the fishing line. Its whole body began to tremble and its eyes began closing, as if it were going into shock. I talked to it and told it that it would be okay. Stroking its feathers, I gently tried to open its beak.

The fishing line was tangled so tightly that I could open the beak only a few inches. But I saw a three-pronged hook imbedded inside, the fishing line attached. I tried to pull out the hook, but couldn't grip it. Clearly I couldn't save this pelican alone.

Louise was swimming just offshore. "I need your help!" I shouted. She immediately swam into shore and jogged over to us.

"I need you to get some scissors from one of those houses up the beach so we can cut the line," I said.

Louise ran across Big Rock Beach and climbed a steep embankment. At the first house, an old woman called out that she was too frail to walk to the door. At the second house, a young woman answered from inside that she was too busy to help. At the third house, an elderly man answered, who immediately and wisely grabbed a pair of pliers and jogged with Louise down to the beach.

The pelican was going into deeper shock. The man and Louise held the pelican, who stood patiently on the sand, letting us work on him. I used the pliers to cut the lines and we carefully pulled them off its wings, breast, beak, and between its feet.

When I opened its beak to remove the hook, we saw there were two additional three-pronged hooks inside. Using the pliers, I pulled out the first one. The pelican blinked and squirmed a little, but didn't try to get away. The second hook took three attempts to yank out. The last hook was so deeply imbedded that I couldn't remove it. The man gave it a try, and in a matter of moments he pulled the last hook out.

We examined the bird's body. All the lines were gone and the hooks were out. We were worried about the gash in its leg, but decided that the saltwater would heal it. Together we carried the pelican to the water's edge.

The bird stood on one leg and then the other. It lifted its wings and tested them. Then all at once, it pushed off the beach and flew above the waves and out to sea.

With a great sense of satisfaction, Louise, the elderly man, and I smiled and applauded each other. Soon after, Louise and I climbed back in the water and continued our swim down the coastline. As we neared the finish of our fifteen-mile swim, near Santa Monica pier, a pelican splashed into the water nearby and paddled over to us. We looked closely and saw a gash in its leg. It was the same pelican.

The bird paddled with us to the pier, then left us to join a flock of pelicans flying north. We watched the birds glide magnificently above the breaking waves, riding the warm afternoon air currents, until they were out of sight.

Two months later, Louise swam across the Catalina Channel in just over fifteen hours.

At age fifteen, Lynne Cox shattered the men's and women's world records for swimming the English Channel. After her historic swim across the Bering Strait, President Reagan and President Gorbachev toasted her at the signing of the first INF treaty. She was named Los Angeles Times *Woman of the Year in 1975, inducted into the Swimming Hall of Fame in 2000, honored with a lifetime achievement award from U.C. Santa Barbara, and named one of* Glamour Magazine's *"Women of the Year 2003." She chronicled her life as an extreme athlete in* Swimming to Antarctica: Tales of a Long-Distance Swimmer. *Her work has also appeared in* The New Yorker, Los Angeles Times Magazine, *several Travelers' Tales books, and other publications. She lives in Los Alamitos, California.*

*

I could feel the possum studying me, though it remained as still as stone. It was amazing, really, the two of us eye to eye, facing each other across the huge divide of our separate species. I felt a sudden urge to speak to it. "Hello," I said in a low voice. "I won't hurt you."

I sensed that it understood, though not from my words. Some other language ran between us, a language of gesture and scent, perhaps....

All around us, I could hear the low twittering of birds, things rustling under the trees. They were tiny sounds, sounds I probably would not have heard if I were not then as still as the possum. I wondered how many other creatures were watching me, watching this little drama unfold. I imagined them peering out from burrows, from rocks, from behind and over tree trunks.

Native Americans believe that animals choose to show themselves to humans, so that humans can learn from them. Perhaps the possum had shown itself to me on purpose, wanting to teach me something. Perhaps if I could be still enough, watchful enough, I would learn what it was.

—Simone Poirier-Bures, "The Face in the Tree"

ALICE WALKER

* * *

Am I Blue?

"Ain't these tears in these eyes tellin' you?"

FOR ABOUT THREE YEARS MY COMPANION AND I RENTED A SMALL house in the country that stood on the edge of a large meadow that appeared to run from the end of our deck straight into the mountains. The mountains, however, were quite far away, and between us and them there was, in fact, a town. It was one of the many pleasant aspects of the house that you never really were aware of this.

It was a house of many windows, low, wide, nearly floor to ceiling in the living room, which faced the meadow, and it was from one of these that I first saw our closest neighbor, a large white horse, cropping grass, flipping its mane, and ambling about—not over the entire meadow, which stretched well out of sight of the house, but over the five or so fenced-in acres that were next to the twenty-odd that we had rented. I soon learned that the horse, whose name was Blue, belonged to a man who lived in another town, but was boarded by our neighbors next door. Occasionally, one of the children, usually a stocky teen-ager, but sometimes a much younger girl or boy, could be seen riding Blue. They would appear in the meadow, climb up on his back, ride furiously for ten or fifteen minutes, then get off, slap Blue on the flanks, and not be seen again for a month or more.

There were many apple trees in our yard, and one by the fence that Blue could almost reach. We were soon in the habit of feeding him apples, which he relished, especially because by the middle of summer the meadow grasses—so green and succulent since January—had dried out from lack of rain, and Blue stumbled about munching the dried stalks half-heartedly. Sometimes he would stand very still just by the apple tree, and when one of us came out he would whinny, snort loudly, or stamp the ground. This meant, of course: I want an apple.

It was quite wonderful to pick a few apples, or collect those that had fallen to the ground overnight, and patiently hold them, one by one, up to his large, toothy mouth. I remained as thrilled as a child by his flexible dark lips, huge, cubelike teeth that crunched the apples, core and all, with such finality, and his high, broad-breasted *enormity*; beside which, I felt small indeed. When I was a child, I used to ride horses, and was especially friendly with one named Nan until the day I was riding and my brother deliberately spooked her and I was thrown, head first, against the trunk of a tree. When I came to, I was in bed and my mother was bending worriedly over me; we silently agreed that perhaps horseback riding was not the safest sport for me. Since then I have walked, and prefer walking to horseback riding—but I had forgotten the depth of feeling one could see in horses' eyes.

I was therefore unprepared for the expression in Blue's. Blue was lonely. Blue was horribly lonely and bored. I was not shocked that this should be the case; five acres to tramp by yourself, endlessly, even in the most beautiful of meadows—and his was—cannot provide many interesting events, and once rainy season turned to dry that was about it. No, I was shocked that I had forgotten that human animals and nonhuman animals can communicate quite well; if we are brought up around animals as children we take this for granted. By the time we are adults we no longer remember. However, the animals have not changed. They are in fact completed creations (at least they seem to be, so much more than we) who are not likely to change; it is their nature to express themselves. What else are they going to express? And they do. And, generally speaking, they are ignored.

After giving Blue the apples, I would wander back to the house, aware that he was observing me. Were more apples not forthcoming then? Was that to be his sole entertainment for the day? My partner's small son had decided he wanted to learn how to piece a quilt; we worked in silence on our respective squares as I thought....

Well, about slavery: about white children, who were raised by black people, who knew their first all-accepting love from black women, and then, when they were twelve or so, were told they must "forget" the deep levels of communication between themselves and "mammy" that they knew. Later they would be able to relate quite calmly, "My old mammy was sold to another good family." "My old mammy was __ __." Fill in the blank. Many more years later a white woman would say: "I can't understand these Negroes, these blacks. What do they want? They're so different from us."

And about the Indians, considered to be "like animals" by the "settlers" (a very benign euphemism for what they actually were), who did not understand their description as a compliment.

And about the thousands of American men who marry Japanese, Korean, Filipina, and other non-English-speaking women and of how happy they report they are, "*blissfully*," until their brides learn to speak English, at which point the marriages tend to fall apart. What then did the men see, when they looked into the eyes of the women they married, before they could speak English? Apparently only their own reflections.

I thought of society's impatience with the young. "Why are they playing the music so loud?" Perhaps the children have listened to much of the music of oppressed people their parents danced to before they were born, with its passionate but soft cries for acceptance and love, and they have wondered why their parents failed to hear.

I do not know how long Blue had inhabited his five beautiful, boring acres before we moved into our house; a year after we had arrived—and had also traveled to other valleys, other cities, other worlds—he was still there.

But then, in our second year at the house, something happened in Blue's life. One morning, looking out the window at the fog that lay like a ribbon over the meadow, I saw another horse, a brown one, at the other end of Blue's field. Blue appeared to be afraid of it, and for several days made no attempt to go near. We went away for a week. When we returned, Blue had decided to make friends and the two horses ambled or galloped along together, and Blue did not come nearly as often to the fence underneath the apple tree.

When he did, bringing his new friend with him, there was a different look in his eyes. A look of independence, of self-possession, of inalienable *horseness*. His friend eventually became pregnant. For months and months there was, it seemed to me, a mutual feeling between me and the horses of justice, of peace. I fed apples to them both. The look in Blue's eyes was one of unabashed "this is *it*ness."

It did not, however, last forever. One day, after a visit to the city, I went out to give Blue some apples. He stood waiting, or so I thought, though not beneath the tree. When I shook the tree and jumped back from the shower of apples, he made no move. I carried some over to him. He managed to half-crunch one. The rest he let fall to the ground. I dreaded looking into his eyes—because I had of course noticed that Brown, his partner, had gone—but I did look. If I had been born into slavery,

> *A*lbert Schweitzer said, "We need a boundless ethic that includes animals too." And at the present time our ethic, where non-human animals are concerned, is limited and confused.
>
> ◆
>
> —Jane Goodall, *Through a Window: My Thirty Years with the Chimpanzees of Gombe*

and my partner had been sold or killed, my eyes would have looked like that. The children next door explained that Blue's partner had been "put with him" (the same expression that old people used, I had noticed, when speaking of an ancestor during slavery who had been impregnated by her owner) so that they could mate and she conceive. Since that was accomplished, she had been taken back by her owner, who lived somewhere else.

Will she be back? I asked.

They didn't know.

Blue was like a crazed person. Blue *was*, to me, a crazed person. He galloped furiously, as if he were being ridden, around and around his five beautiful acres. He whinnied until he couldn't. He tore at the ground with his hooves. He butted himself against his single shade tree. He looked always and always toward the road down which his partner had gone. And then, occasionally, when he came up for apples, or I took apples to him, he looked at me. It was a look so piercing, so full of grief, a look so *human*, I almost laughed (I felt too sad to cry) to think there are people who do not know that animals suffer. People like me who have forgotten, and daily forget, all that animals try to tell us. "Everything you do to us will happen to you; we are your teachers, as you are ours. We are one lesson" is essentially it, I think. There are those who never once have even considered animals' rights: those who have been taught that animals actually want to be used and abused by us, as small children "love" to be frightened, or women "love" to be mutilated and raped.... They are the great-grandchildren of those who honestly thought, because someone taught them this: "Women can't think," and "niggers can't faint." But most disturbing of all, in Blue's large brown eyes was a new look, more painful than the look of despair: the look of disgust with human beings, with life; the look of hatred. And it was odd what the look of hatred did. It gave him, for the first time, the look of a beast. And what that meant was that he had put up a barrier within to protect himself from further violence; all the apples in the world wouldn't change that fact.

And so Blue remained, a beautiful part of our landscape, very peaceful to look at from the window, white against the grass. Once a friend came to visit and said, looking out on the soothing view: "And it *would* have to be a *white* horse; the very image of freedom." And I thought, yes, the animals are forced to become for us merely "images" of what they once so beautifully expressed. And we are used to drinking milk from containers showing "contented" cows, whose real lives we want to hear nothing about, eating eggs and drumsticks from "happy" hens, and munching hamburgers advertised by bulls of integrity who seem to command their fate.

As we talked of freedom and justice one day for all, we sat down to steaks. I am eating misery, I thought, as I took the first bite. And spit it out.

Alice Walker won a National Book Award and the Pulitzer Prize for The Color Purple. *Her other books include* The Third Life of Grange Copeland, Meridian, Possessing the Secret Joy, The Temple of My Familiar, Anything We Love Can Be Saved, By the Light of My Father's Smile, The Way Forward is with a Broken Heart, *as well as numerous collections of short stories, poetry, and essays.*

★

We put them on tethers and leashes,
in shackles and harnesses, in cages and boxes,
inside fences and walls. We put them in yokes
and muzzles. We want them to carry us and pull us
and haul for us.

And we want some of them
to be our companions, some of them to ride on our fingers
and some to ride sitting on our wrists or on our shoulders
and some to ride in our arms, ride clutching our necks.
We want them to walk at our heels....

We know we are one with them,
and we are frantic to understand how to actualize that union.
We attempt to actualize that union in our many stumbling,
ignorant and destructive ways, in our many confused
and noble and praiseworthy ways.

For how can we possess dignity
if we allow them no dignity? Who will recognize our beauty
if we do not revel in their beauty? How can we hope
to receive honor if we give no honor? How can we believe
in grace if we cannot bestow grace?

> —Pattiann Rogers, "Animals and People: The Human Heart
> in Conflict with Itself," *Orion*

A Desert Affair

In the Sinai, at the edge of no return.

THERE IS AN HOUR IN JERUSALEM WHEN ONE CAN ALMOST SMELL the burnt offerings. When the sky, purple, orange, sage, cracks open for a moment to allow in the day's load of prayers and curses, then closes up again, majestic and mysterious as the lights come on below the ancient walls, and cars weave down the thin roads that lead out of the city, and silence blows in from the east.

At this hour, I would usually pull a chair outside the small cottage I had rented and watch evening approach, or take a walk down to Mishkenot Shaananim to watch dusk soften the just-lit walls, to hear the bells of mules in a nearby village mingle with the unintentional medley of opposing prayers.

It was 1976 and I was 21 and living in Jerusalem with the conviction (that one can only have at that age) that I had found my place in the world, had stumbled upon where I was supposed to be.

I had fallen completely and passionately in love with Jerusalem with its strange golden light, its babel of languages, its bougainvillea and almond blossom, its disputed and thrice-claimed god. I had fallen in love, too, with the country around it. Had I been asked to explain it, I would have said that it was as if I had stumbled upon in those teeming streets, by the turquoise sea and in that shimmering heat, the maelstrom of some recurrent dream.

Whether it was the East with its sultry ways, its lid full of half-turned instinct and mystery, or whether it was the thrill of having left behind the life that had been prescribed for me, all I knew was I wanted to be a part of this beautiful and complicated place, to move in its sultry rhythm, to learn its veiled Levantine ways.

So that when I heard everyone talking about the Sinai desert that lay hours south, I knew that I needed to go. Travelers described dunes alongside a brilliant blue sea, Bedouin on camels, beautiful reefs. In the few weeks that remained before classes began, I gathered together a few new friends and headed for the great hills of sand, for the ancient tongue of sea said to lick like a memory at the banks of two lands.

In the third month after the children of Israel had left Egypt, they came to the wilderness of Sinai. They set out from Rephidim and entered the wilderness of Sinai, where they encamped, pitching their tents opposite the mountain.

♦

—Exodus 19:1–2

We left Jerusalem at midnight to avoid the heat, five of us piled into an old green Renault. The sleeping countryside sped by us; Arab villages, some small Israeli towns, a few kibbutzim, then the dusty welcome of Beersheba, after which there were only a few scattered lights dotting the large, dark stretches of the Negev. About an hour out of Beersheba, we pulled over to the side of the road so that our only licensed driver could have a short sleep. I walked down the road for a little while, breathing in the night air of the Negev. The darkness was thick and silent but I could smell the desert, knew that around us were the pink sculpted hills of the Arava.

As dawn broke, we continued on, stopping as briefly as we could to grab breakfast in Eilat, eager to leave its "skyline" of five star hotels, its tourist boats and shops. Then we continued south; to our right, the dry red mountains of the desert, to our left, the glittering sea.

What we finally arrived at was this: Nothing but dunes, shifting seething dunes, rolling softly to the sea, crashing up against great palms that hung with drunken fruit and shade. The water was stretched as far as one could see, clear and sparkling with its coral reefs, its brilliantly colored fish. The sea was bordered by soft burning sand that would scorch the soles of your feet if you dared to venture out during the day from your homemade tent, or your small circumference of palm tree shade. Across the water, like a picture out of focus, the light pink haze of mountains that lined the coast of Saudi Arabia.

This was Nueiba. It housed—at that time (it is now, once again, part of Egypt) an Israeli *moshav* that grew watermelons, the probability of a hidden army encampment, and then between the sea and the ochre colored range of desert mountains, a long stretch of sand that rose into soft sculpted dunes, dotted here and there with tall palm trees. We decided to stop here. Others traveling down to the Sinai went on, on buses, motorcycles or hitchhiking, to the Bedouin fishing village of Dahab, to the hallucinatory reefs of Ras Mohammed, or inward, to the monastery at Santa Katarina. But Nueiba was where we wanted to be.

It was the mid-seventies and the sixties were just arriving here. And with its voluptuous sands, its seemingly hash-induced mirages of Bedouin women in long colorful trails by the water's edge (no mirage; they appeared and disappeared at various times of day, emerging in groups from their hidden tents to cool the soles of their feet at the edge of the Red Sea), this desert was luring us, along with scores of Scandinavians and Europeans, to leave our lives behind and learn its ways. To learn the soft, almost imperceptible way the dunes reshaped themselves in the late afternoon, the way the pink light lifted in a haze off the mountains, the way dates, hanging like desert gold, would fatten and wrinkle, then fall from the tall palms from which they hung. The taste of coffee at the end of the day, cooked in a blackened Turkish coffee pot, desert bread, as biblical and full of sand as thousands of years ago. The terrain of prophets and outcasts and lovers who wanted, however briefly, to leave their bodies.

We left our car at the parking lot that adjoined the gas station and small café run by the *moshav* and walked for an hour and a half into the dunes, following the sultry curve of the water. At first we passed large tents with every convenience, gas stoves, even televisions. Then clusters of young people speaking German, then French, then the soft sparsely inhabited "hill country" of the dunes. This was where the serious desert travelers came, many of whom had come here for a few days or a few weeks and gotten hypnotized; ended up living in tents made of anything they could find, or settled for a year or more between the branches of some huge and sprawling palm.

We found a palm tree among the dunes that was so large and strangely shaped from years of desert winds, that it almost seemed like two palms growing from the same cluster of roots. We unpacked the various colorful sheets we'd brought and constructed a "house" a few feet from the tree to protect us, where the tree wouldn't, from the seething sun, the night winds, the late afternoon's mist of sand. And then we settled each into his or her own silence. With every day, we spoke less and less. This was not a decision but a response to the extraordinary silence around us.

Every day I stretched out on a thin colorful cloth on the sand, first in the early morning's still gentle sun, then for hours, under the large leaves of the palm, clinging to every last inch of shade.

For days I just lay in the lap of the desert's strange and rustling silence, listening for the nomad's secret footfall, the shift of dunes, the play of waves. Until I knew, as the motionless Bedouin knew, as those before me who had in that starkest wedding, met the most ancient sparks of their souls, that if one chose, one could sleep here the sleep of centuries. That the sun rose and the sun shone and the sun remained for most of one's life baking its great lengths of sand and that one lay in it, not chosen, not spared, but without a will— half-cactus, half-rock, all thought falling away like wizened fruit, all abstractions and all previous truths dissolving in a world grown thick and real. That one grew slowly dull and parched and that still the sun shone and shone. That one hid in the thin shade of the trees, pressed one's face against the darkening bark and that still the sun mercilessly shone. That water grew precious and language scarce. That now and then a specter of breeze lifted mirage-like from a distant dune and one turned one's face slowly right into it, lifted one's face gently right into it.

That each day it would come to this. The morning with its rustling sea, its shifting sands, its quickened breeze would slow daily into this gaping and chimerical stillness. The Bedouin children would dissolve from view, the flapping tents stand still and full, the dunes which only hours before had not been able to keep their form would stiffen like sphinxes by a plate-like sea, not a grain evolving, not a scorpion's slide breaking across the trailless sand.

And then the day would draw to a close. We would wake up from a heat-drugged sleep, feel a breeze lifting, see the palm leaves above us begin their delicate dance. We would pass around the precious jug of water, then start a fire for the afternoon tea, as the huge and biblical sun fell lower in the sky, then plunged angrily into the water. The colors of the sky would deepen, a fiery orange, then pink, then only a golden veil rippling over the face of the water.

Then night would arrive with its great web of stars which loomed so close, so large, you felt you had only to reach up and catch some in your palm. We would wander around the sur-

---

———) ———

*W*hole days passed without words, empty and desolate. The wind that came seemed uneasy and mysterious. In the hot sun, I could see images of bones and days cracking up before me. I could feel myself changing, slowly changing, pieces falling away, turning to a fine clay dust, like an archeological clay relic exploding in slow motion.

◆

—Irene-Marie Spencer,
"The Old Mill"

rounding dunes collecting branches, bits of desert brush, then we'd light our night fire, sit quietly around it, or drift off on solitary walks across the dunes or down to the rustling water.

I would usually wander down to the water. Leave my *jalabieh* on some rocks and swim beneath the thick net of stars, beneath the strong beam of moonlight lighting the dark pools round my arms, then the parched hills of Saudi Arabia. And what I remember thinking one night, if, in fact, it could be called thinking, that merging of thought and sensation as the moonlight danced around me, illuminating the gills of the water, the mountain crags, the still space, was that I had arrived surely to the edge of my senses, was reeling at the very edge of my senses; that I was floating suspended somewhere between heaven and earth.

It was a week and a half into our stay when we experienced that strange and moonless night. We were beginning to grow aware that soon we would need to go back to Jerusalem. That we would need to reenter our city selves so as to be able to return to what awaited us: schedules, classes, university.

As if in preparation, the friends with whom I was traveling began to grow restless, to take long walks back to the small café at the entry point, to return with tales of other travelers, with food and small treats they had bought. Only I had no desire to do so. I was unwilling to move away from this wonderful silence, this rhythm of the desert that we had entered, that followed unquestioningly the imperatives of survival, the position of the sun in the sky.

The day that ushered in that particularly dark and eerie night had passed like many others. We had swum for hours in the cool waters, hidden from the looming midday sun, gathered branches for the evening fire. The few who had hiked back to the café had returned with fresh water and supplies.

We had spoken briefly about the peculiar lift of the wind, about the wear our "house" had suffered, about how our bright cloths had softened, succumbed slowly to the color of sand.

And then the strange arrival of night. It had approached from the peaks of Saudi Arabia, rumbling with the coming wrath of its god. An odd and ominous night in the way that it had crawled towards us—moved with still purpose towards us, hung there like the pillar of fire that it had once been. Then devoured our arms, our legs, our things; devoured the sand, the waves, the trees.

The friends with whom I was traveling decided suddenly to head back up the coast for the night, in search of food and light, some reminders of "civilization." I offered to stay behind to guard our meager belongings, our little house, our precious tree.

Before they left, they asked me again if I was sure that I didn't want to join them. I was sure. Although it was a little unnerving to see them about to go, I knew that it would be as good as leaving the desert if I went with them, that when we returned it would not be the same.

They gathered themselves up and left. As soon as they had taken a few steps, the night swallowed them, erased them immediately. I could neither hear nor see them. I looked around, but could see nothing. All I could hear was the sound of the sea some distance ahead, its primordial waves rushing and retreating in an invisible line of sound up ahead. I got up and took a few steps. I couldn't see the dunes that I knew were there. I knew their contours only by the way they forced my feet up or down as I crossed their surface. I retraced my steps to our tree and then lay down on the sand, sinking softly and blindly into it. As if to reassure myself of what was still present, I reached for the lines of my body, then ran my hands through the cool night sand and felt a strange exultation as I realized that I was truly alone in the desert—in this vast invisible night desert and it was a black dance, a cauldron of souls.

I remained there for a long while in the most complete darkness I had ever known, my body sculpted into the sand, a night wind dancing across my face. And I knew then that this was the way I wanted to live—that I wanted the courage to live like this. That I wanted to explore all the unknown worlds that lay yet buried at my feet, to unearth their wisdom, to devour their wisdom, until it entered my soul, until it was lodged in my armor, jeweled and light.

This is what I remember thinking when suddenly a fire sprang up—several dunes from where I was lying. A defiant rite, a primordial laugh, it burst suddenly into the impenetrable darkness. What I could see was a cluster of bushes, a house made of wood and brilliantly colored cloths and three men of indeterminate age who had noticed me and were looking in my direction, and who began beckoning me to join them, to come.

It was a strange intimacy that held us for a moment staring at one another across the patch of light that unfurled like a path between us. A strange and unsurpassed intimacy. I took in their long blond hair, their desert robes, their house made of cloth and wood. Then I rose and began walking slowly towards them. The dunes were soft beneath my feet. With every step, I felt the sand recording then erasing my footprints. But as I began to draw closer to them, to approach them where they waited like a crevice, like a footpath, like a wild unknown, when I saw the flames licking at them, illuminating them like ancient shadows, like prophets, like survivors of god, I felt a bit afraid despite myself. They were, I could see now, dark, unfamiliar creatures of the desert to whom language had been lost for years. Who had renounced the world as I had known it but had woken every day for years to the sound of the rushing sea outside the makeshift walls of their house that hung of canvas, that rattled in wood, that held on its skeletal walls a button found, a piece of glass. Language had seeped out of them for years and it had left them muscled, elemental, sparse. Approaching their silent faces that night, I knew that they had lived far too long, seen far too much in this primitive place.

But still I came up to them, to their trailing beards, their sexless skin, their silence and their Bedouin understanding of a world, that once like I, they hadn't known. They were sitting by their fire, cooking tea in a pot black with years of black. Three men with dark skin and distant eyes. German once, Scandinavian perhaps, now citizens of silence, of sand, disciples of a desert god who still visited this land with historic wrath and from whom they hid between great dunes, in makeshift houses, in silent tents.

They received me like the Bedouin would receive a night

traveler, with a cushion and a pot of tea rattling on its bed of sticks. They seemed to have no need to find out who I was; it was as a weary traveler that they received me though they'd seen my nearby bed of sand. They patted some bright cushions around me, they threw more sugar into the tea. They brewed it dark, it smelled strangely sweet and unfamiliar, and then there was a rustling just behind me, and turning—a woman such as I'd never seen—whose body hung with the remnants of centuries, of Arabian trade routes, of harems, of kings. A woman whose eyes were glowing as if in league with the larger usurpation, she had sucked all the light from the universe, hung it about herself like a jewel, then ignited the fire that had swept the dunes, that had fallen about me like the net of a princess wanting play.

She was standing in the doorway of their house that hung of canvas, that rattled in wood, with her eyes commanding a space and the men gently slid over and created a space for her next to me. I was filled with wonder at this strange and beautiful woman, whose wrists and ankles dangled with tiny hammered bells, who was swooping down like a bird next to me, pouring me some thick sweet tea. I could smell fjords left behind, long winters, cold streets and desert all mixed together. We sat drinking the dark sweet tea from tiny chipped porcelain cups, watching the dancing flames of their fire as it consumed the dry desert brush they were burning, that was crackling and sending sparks over the sand. No one spoke. I remember wondering how long they'd been living like this, who they once had been, what lives they would return to if they ever left this nomadic existence. But pretty soon my head began to grow heavy, to grow sweetly tired and heavy, and I closed my eyes on a world that seemed to have stopped and lay my head on someone's lap, I wasn't sure whose lap. Someone's hands came to stroke me gently, as one would putting a child to sleep. They smelled of Vikings, they sounded like the sea, they had a rhythm that was the rhythm of wind. They spoke of nothing. They wanted nothing. Their rhythm felt like the cyclical dreams of the sea.

*

When I woke, the night's thick blackness was lifting like a sub-
stance, growing like a painting out of the sea. I was lying by the last
embers of a fire, a cloth thrown over me, a Bedouin cloth with
brilliant flowers and withered seams. In the doorway of that sand-
swept house that hung in canvas, that rattled in wood, that looked
again like it held no one, knew nothing but the wind shaking it at
its foundations, sat a small Bedouin boy with a beautifully carved
stick in his hand. He was watching me as if he'd been waiting. He
pointed to the weather-beaten shack, now stripped of its bright
cloths, its adornments of trinkets and shells.

"Mine," he said as he continued pointing to the house.

I peered at the house. There was no sign of them. I felt a sudden and inexplicable sadness, as if I might have joined them. As if
I might have had the courage to renounce the life I was supposed
to have and join their wandering from place to place, drape around
me the riches and silence of the desert, live for a while in a soft
valley of dunes, then move on like the Bedouin.

"They go," he said in his rudimentary English. "Mine," he
repeated, pointing again at the house.

"Do you know where they went?" I asked him in English, then
in Hebrew.

No, he shook his head.

"Are they coming back? Might they come back?" I asked, realizing the silliness of my question even as it was escaping my lips.

He smiled and raised his gaze to the sky. *"Inshallah,"* If it is
God's desire, he said.

I smiled at him and began to head back to where our things
were piled, dusty and colorful a few dunes away. When I turned
around for one last look, he was standing in the doorway of the
house, twirling his beautiful stick like an angel at the mysterious
and now empty gate of Eden.

Tehila Lieberman's work has appeared in Salamander, *the* Colorado
Review, Salon Magazine, Literary Latté, *and* Sideshow. *She is a
winner of the* Colorado Review*'s Stanley Elkin Memorial prize for*

fiction and has served on the board of directors of the Writer's Room of Boston. She lives in Cambridge, Massachusetts.

✳

Summer in Crete was blue and silvery-green, rocks and olive groves and sea. An aroma of wild oregano and thyme lingered through the long hot afternoons. Backpacking travelers found easy shelter on the southern beaches and in the coolness of shallow caves. Villagers fed us their fish and olives in nearby *tavernas.*

That was before the wind began. The Etesian blasts into Crete from the north. The Sirocco begins in Egypt and Libya to the south, visiting Crete on its path to Italy. Cretans mention the word *meltemi* and name hotels and cafés after it.

It arrived in the night like a marauding creature, and routed me from my sandy home. Swirling sand stung my skin, parched my throat and blinded me; wailing filled my ears. Palm trees were bent over double to the ground, like rubber bands about to snap. The landscape was drained of all color. All my senses were alert and electric with an instinctive fear of nature I had never known before. We covered our heads like Bedouins and sought shelter in the town.

—Lynn Shirey, "Meltemi"

PART TWO

SOME THINGS TO DO

DENISE M. SPRANGER

Diving the Jungle

In Mexico, two women share their strength.

EVEN IN MAYAN TIMES THERE MUST HAVE BEEN SKEPTICS. ONES who did not succumb to trance. Did not find a convincing correlation between the letting of blood and the appeasement of the gods. In modern times we have similar outcasts. They are usually the ones who find absolutely no thrill in American football. I've always known my true ancestors, whether they be Celts, Sumerians, or ancient Maya. They were those few who hovered at the edge as the flames leaped and the great spirits danced among the living in the sacred frenzy of sacrifice. In the midst of this pure, primal faith, in the current of wisdom that flowed between this world and the next, a silver blade was passed from hand to hand. A gift of blood demanded. In this bold transcendence beyond physical suffering, my ancestors, keeping a sharp eye on the way out, said, "None for me, thanks!" Maybe this is how the tribes determined who would be sacrificed that day.

The morning that I was planning to dive the cenotes of the Yucatan I had to face that I was, perhaps, letting my ancestors down. I would plunge into the dark waters in the jungle a willing victim. Fed by the massive underground river system that veins the Yucatan Peninsula of Mexico, these freshwater pools, or cenotes,

71

provided the ancient Maya with a means of survival and, as they believed, a window to the Under World. Divers began exploring these rivers in the late 1980s, at last finding a link to the sea in 1995. When I learned it was possible to follow a portion of the course they had charted, I knew I must do it. I had to.

New to scuba diving, but practiced in claustrophobia, I was the first to arrive at the dive shop where I would meet the priest of all diving rituals, the dive master. Trying to appear casual, I paced between the racks of neon colored wetsuits, masks, and assorted paraphernalia as I plied the woman at the counter about two things: light and space. One should really not expect to find much of either in an underwater cavern, but one can hope. Just as I was contemplating a more relaxing career in sky diving, the dive master entered the room with the five others in our group.

Our leader, Luis, was a small man, a Mexican whose compact frame seemed perfect for negotiating narrow and hazardous spaces. Around his shoulders bright yellow hoses were coiled. Hooked to his belt were several flashlights, varying in size and shape. For all his commando appearance, he smiled easily as he shook our hands and introduced himself. He had the manner of one who was eager for a stirring game of volleyball more than the experienced cave diver who would guide us through the perils of watery canyons. I suspected that this was a practiced attempt to calm the less certain. While he gathered our gear, we shuffled our feet, feigning confidence. The men did this by telling war stories from a litany of previous dives. Shipwrecks, unpredictable currents, the inevitable sharks, and treacheries of faulty equipment. Marta, a German woman, kept quiet as her boyfriend, Joseph, compared the specs of his dive computer with the ones in the glass case. Like myself, Marta had begun diving only several months before. She lifted her long red hair and applied sunscreen to the freckled skin of her neck.

As we helped Luis load tanks into the back of the van, he discussed the logistics of our dive. From this I learned one unwelcome fact. I had wrongly assumed that cavern diving was defined by the presence of an overhead airspace. This is not the case. A "cavern" merely promises a visible light source either behind or in front of you, thereby denoting an exit route, however distant that might be. If you were to turn a corner and have that light blocked, it would then become a "cave," requiring special certification to dive. While I was practically giddy about the existence of light sources, I was a bit squeamish about the absence of that nice cushy layer of air over my head. I hadn't realized that the tunnels connecting the cenotes are completely submerged. I suddenly regretted scoffing at that wise and lovely game of golf. Wistfully, I considered those green, wide open lawns in the full light of sunshine.

As the van bumped along the jungle back roads, I remembered the first time I had ever seen a cenote. I was twenty years old and traveling with friends through southern Mexico. While visiting the temples at Chichen Itza, we took the dirt path to the cenote, referred to by archeologists as the "cenote of sacrifice." Dredging its deep bottom they had found the skeletons of children.

From what they can surmise, young boys were sacrificed to the gods in a prayer for rain. They discovered the vests made of jade that the boys wore as they stepped from the high wall that enclosed the deep, clear water. There was something ominous, yet inviting, in the emerald surface gleaming in the heat. The Maya had believed that these boys hadn't died but had traveled to another world through this opening. As I stared into the sacred waters, I offered my own prayer that they were right.

Laboring over the rutted road, the driver slowed, then swung the tires through a break in the trees. Dust flew as we came to a halt in a rocky clearing; Luis jumped out and beckoned us to follow him. Stone steps wound down a hidden hillside in an overgrown glade. As our eyes grew accustomed to the light we could make out an immense shelf of rock lined at its base with a thin blue pool of water, barely twelve feet across. Small black catfish swam through the rocks that shaped its edge. Vines hung from the boulders above, their leaves just grazing the water. Here the cool air wrapped the skin in moss, filled the nostrils with the scent of a secret.

Luis pointed to the blackness that rested in the shadows beneath the looming rock. "That is where we will go," he said. "We will follow that yellow rope, can you see it? It will lead us to another cenote. There we will ascend in a cavern, and beyond that, another." I peered into the still water until I could make out a line of yellow disappearing into an inky darkness. A darkness not of absence, but presence. Sentient. Articulate. Aware. My rib cage constricted. Cold and smooth against my chest and back, I felt it. The garment of terror; the jade vest.

I looked up to see everyone lugging the equipment down the path. Like a captive enslaved by the will of others, I joined them. In a few short minutes our gear stood ready on the rocks. Desperate as a politician on the eve of an election, I practiced my speech. "No, I'm terribly sorry. Really, I am. I'll pay for it anyway. Of course. But I can't do this." Already I could see myself curled up in the van as I awaited their return. A dry, pathetic ball of cowardice sweating on a vinyl seat less than fifty steps from one of the great wonders of the world. But alive, yes, and breathing.

While some dangers afford the luxury of a minute or two before the onset of panic, mammals tend to react almost instantly to the loss of air. My first diving instructor told me that you have about ten seconds to make one decision: maintain control. Any other choice will send you bolting to the surface, an instinct which may prove fatal.

As flashlights were passed around and fin straps buckled, I saw my ten seconds slip into the gaping hole under the rock with tidal force. I

> ———)———
>
> The Tlingits tell the migration story of the Killer Whale Clan, Duxawadey. As the clan moved south down the Stikine River from Alaska's interior, it encountered a glacier which blocked its way. Two brave women asked permission of the clan leader to explore a route beneath the glacier. Granted permission, they made a raft of tree branches covered with swans' down, and on this raft they floated under the glacier to emerge safe on the other side.
>
> ◆
>
> —Sheila Nickerson,
> *Disappearance—A Map:*
> *A Meditation on Death and Loss*
> *in the High Latitudes*

could no more control them than I could mop up the flood of eternity with a paper towel. I steeled myself to present my speech. I would not risk the life of the dive master who would be burdened with trying to save me. I would not infect the others with the virulent disease of panic.

Luis was breaking the group into two teams; it was unsafe to lead more than four of us at a time. Before I could stammer my regretful apology, Marta spoke. "Perhaps the rest of you should go together," she said, "Joseph and I can go alone with Luis. I may have to turn back. I don't think I can do this."

I sensed that I was not the only one who admired her courage. It takes a lot of guts to admit you're afraid, to stand in the full view of strangers with your own naked limitations. Though the others grew quiet, a tension lifted; postures relaxed. The secret was out: we were human. In one long breath, I exhaled my fear. My ten seconds rushed back to me.

I looked Marta in the eye. "Let's dive together," I said. "I'm a new diver too. I'm completely claustrophobic. But we can do this. We'll concentrate on the light. If either of us needs to go back, we will. No pressure."

She looked at me for a long moment and the decision was in her eyes before she spoke. "All right," she said, "we'll do it." Her boyfriend chose to dive with the other men, trying his best not to appear anxious to do so. Having conquered all those shipwrecks and sharks, "turning back" was no longer an option. Mumbling something about "ladies first," they offered us the first dive into the cavern. I thought it an odd take on chivalry, but we agreed.

So it was that Marta and I descended into the cool water and followed Luis into the midnight that sleeps deeply in the earth beneath the day. Without currents to oppose us, we slipped effortlessly through liquid darkness. Floating downward toward the sparkle of the light that Luis shone, the cavern revealed itself. Immense. Glacial. Prehistoric. As if in candlelight, the cathedral of the Under World.

Luis directed an arc of light upon the walls. Gaping cracks grinned with the jagged teeth of stalactites. Forms, improbable, defying gravity, jutted, arched, soared. Lances of stone sprung from the floor. Poised in a kinetic stillness, even the walls gave evidence of motion. Perhaps our minds were too urgent, our lives too brief. The pace of the millennia eluded us.

Drifting through this twisted geometry, I was alarmed to see up ahead two leaning columns of fluorescent blue. It took me several moments to realize that they must be made of sunlight. Streaming from two holes in the roof of the cavern, fantastic blue rays pierced the water, brilliant and sharp as blown glass.

I checked below me for the yellow rope. It veered from boulder to boulder as it bent to meet the angles of the walls. I glanced over my shoulder to see the beginning of our journey; there, suspended in the distance, a shining opal of light. It was there that we had descended. From another world, another lifetime.

Between the luminous shafts of cobalt we made our ascent into the first cavern. Passing from the deeper saltwater into the layer of freshwater, a strange phenomenon occurred. The room above us appeared to be draped in a translucent membrane. An oily skin lay between us and the bowl of air at the ceiling. It was as if we were inside a vast impermeable bubble looking into another. "A trick of the light," I told myself, struggling with the overwhelming sense of confinement in this shrouded cocoon. I turned to Marta and saw that her widened eyes mirrored mine.

My face broke the surface just after Luis. His dripping hair plastered to the sides of his forehead, he pulled the mouthpiece from his lips.

"What do you think, *señorita*?" he asked.

"My God," was all I could utter.

Marta emerged beside me; I saw her searching for the same thing I had. Yet our bubble had vanished; it did not exist. I noticed Luis smiling. Our blue columns had also disappeared, dissolved into the saffron light leaking through the ceiling.

As we bobbed in the circles of light, Luis pointed up to the birds which flitted through the openings and alighted on the delicate brows of limestone. "See them," he said, "they are the owners of this place." Molested by no other living creature here, they came to drink, to nest.

We descended once more to continue our dive; the next cavern was filled with bats, not birds. They clung, inverted gargoyles, from the tips of drooping stone. Beginning to feel the cold now, our faces shivered above the water. Luis assured us that we were only minutes from the entrance. In the maze of stone, darkness, and light, I hadn't noticed that the yellow rope had looped back upon itself. We sank slowly to a broad shoulder of stone; light filtered below as if under a threshold. Luis gestured expansively for me to precede him; I dove under rock and was born into light. The silhouettes of the four men who waited for us shimmered in the brightness.

The men followed Luis into the cavern; it was now our turn to wait. Marta and I rested on the curve of boulders as the vines swayed in the breeze. She was concerned about Joseph; she could tell he was nervous. "He left his flashlight," she said, "and he was fidgeting with the buckles of his gear."

"He didn't mention any anxiety," I offered, hoping to comfort her.

"No, of course not," she said, "he would never mention such a thing."

We discussed our experience in the cavern; each of us grateful for the strength that the other had inspired. We marveled at the mercurial proportions of time; our dive had lasted just 40 minutes. Yet before long we fell into small talk, yielding to a keen thirst for the superficial. As we laughed over such vital matters as how unfairly red hair turns to gray, it dawned upon me that this, too, was a tradition of the cenotes. While the mysteries of ritual and death intrigued us, the richest gift of these pools was that of life.

On ordinary days the women would come to fill their clay pots with water. As their children splashed in the shallows, they might have lingered. Sometimes, they surely laughed. They may have even seen the birds rising, as I did now, from the ceilings of buried caverns cloaked in leaves.

My spiritual ancestors preferred those days, free from ceremonies heralding the mutilation of kings or the drowning of princes. When the only sacrifices required contained a simple glory: the taste of clear water that they carried to the village. Or sharing sunlight, fresh as mango, in the sweet relinquishment of fear.

Denise M. Spranger is a writer and painter living on the high desert that surrounds Taos, New Mexico. Scuba diving being difficult to practice in the desert, she finds herself traveling often to far and exotic places.

✳

Underwater, the wind doesn't whistle. Scuba bubbles are the loudest things you hear. Sunlight filters down onto—no—the sunlight goes away. A cloud? An errant ocean liner? You look up. You stop. There's no way to take it all in. It goes from the bottom to the surface; it's thirty, forty feet high. Wait. It's moving. It's alive. It's...it's...fish.

An enormous school of fish, scad to be exact. A single scad is silvery, about six inches long. Fifteen thousand scad are an undulating solid wall, moving through the water like a slow-motion whip. You float not ten inches from it and the wall flows past. One kick and you're inside, swallowed up, absorbed, no right or left or up or down. Just fish.

—Daisy Scott, "Immersed"

CAROL DROGE CLARK

✦ ✦ ✦

Hang Gliding Big Sur

Three thousand feet is
a long way down.

I HAD PREPARED WELL FOR MY FIRST HIGH–ALTITUDE HANG gliding flight at Big Sur. I'd trekked my glider up the side of the sand dune training hill at Marin County's Dillon Beach for count-less take-offs and landings, gradually working my way up over six months to the 200-foot summit. Then I learned to negotiate traf-fic 100 feet above Fort Funston, on the San Francisco coast, where I made graceful 180 degree turns to soar the ridge lift along the cliff's edge. In those days, there was a large group of pilots who went away almost every weekend to mountain sites to fly, so I went along as a driver on several trips to watch and learn before I did it myself. The launches at Big Sur, the current choice for first high-altitude flights, were about 3,000 feet above sea level. This would be a major step up from my previous flying experiences, even in Big Sur's standard "glass" air where there wasn't a bump in the sky. It was still mighty high off the ground.

I learned to read the wind conditions on those trips. The senior pilot would usually make the call and act as wind dummy unless some red hot decided to fling himself off the hill first. We'd all watch the birds—the real experts. If they were getting trashed out in front of launch, we knew that it was pretty rotory and that, in fact, the wind was coming from the backside instead of straight up the front as it appeared to be. Tricky stuff, wind.

Big Sur. This was my rite-of-passage flight. As familiar as I was by then with the area, I'd been terrified on the last part of the four-hour drive down from San Francisco. Palms sweaty, making the steering wheel slippery, I'd distracted myself by looking at the incredible coastline stretched out before me. Negotiating the curves helped distract me, too. Driving was like flying. It was all balance.

California's Highway 1 coastline has always seemed like a big sheet cake on which the Creator carved out little points, curves and swirls. The Pacific Ocean rushes up to the short cliffs, usually leaving no beach at all. In some areas, the surf hits a partially submerged rock and sprays up suddenly, sparkly white against the greenish blue of the water. Pristine. Unspoiled. I love the way the west side of the highway flattens out into mesas, contrasting sharply with the 3,000 foot mountains on the east side.

I finally arrived at the landing site in Pacific Valley. No gliders. No hang gliding trucks. Everyone was on top already. The landing area windsocks were blowing slightly from the west. Good direction. I took the steep, curvy dirt road up the mountain, getting vertigo at some of the sharp dropoffs. Funny how I could have a pronounced fear of heights and still love being in the air.

The drive to the top takes nearly an hour as it winds through areas where the trees have canopied over the road, their leaves dappling the ground with shadows, past peaceful meadows, then up on the ridge for glimpses of the ocean and the fog-banked horizon. And massive potholes all along the way that required careful negotiation.

I stopped at Plaskett, my favorite because of its steep launch. After parking the truck behind the others, I shouldered my glider and harness bag for the short walk. Weegie and Wally and a dozen other pilots were already at launch, feeling the wind and reading the conditions. Hugs all around. Weegie tucked a coppery curl behind her ear and gave me a visual check to see if I was okay. I smiled at her with more confidence than I felt.

"Ready?" My old friend smiled back at me.

"Yup." I gave her a brave smile.

"Let's get set up, then." I found a spot to assemble the glider that would put me in the second or third position and then stood at launch for a moment, palms out, feeling the breeze ruffle my long dark hair and tingle my hands. Turning my face slightly left and right, I could feel the exact place where the wind hit me full on, and determined for myself that it was coming out of the west from up here, too. Lightly. That required a good strong launch. I centered myself and visualized my flight path before going back to attend to the matter of setting up the craft that would get me from here to there.

"Lookin' good," I thought to myself as I went around the assembled glider, checking connections, sighting down each leading edge, sliding my hands along the tubing to see if any dents had mysteriously grown there, pulling on the hang strap. I attached my variometer to the left downtube so I'd be able to tune into any lift or sink on the flight, and set my wrist altimeter to 3,000 feet above sea level.

"Weegie? Do a preflight for me?" She had just finished setting up her glider, too, so I wandered over to her.

"Sure. Hey, are you okay? You're awfully quiet."

"Sure," I grinned. "Should I be nervous? This is just three grand. Piece o' cake. It's not Mount Everest." Weegie gave me one of her looks and we both laughed.

"Want me to do yours while you do mine?"

"Sure."

Five minutes later, we'd each assured the other that our gliders wouldn't fall apart in the air, we'd given each other hang checks just to make sure the clearance over the bar was adequate, and we were standing at launch again, arms laced over each other's shoulders, checking the conditions.

"Still looks good."

"Yeah. It'll be a glass ride, but that's good for a first time."

"Yup."

"Ready for a good run off the hill?"

"Just about. I want to see at least one wind dummy go off first, though." Just as I said that, Wally started carrying his glider toward us.

"Speak of the devil."

> ——— ☽ ———
>
> elow, the town of Mont-Saint-Pierre resembled a toy village, tiny cars glinting in the sun and people going about their business on terra firma. And down, straight down, was the bare gray and white rock of the mountain.
>
> Not me. I backed away from the precipice. "Paul, I don't know if I can do this," I whispered to my husband, who was trying to conceal his horror at the thought of me hang gliding.
>
> "I wouldn't do it," he said.
>
> "Do you think I'm crazy?"
>
> "Well, I just wouldn't do it," he reiterated.
>
> ◆
>
> —Jill Schensul, "Flying Like an Eagle—OK, Well, Maybe a Chicken," *The Bergen Record*

"Thought I'd show you one more time how it's done." Wally grinned, then looked at me and said, "You'll be fine. You know what to do. You're ready for this. So do it and have a good time."

I held the nose of his glider while he did a hang check, then got out of the way quickly because I knew he wasn't one of those who dawdled at launch. Sure enough, he yelled "Clear!" glanced at me to make sure I was behind the wing, and then started running down the slope. One, five, seven steps to get off. Good launch! We cheered as we watched the glider lift from the take-off speed. He headed out without further lift and in a few minutes was a dot over the ridge to the left.

I took a deep breath, put on my helmet, flipped on the vario, hooked my harness to the carabiner, and did a hang check while Weegie held the nose. I stood up with my hands wrapped around the downtubes and picked up the glider.

"Have a good time, sweetie," Weegie said. She moved behind the glider and I waited a moment for the wind to shoot up a little stronger. I wanted all the help I could get. My launches were pretty clean, but a no-wind launch means little room for error—the less wind there is, the longer and faster you have to run to lift off. And if the wings aren't level when you're running, arrrgggghhhhhh—a spin back into the hill, or worse. I took a couple of slow, deep yogic breaths, steadied the glider, pointed its nose at the appropriate angle for takeoff, and ran my tail off down the slope. My feet were still moving even after I was airborne. It was a good one.

I was in the air! My heart did a little dance of joy as I felt the glider rise from the takeoff speed. I headed out toward the ridge on my left, cutting over the top of the dead tree, and felt the glider lift slightly with the resident thermal there. This was a new sensation. Funston ridge lift was smooth, consistent, usually not a bump in the sky. My variometer beeped to let me know what my body already knew. I was going up! I turned my head to look up at my wings and then back to see the little knot of pilots watching me. What a glorious feeling to be in the air with the warm wind on my face, free as a bird.

I was coming up on the ridge now. It ran east to west, ending just before Highway 1, brown this time of year with some oak trees dotting it. I shifted my weight and turned right when I hit the center of the ridge and flew along it. The vario started going off again. I had expected a little lift here, but the vario continued to beep and I continued to climb. Strange. This didn't feel like a thermal. I glanced out at the ocean, which had been smooth and flat when I had launched. It was now covered with whitecaps. Uh oh. High winds. I knew about those—and about the rotors they produced on the landing plateau. Another pilot, an experienced one, had broken her jaw the previous year coming in through the rotor, hard. My stomach knotted. Now what?

I was still climbing. I looked at my altimeter and found that I was almost at 3,000 feet again. What in the world am I doing up here? I thought. My stomach knotted. I looked at the windsock in the landing area. The cone of bright orange nylon was sticking straight out, indicating wind out of the north-northwest. Wally's glider was in the landing area, tucked up against the fence next to the parking lot, not yet disassembled. Apparently the wind had come up suddenly, as it sometimes did.

My mind was working at warp speed, reviewing my choices. I knew I couldn't land on the regular spot next to the windsock. That was rotor territory for sure. Tuck it in close to the fence? Risk getting rotored anyway, coming down through the trashy air?

The beach. The beach was my only alternative. Fortunately, it was low tide. The beach below the landing area was small, but doable, I thought. I'd had to do spot landings for each of my three hang ratings, so I was fairly confident that I could put it where it needed to go. Maybe. This was a new site for me, I cautioned myself. And the beach was awfully small. No point in getting cocky or whining, psyching yourself out even more, I thought. Might as well just *do* it.

I pulled the glider's nose down and started descending a little while I picked up speed. I reached over and turned the vario off. I was at the end of the ridge now, about to cross the highway. When I crossed it, I felt the marine layer against my skin. Cool with a little wispy fog mixed in. Little droplets of moisture. It felt good against my forearms although it made me shiver. I kept the glider straight and level, and flew through some major air bumps over the landing area plateau to the cliff edge. Lord, that beach was small. Well, I'm committed now, I thought. No turning back. No broken jaw for me. I flew out to the point and looked down at an indentation in the rock. I could see water surging into it from the side and then a miniature geyser erupted out of the indentation just as I flew over. That's a good sign, I hoped.

I was still too high to start the final turn. I'd overshoot and land in the drink if I did, so I did 180s back and forth from the rock to the edge of the beach for awhile until my sense told me it was okay to make the long approach. I came in fast then, pulling in the control bar, cutting through the bumps in the air, and before I knew it, my toes had touched down. Safe. Safe. SAFE!

Tears sprang to my eyes. I was so grateful that I hadn't hurt myself on that landing. Hadn't thumped it in at Funston like Lee

Sterios. Hadn't overshot into the ocean at Pacifica and drowned like Jim Geiger. I was alive. Safe!

I unclipped from my glider and then turned it tail into the wind. I was shaking from all the adrenaline and felt like I had to throw up. Instead, I sat down on the sand and cried. A big wail followed by a long sob was drowned out by the wind, thankfully, because by then Wally and some spectators had reached the cliff edge and were coming down to see if I was okay. I collected myself quickly. Didn't want them to see me act like a sissy girl, I had thought, and greeted them with a smile.

"Piece o' cake," I said. They all laughed, knowing how traumatic coming in for a landing must have been. Wally gave me a lopsided grin.

Later, around the campfire, we all traded stories about the scariest flights we'd had. They had witnessed mine: My first high-altitude flight off Big Sur.

Carol Droge Clark is an adventurer and outdoor enthusiast, a hang glider pilot and instructor (retired), and owner of Winged Adventure, an importer of native crafts and folk art from Latin America. An author of fiction, nonfiction, and poetry, she lives in Northern California. She would like to dedicate this story to Michael.

✳

I have been taking blind leaps all my life, metaphorically, less often literally, but as I ascended the bungee jump bridge, I could find no metaphor for the sheer silliness of what I was about to do.

Two young travelers queued up ahead of me, returnees from the day before who hadn't gotten up the nerve to jump. Pale with panic they clasped each other's hands, mumbled mantras, and finally plunged into the abyss, thrashing and wriggling like caught fish on a line. Then it was my turn. I mustered dignity. As two hulking Kiwis secured the bungee cord to my ankles, I forced myself to breathe deeply, aware suddenly of the pit of my stomach.

Fun, this had ceased to be.

I positioned myself at the edge of the plank and leveled my gaze on the horizon. I willed my body steady. Why the hell I was about to hurl myself off a 230-foot-high bridge, I couldn't have said in that moment, having already gone mute from the lips inward.

Clench-jawed, I lined up my feet, took one more greedy breath, and jumped.

My flight was brief, a split second letting-go of everything that bound me to the Earth: gravity, mass, caution...tomorrow. Disembodied, I soared through the molecular confetti of my being into a fantasy landscape of streaks and swirls. Unseen angels called my name. I remembered the taste of fingerpaint.

Then—boing!—the cord snapped me back, straining every bone joint, whipping hair into my gaping mouth. Laughter—my own or someone else's? Scrubby riverbanks, dribs and drabs of cloud a blur around me as I bobbed, spun, and finally dangled upside down by my ankles. Slowly the riverbed came back into focus. Hands reached up to ease me down into a world transformed: rocky where the sky had once been, blue along the bottom. It was all new, all waiting, and I was swinging low on my elastic lifeline, eager to begin again.

—Germaine W. Shames, "World's Highest Bungee Jump"

SARA FRASER

The Catch

Fishing alone off Ireland's coast,
a young woman confronts
her hunter's instincts.

THE OCEAN THAT LICKS THE SHORES OF CONNEMARA IS RESTFUL. The row of bars and restaurants that huddle at the hem of the hills, casting their gaze across the lane, over the stone wall, and onto Roundstone Harbour, have their windows and doors open. There is a slight breeze that caresses my skin. It has just enough enthusiasm to lift the very ends of my hair from my shoulders, twist them a little and then release them; the wind is exhausted and lies in wait for something over the ocean, to the west, to fortify its vitality. Maybe tomorrow it will again lift my hair from the roots, shake my clothing, course beneath the fabric of my sleeves to try to freeze me or drive me back indoors. But not today. Today I am going fishing.

I have never caught a fish before, although I have gone fishing. I used to spend long unemployed afternoons resting a pole against the railing of a pier near Malibu. Once I got a bite, and a couple of the retired men who also spent their days there had to drop tuna sandwiches and fishing poles and run to my aid. I made a half-crow, half-cow squawking and moaning noise as the pole flew this way and that in my white-tense hands. The men were too late to help. I breathed a sigh of relief as the fish got away and I was left

87

giggling in the half-crazed way of someone who realizes that she has just made a fool of herself and is trying to make light of her embarrassment. The men retreated back to their sandwiches, disappointing the seagulls who had been inching towards them, and I decided to spend the rest of the day reading Want Ads.

But I remember the rush of the tensed line. After days of having the glimmer of excitement extinguished by the sight of a bush of seaweed or a plastic bag attached to my hook, the dread and the thrill of being connected to a living thing by a filament of plastic wire was unforgettable. Me, in the sun, part of the sky. The fish, madly wrestling the foreign object lodged in its mouth. The battle within me, between pure good and pure evil, between the thrill of murder and a retreat in pacifism, would have seemed ridiculous to the men with their buckets of fish and coolers of beer. They and I were there to relax and catch fish. Whoever was lucky would bring home dinner, gutted and plopped into a bucket. I loved the days of waiting for a bite. I loved the apprehension, the possibility, but I didn't want to have to kill anything. With hindsight's ability to let the air out of distended notions, I realize that the battle inside me wasn't really so severe. For I don't believe that actually catching a fish would constitute evil, or even selfishness. I tell myself now, as then, that I was fishing because I needed to eat. That it is more humane to catch a fish and eat it than it is to buy the thing shrink-wrapped from the top of a pile of shaved ice at the grocery store.

The boat is waiting at Roundstone Pier. I try to look like I know what I'm doing for the benefit of the watching buildings, the vacationing couples who are eating fried food at tables outside of them. I drop rod, tackle bag, and myself into the boat and untie it. I have promised to make a fish pate for my hosts on the island of Inishnee. I am more challenged than they know by the prospect of catching the fish myself.

The sun is about two inches from the tops of the hills when I start the motor and maneuver this squeaking indentation out over the blue skin of the harbor. The light is an infusion of squash soup and curried onions by the time I get to the middle, and it smells like purple salt. Soon the shadow that darkens the hills to the west will reach me. And the small village of Roundstone, the last hold-out of reddening light, will give up the fight and surrender to darkness as well. I can no longer hear the gravelly voices of the men who have begun to enjoy the evening with a pint at the sea wall. Soon the first of the young people will arrive, clustering in the lane, showing off their tans in white cotton sweaters and faded jeans. They will pour their voices into the air, watch each car as it creeps past, lean in the window of the driver's side, negotiate times to meet in which bar. I can only imagine it, remember it from previous nights. I can no longer make out the people by the sea wall or the couples at tables on restaurant porches; they are silent specks. I can see hills to the west. Hills to the east and ocean to the north. I cut the motor and can hear only air, pausing to rustle in my ear, examine my neck. Small hills of sea rock me slightly back and forth. I don't have to cast vary far; the water burps delicately as it swallows the end of the line.

The little boat leaks slowly and has to be bailed out every once in a while. The line lives in both worlds, an explorer of the mysteries of underwater; it tempts calmly with a series of colored feathers, returns to report back. Nothing yet. What I am expecting is mackerel. Small fish, nothing overpowering. The harbor is reportedly overflowing with them. They are supposed to jump into the boat, commit hara-kiri and throw themselves into a bucket. I hope this is true; I am not looking forward to killing them.

The boat has drifted close to the western shore, and I can hear something. Hail stones or hands clapping. It is

> "*F*ishing is flexibility," Flor calmly remarked. "You flow, you drift, you troll, you go in circles, you rock, you yield to the currents. Fishing is a feeling, no matter what country you're in. In fact," she added, "fishers are people without a country. They belong to whatever body of water supports them."
>
> ◆
>
> —Brenda Peterson, "With Fish and Friends," *Sierra*

fish. They are jumping close to the rocks. It seems that they must be doing this out of pure glee. They are an infestation, a school-yard at recess. I am mesmerized by their activity when I feel the tug on the line. My hands tighten instinctively on the handle. I am Ahab and have caught sight of Moby Dick. My stomach clenches, my throat closes. I am a warrior at the moment when the first of the enemy troops is seen advancing through the canyon by the lookout. I have just lifted the card under the queen to reveal an ace. I have been told something about my future, and about the essence of the soul of the earth. Something I suspected is proven true. My head is clear and focused, I know what I have to do. My fears of dropping the rod into the ocean, of falling overboard in confusion and apprehension are suddenly forgotten and ridiculous. They are from a different age. I reel in the fish.

I am hoping for two or three, because that is plenty. There are five. They are frantic, the line is bounding between them like a jumprope. They are sliding all over in the water at the bottom of the boat. I have no time to bail it out. My calm is gone and I am as afraid of them as they are of me. All I can think of is that they can't breathe, and that they have hooks stuck in their cheeks. I can barely breathe. My fear is unreasonable, like the fear of a pet-store mouse, loose in the kitchen, or of under-the-bed when the lights are out. I am making noises of fear, wishing it all were over. The power of excitement has turned to wholehearted regret. If only they would stop jumping. If they would just relax. Okay, I breathe, okay.

I take one, hold it tightly around the middle, my fingers hold-ing the head still while I carefully remove the hook. The fish is the size of a telephone receiver. It slides out of my hand and back to the bottom of the boat; I jerk back, catch my breath. There is blood now mixed with the water, and the fish is still heaving itself back and forth, its tail flapping. The others have calmed down. Maybe they have surrendered, maybe they are breathing well enough in the slowly leaking, bloody boat bottom. The first one has slid far away and I grab another, remove the hook, throw it back and it slides into the water like a diver.

I throw another back and keep three. Before I kill each one, I look at its eyes and tell it I'm sorry. That I hope there is life after death; that I hope it will fare better next time. I have to smash its head. But I tell myself it is the natural order of things. I am sure that when I pick up each fish, there is fear in its eyes. Either it is trembling or I am. The violence of the act is absolute. But when they are dead, the guilt, the shame, the fear, the anxiety, all disappear. They are like any other fish that you might buy in the supermarket. Just a resemblance of

> ──── ☽ ────
>
> *I* take fish personally, the way I have my life, like a sacrament. This is my body. Eat of it. This my blood. Drink. I imagine this reverence is what they want of me.
>
> ♦
>
> —Lorian Hemingway, "Walk on Water for Me," *The Gift of Trout* edited by Ted Leeson

their former life. Except that I was there in the interval, I killed them. The playground of fish are still jumping. They don't know yet, or don't mind, about the loss of these three. Or maybe there is a small vigil at the bottom. I yell an apology to the flapping noises and start the engine. Either through real insight or through psychological survival equipment, I think that I am forgiven, that I have taken my place in the natural world. That I am a predator, but not a greedy one. I have been given a gift, and it will sustain me.

The three fish are quiet in a plastic bag as I return from the hunt through the clear darkening air. The motor sneezes me east to Roundstone as I scoop up water in a plastic cup and pour it over the side. Stars switch on, one at a time. People are drinking pints, laughing, talking. My hosts are coming to meet me from the bar across the road, have bought me a black pint of Guinness with an oatmeal froth.

I smile and wonder if they can see the change in me. I have killed. The knowledge will become a location within me, a small bit of a tiny person beside the sea. The rod is at the bottom of the boat, the line is tangled around my feet that are housed in big, borrowed Wellingtons. The salt is in my nostrils. I wipe scales on my jeans and face the breeze as the boat bucks at the side of the dock.

Sara Fraser lives and eats fish in Somerville, Massachusetts. She hasn't touched a cow or a chicken in ten years.

★

Like me, the boat had been on its way home, the outbound part of its journey spent. The first hour out of Palm Beach had been a rush—fighting waves which blocked our exit from the harbor, snagging a few sharp bites, collectively "oooohing" the spectacular low arc made by a king mackerel on the horizon.

Now two hours out, our lines hung limply on the rapidly warming surface of the late winter Atlantic. My husband of thirty years and I settled into our familiar pattern of accommodation, accepting as inevitable this time of quiet rods and slowly dissolving expectations.

Then the fish hit my line.

"Play it out, ma'am" the young helper breathed at my side, as the fish streaked for the open sea. Using all the skills I'd picked up mothering teenage sons, I gave this fish its lead. Then, feeling resistance drain, I lifted the tip of the rod high and reeled in furiously. For twenty minutes, I gained precious yards, only to give them back in the sailfish's next run for independence.

Despite muscles that burned, my hands held tight and cranked the reel like life itself. "Jump, just jump," I whispered in a kind of prayer I was sure only it could hear. Suddenly, not ten feet off the back of the boat, a slender eight-foot column of fish sailed into the sky, twisted once, and dropped soundlessly back into the sea. Its only wake was the one now planted indelibly in my mind.

As we cut the line, the helper turned, clapped me on the shoulder, and announced, "You're a bill fisher now."

I thought of all the transitions that had passed beneath my boat these last fifty years—daughter to mother, bride to corporate wife, teacher to trainer, size 10 to full-figured. Out a middle aged woman; back a bill fisher. I'll take it. It feels good, and there are still lots more fish out there.

—Judith M. Huge, "The Middle-Aged Woman and the Sea"

LESLEY HAZLETON

⋆ ⋆ ⋆

No Road? No Problem

*Off-road driving demands more
finesse than machismo.*

THE SCENE IS EVERY ENVIRONMENTALIST'S NIGHTMARE. AT THE edge of the Anza-Borrego Desert State Park, east of San Diego, a section has been set aside for off-roading. A veritable Mad Max collection of wheeled machines tears up the terrain here—every driver a Road Warrior with a Gibson-Schwarzenegger-Stallone movie playing in his head.

The vehicles are giant-tired internal-combustion fantasies. The exhaust pipes and air intakes look as if they're on steroids. Many of the machines seem pirated from parts of other vehicles, and most of them are painted in either Day-Glo colors or Darth Vader black. The favored accessory is a skull-and-crossbones pennant flying from a mast.

The drivers live up to the stereotype of off-roading with a joyful defiance, and then some. So I was prepared for the worst this summer when I joined a small group of off-roaders on the famed Rubicon Trail. A 26-mile stretch over the High Sierras, the Rubicon is the granddaddy of all dedicated off-road trails, the ten in difficulty on the scale against which all others are measured, and the one you are warned never, ever, to attempt in one vehicle traveling by itself.

So why was I there? Bragging rights, I suspect. A touch of female machismo. But above all, the assurance that the trail wound through stunningly beautiful country. If things got too Mad Maxish, it would be a pleasure to just get out and walk.

We drove up from Lake Tahoe early in the morning, a convoy of ten Jeep Wranglers ready to drive the toughest 9-mile section of the trail into Rubicon Springs. At Loon Lake, about 8 miles west of Lake Tahoe, we met up with our guide, Mark Smith. He is a founder of Jeep Jamboree, which arranges off-road gatherings, and the gray-haired guru of off-roading. With Mark was his grand-daughter, Sadie. Delicate and shy, just seventeen years old, she seemed far too innocent for this sort of thing. But Sadie, Mark announced, would be driving the lead vehicle. The men around me went quiet. Farewell all thought of testosterone excesses. Sadie Smith's very presence was a perfect rebuttal of machismo. And my, could she handle a Jeep.

Ahead of us, her vehicle seemed to have the grace and ability of a mountain goat, while we sweated in terror at the very idea of negotiating what reason said was an impassable trail, and what the eye often said was no trail at all. If I hadn't just seen her drive up what looked like a vertical stab of rock and disappear from view, I'd have sworn it couldn't be done.

But we learned. In low gear with four-wheel-drive engaged, we let the vehicles creep over boulders, through streams, up and down intimidating inclines. And we did so at an average of exactly one mile an hour.

It was a perfect reversal of all my expectations. Forget speed, forget time. Get hung up on power, and you'd find yourself "high centered" on a boulder, with the wheels off the ground and no way to move without a tow rope. Just the gentlest pressure on the gas pedal here and there was enough.

So it was quiet. There were no engines being gunned, just the occasional groan of brakes or grating of the skidplate on the Jeeps' underside against rock—and as the day went on and we became more skilled, not even that. And one mile an hour was the perfect speed for this high mountain desert rimmed by snowcapped peaks, where pines grew up through glacier-smoothed granite, manzanita flowered in the cracks, and mountain lakes offered dark water velvety with minerals for sun-hot travelers.

It was dark when we pulled into Rubicon Springs, where the Rubicon River runs cold and fast in a series of falls and pools, so I was up before dawn, exploring. The rising sun found me a half-mile or so from camp, perched on a good rock in the middle of a waterfall, thanking the sheer good fortune that had brought me here despite myself.

All the moralizing about sport-utilities and their use and abuse—about irresponsible off-roading or boomers' status-seeking—fell into irrelevance. The Jeeps, I reflected, are modern American versions of beasts of burden. Like mules and camels, Llamas and yaks, they carry more than humans can, and go farther than human legs. They'd brought me into this hidden valley, and they'd bring me out again. At that moment, in that place, it was that simple.

But there was still an element of the absurd: I could have walked the Rubicon Trail in a third of the time it took to drive it. It wasn't until a month or so later, at the other end of the West Coast's mountain chain, that off-roading finally made sense.

I was in Alaska's Kenai Peninsula, driving a Ford Explorer with three passengers and no fixed itinerary. At least there had been one, more or less, until we spotted what looked like an interesting dirt-trial.

We spent the next hour or two snaking through a narrow valley, following and occasionally fording a stream. Moose watched us pass by. Occasionally we'd wonder if we shouldn't turn back, but the sun was shining and the Explorer was handling fine, and a lazy curiosity led us on.

Some 12 miles in, past a series of high waterfalls, the trail abruptly changed. We began a long, rocky switchback ascent, steep and uncompromising, with streams trickling over it. Compared with the Rubicon, it was smooth sailing; without the Rubicon experience, I never would have tried it.

High above the valley, the trail ended at the rough remains of a gold miner's hut. The remnants of workings were nearby; a rusted bed frame lay inside the low stone walls. I pitied the mule that hauled it up there.

Yet the ground still rose steeply in front of us, so we left the Explorer and clambered up over spongy lichens and moss until we were so high we could have been eagles or glider pilots poised to soar down over the valley. We spread our arms wide and leaped around like kids up there, and that's how we found ourselves standing on the rim of a small crater filled with a turquoise-blue circle of water no more than 200 feet wide.

Without even realizing it, we had climbed into the mouth of a volcano, half blown away in an eruption in the distant past. A volcano so small and insignificant in this part of the world that it didn't even warrant a name on the state map. Our own private volcano. And we just stood there and laughed as the late afternoon wind gathered strength behind us and carried our laughter back down.

Trails take us into the back country, and unless we take righteous delight in hiking mile after mile with a full pack and uncertain destination, a sport-utility is a great way to get there. But to get to its heart—to that small circle of turquoise inside the caldera—you need to switch off the engine, leave the trail and walk. In the end, blessedly, it still comes down to you and your own two feet, listening to the silence, in amazement at the very fact that you're here.

Lesley Hazleton is the author of eight books, including Mary: A Flesh-and-Blood Biography of the Virgin Mother; Jerusalem, Jerusalem; *and* Where Mountains Roar. *Her work has appeared in numerous publications including* The New York Times, Harper's, Parade, Esquire, Vanity Fair, Mirabella, *and* The Nation. *She lived in and reported from Jerusalem for thirteen years, and now lives in Seattle.*

★

I have my own motorcycle now. I've got my motor running.

Moto Guzzi makes 650 cc with a comfortable faring and a stride low enough for a woman, say 5'1" to 5'4".

I can go as fast as I want to. Once I was riding so fast my wheels left the ground. I've ridden to Canada and home again, and down into old colonial Mexico, yellow-lining at 100 mph more than once. Now when I dip into hollows, I control the speed. My stomach flies as on a roller coaster just as the icy air hits my face.

Sometimes I feel like I'm part of the weather or a piece of the landscape. I've ridden in freezing rain and driving gales. I've crouched beneath a fast-eroding embankment to hide from a tornado in the Texas Panhandle. I've been bruised by hail while trying to find shelter in the middle of a petrified wood forest on a vast, empty plain. I've ridden in snowstorms where there are no motels, and rainstorms above tree line. I've ridden under dreary, dappled skies directly into blinding electrical storms.

On a motorcycle, I am alone and responsible for myself. Time assumes a new quality. An hour passes like five minutes, a hundred miles like ten. I forget all the worries I left at 4:00 p.m. I pass from town to town as though on a magic carpet.

—Robbie Ray, "Woman on Motorcycle"

TRACY JOHNSTON

⋆ ⋆ ⋆

Rafting the Boh

A woman voyages down the
wildest river in Borneo.

WE ENTERED THE GORGE ALMOST WITHOUT REALIZING IT.
Suddenly the canyon was narrow and at times the tree canopy
completely enclosed us. The walls grew steep and a thick tangle of
vegetation spilled down to the highwater mark. Mostly, the river
flowed right up against the walls of the gorge; occasionally, it
skirted piles of boulders. As Mimo and Sylvie had warned, there
were no beaches or sandbars.

That morning rapids were not the problem; boredom was. We
were moving downriver at about twenty yards an hour. Since no
one knew what lay ahead, the guides had to stop at every rapid and
scout it. That meant we had to get the boats into an eddy, tie them
to a tree or rock, and wait while Dave, Mike, and Gary took off
downriver to study the white water and come up with a plan for
running it. It was hard work for them, and tedious for those left
behind, but it was absolutely necessary. Boredom is the enemy of
caution; we needed to be careful.

Even though the river looked calm, it was big, and something
as simple and inevitable as a drop in the gradient or a rockpile
could create a deathtrap. We might turn a corner and discover a
twenty-foot waterfall, or slide into a keeper hole and get trapped

by a back-wave. My own particular nightmare was a sieve, where the current strains through a pile of rocks or debris underwater. You can be pressed flat up against a sieve and held there forever.

The rest of us stayed behind on these long scouts mainly because we couldn't keep up with the guides, who would literally run over the rocks and boulders, pick their way across what seemed like sheer vertical rock walls, and climb up and down the gorge, traveling from rock to mud to jungle at a breakneck pace, occasionally stringing ropes and rappelling. At times they had to hack their way through wet creepers and vines with machetes, which they also used to whack the leeches off.

When we stopped for lunch on some rocks, we had our first taste of Dave Heckman's river cuisine: peanut butter, jelly, Kraft processed cheese, and some pale slabs of pressed animal product that tasted more or less like candy-coated industrial carpet. "Deng deng," Dave called it.

"Jesus," said Raymond with genuine annoyance. "I could have done better than this in just a couple of hours in Jakarta."

The rest of us teased Dave more gently. We were becoming a determinedly amiable group.

After lunch the guides came back from a long scout and motioned us to get into the boats. Gary told Sylvie and me to unstrap the white plastic helmets and put them on. "This is a big one," he said. "There are two big drops, about twenty feet, but it's impossible to portage around it and we think we can run it." Later he told us that when they were scouting, Dave had said, "Let's run it before we get scared."

So Sylvie and I buckled up, grabbed the ropes around the side of the raft, and prepared to do the only thing we could: hang on. This might, after all, be fun. We were going to take the rapids with a very good boatman; it could be like sitting on the shoulders of a competition skier as he made a difficult run.

And we hung on, all right. We braced our feet and hung on as we glided around the bend, still in calm water. We hung on when we spotted the paddle boat ahead of us in the white water and saw it hit a wave, fly up in the air, and land upside down. We hung on

as Gary positioned us at the top of the run, and we hung on as we
bounded down a chute, ended up too far to the right, and hit a
rock wall at a 45-degree angle and began to fly. We were still hanging on in midair as the boat started to turn all the way over.

I let go and took a big breath before I plunged into the water....

After my initial rush of terror and panic, time cart-wheeled slowly as I spun helplessly at the bottom of the Boh, pounded into place by great walls of water. For a while I tried kicking and flailing my arms, trying to get upright, but it soon became clear that I didn't really know which way was up. Gradually I realized that I was more in danger of running out of breath than plunging downstream and hitting rocks, so I stopped fighting the river, stopped trying to get upright, and told myself to relax. Gary had said something about going into a "reptilian mode" underwater, and I remembered that and let myself go limp, hoping one of my legs or arms would catch a current and shoot me downriver.

Even at the time, I found it remarkable that I had coherent thoughts. I wondered if it was Sylvie's foot I felt when I first fell out of the boat, and whether or not we could have avoided the flip if all three of us had highsided. I debated the pros and cons of gulping more water and determined that for some reason it seemed to have helped when I did it earlier. I even had time left over to re-member my most recurring childhood nightmare: I would be

As we sallied forth, the names of the five remaining rapids worsened. Bumper Car, Table Saw, Widow Maker...each rapid threw our raft just a little higher in the air, each bounce sent more cold water rushing into our raft, each encounter with a large chunk of rock rattled my skeleton. My raftmates squealed with exhilaration. I said silent Hail Marys.

◆

—Kathryn Lively,
"Deliverance from Paranoia:
Riding the Wild Ocoee"

playing in the sand on a beach in front of an amusement park, and the tidal wave would rise way off in the ocean and get bigger and bigger until finally it curled up over my entire world—the beach, the hot-dog stands, the couples on the boardwalk, even the Ferris wheel. In my dream I would run away from the wave, up the beach and down a street until I felt water licking at my feet, and then I would turn around and feel myself being sucked backward, up, up, up the funnel of the wave and over the tops of the houses.

Perhaps this time I wasn't going to wake up, I thought. Perhaps this time I'd crash and end up draped over a pile of rocks like an old nightgown.

All of a sudden I shot up toward the light and my head broke water. I gasped some air before I was sucked under again, but now I was careening downriver, tumbling and tumbling, like Alice falling down the rabbit hole. Then the nightmare started all over— I ran out of air; I couldn't reach the light; my lungs felt like they were going to explode. I remembered, finally, to blow out some carbon dioxide, but then I gasped again and choked down more water. It worked! Of course! I thought. Frothing water is full of air.

Then the water around me began to darken, and I realized that instead of rising to the top of the river, I was being pushed down. It occurred to me that there might be a series of rapids, not just one, and that I had missed the first eddy and was now in a part of the river the guides hadn't scouted. But just as I had this thought I popped up above water again, and suddenly, almost like magic, I was out of the rapids and in calm water. It was a small eddy, and after a few strokes I stood up, thigh deep in the water, heaving, coughing, blowing water out my nose, and trying to hold on to a slippery rock. I looked up and saw an upturned raft bouncing down the other side of the river with Gary climbing on top of it and Sylvie trailing behind, holding on to the bowline. I watched them go around the bend.

And then I was all alone. Behind me was a steep rock wall. My instinct was to swim to the other side of the river where I could get out of the water and make my way downstream over some boulders. But I knew I probably couldn't make it across before I rounded the bend, and since there might be more rapids ahead, or a waterfall, I made myself wait.

I waited long enough to relive the rapids I'd just been through; I'd spilled at the top of the first waterfall and had gone down it and then down the second one. Then I waited while I tried to think of what to do next. If the boats had all flipped and no one had been able to get out of the river for a mile or so, the guides might not be able to get back to me.

Or maybe someone had gotten hurt and there was no time to hike back upstream.

Maybe I'd have to wait where I was until they got off the Boh and down the Mahakam far enough to call for some kind of helicopter rescue. I might be stuck where I was for days: thigh deep in water in a part of Borneo that perhaps only ten or twenty people on earth had ever seen, without food or dry clothes or even a place to sit, let alone sleep.

I looked around at the dark green water, the black rock wall in back of me, the rank tangle of trees and leaves and vines over my head. My legs in the water looked like little twigs: my knees were quivering. I felt very much alone.

I smelled the mold already in my life jacket and fingered my arm, which was red with deep scratches, and realized that this loneliness might not be just in my head. It might not be romantic or metaphorical; it might be ugly and real. I might have to try to climb up the wall, find a place to sleep in the jungle, and live on...something. Leaves and berries. I felt as if I were looking down a dark well into my essence, but I couldn't see it. I couldn't see what to do next. I couldn't even see how to get out of the god-damned water.

It had all been very naïve, my idea about how safe it was to go on a river trip with world-class boatmen. I hadn't thought about what would happen if a wave suddenly reached out of the river and flicked over the boat. I'd been on my own in that white water. As had everyone.

And then...I heard a voice across the river calling, "*Tracy, Tracy,*" and I yelled back, *"Here! Here!"* It was warmth, it was music. Whoever had come to get me, I loved him.

It was Mike, in his headband and wire-rimmed glasses, waving from the other side of the river; strong, lovely Mike with his bulging biceps. He tried to tell me something, but the water was too loud and I couldn't hear, and then he held out his palm, indicating that I should stay put, and I smiled and laughed and gave him the okay sign. "I'm fine!" I cried. *"Fine!"*

I was still shaky, but the adrenaline was pumping, and after a minute or so of waiting I became impatient and examined the rock wall behind me with a climber's eye. I saw a route and decided to try it. Moving deliberately, checking my strength, I traversed the wall, making my way downstream, feeling strong and high. I've never discovered anything that requires more concentration than rock climbing—more centering of mind and body, more awareness at every nerve ending—and I felt a rising ecstasy as the handholds materialized, roots appeared around corners, ledges held firm. When I rounded the bend I looked up as if to applause, but there was only the dirty-brown Boh, the river taking another quick curve.

It was an easy boulder hop around the next bend, and then I saw the boats. Two were still overturned, and everyone was busy trying to get them upright. I yelled, but no one heard me, and finally, when I was right across the river from everyone, Dave looked up and saw me waving. He waved back and continued fixing something on his boat.

It was something of an anticlimax, not having anyone falling to their knees with thanksgiving for my safe arrival, but I took it in stride, and finally, after the guides huddled together for a moment, I saw Dave cup his hands and yell:

"We're going to throw you a line. Try and catch it."

I braced myself against a rock, held out both arms, and tried not to think about being dragged across the current. The "rescue line" or "throw line" was a rope in a small canvas bag that uncoiled as it sailed through the air. I watched Gary's throw arc across the river toward me and fall short by about twenty feet. Then I watched

Mike's throw land upriver in the current and sail by far out of reach. The guides went into another huddle, and soon Gary and Sylvie got in our boat and took off. Gary strained against the current, oaring into it at a 45-degree angle, and made it across just a few feet before the river disappeared around a bend.

"I want you to know," said Gary, when I reached the boat, "that I've been rafting for nineteen years, and this is only the fifth time I've flipped a boat."

I was impressed.

While we waited for the other boats to put in, Gary described the rescue. It had been frantic, he said, but well done. Luckily, Mike, Raymond, and John had made it through the rapids safely in Mike's boat, and Mike was ready to throw a line to the paddlers who were coming down in the water. Mimo caught the line and clipped it to one of the boat's metal rings, and Bill grabbed the paddles that floated by him in the water. Then, just as Mike and Raymond were pulling in the paddle boat and the swimmers were safe in the eddy, Gary came down the river on top of his over-turned boat, Sylvie trailing in the water behind him. Gary had managed to reach under the boat and unclip the throw line, which he hurled at Bill, who had just pulled himself up out of the rapids onto a rock. Mike yelled at Gary, "Bill can't hold it up there," but somehow Bill braced himself and did. Then Mike ran up and to-gether they pulled the boat in.

Gary asked if I had seen the MAF pilot who had appeared out of nowhere just after the rescue. He did a wing stand in his Cessna, circled, and left. Amazingly enough, I hadn't.

Sylvie and I exchanged "swimming" stories. She, too, had been pounded underwater, but when she popped up she felt something bump her softly on the head. She opened her eyes and saw that she was in complete darkness; the water all around her was black.

"I knew then," she said, "that I had come up underneath the boat."

She tumbled down the river helplessly for what seemed like minutes, trying to stay upright and swim out from underneath the boat. When she opened her eyes a second time, and again saw nothing but blackness, she gave up.

"I knew that I was going to die. I had already swallowed water, and now I couldn't stop it. I kept swallowing big gulps of water. I couldn't get any air."

She had flipped on the Zambezi River in Africa, she said, but she'd never stayed underwater long. There she had worried more about bashing into rhinos or crocodiles than actually drowning.

"All I could think," she said, "was Shit, I'm going to die because of this stupid river trip."

For some reason I couldn't keep the grin off my face. I was still flushed with the euphoria of having survived. I also wanted a moment to send off an apology to my husband. "I'm sorry, lover," I said to the river and the wind. "No more dangerous rivers. Really."

When we finally took off again and I strapped on my life jacket and grabbed the ropes, my mood abruptly changed. Suddenly I felt numb. Blank. Confused. Gary and Sylvie were also quiet. Sylvie clutched the ropes, and Gary stood up to try to see ahead.

I took my position, legs braced, hands secure on the ropes, but it felt futile. I noticed I was shaking, and suddenly I was cold. I was two degrees from the equator, on calm water, gliding through a tropical wonderland, but everything had changed. As Peter Matthiessen once wrote, the earth had nudged me. This little adventure had turned serious.

Tracy Johnston has written for New West, The New York Times Magazine, Playboy, *and the* Village Voice. *This story was excerpted from her book,* Shooting the Boh. *She lives in Northern California.*

✳

Sputtering and gasping, we check to see if all of our comrades are still aboard..."six, seven, eight." Lunches remain intact. Everyone inhales deeply and smiles as we graduates offer support to the neophytes in the raft behind us, still traversing the passage rites of the river.

"Don't worry, it isn't that bad," someone hollers above the roar.

"You'll make it okay. Hold your breath!" someone else yells.

What liars my boatmates are! I want to warn the oncomers, but there is nothing they can do.

—Dian Overly, "Cruisin' Down the River"

Tracking Lessons

How to wait out a rattlesnake.

I'VE BEEN LYING ON MY STOMACH HERE IN THE MIDDLE OF FRIED Liver Wash since noon; Sam, my search dog puppy, is stretched out in the shade behind me. Tranquil doesn't begin to describe this place. The air is still, not even a whisper in the dry creosote branches, and the sky lies well back on the horizon. Without provocation, a dry lupine stalk drops one of its leaves, and a lizard's tail barely misses it as he scurries across the hot sand, heading for the next shady spot. There's a sidewinder coiled up under a smoke tree a few yards away—she and I have been eyeing each other warily ever since I stumbled across her track, startling her into a defensive posture. When I sat down in the middle of the wash, she watched a few seconds and then quickly moved closer to the base of the tree, carefully adjusting her body backward in short undulating sweeps. Very graceful. Funny how I never noticed that rattlesnakes were graceful before today. My mother would undoubtedly disagree.

When I switched positions, lying down and adjusting my hat to avoid the sun, the sidewinder arched and looked my way crossly, settling down into a full coil. Since then, we have both been sitting here mostly motionless. I brushed a fly off my face a couple times and she rearranged her coils once, but other than that, we've been still as dead mice. I intend to stay until she moves again, so that I can see exactly how she makes those odd J-shaped tracks. Sam, content to stay if I am, is sound asleep.

Far overhead, a buzzard rides what appears to be a decent headwind and circles down closer to see who's newly dead in the wash. I wave to him so he realizes we're not dinner fixings yet, and he good-naturedly wends his way toward the Eagle Mountains. Four Huey helicopters putter their way north toward the Marine Corps Base, and a cactus wren from somewhere nearby shouts her annoyance at the disturbance. Actually, she was shouting before the Hueys came by, so any annoyance is probably all mine. Sam looks up, yawns, rolls onto his back, and falls asleep again. Even the sidewinder looks relaxed now, and as the sounds of the Hueys fade, mindful of the desert's hints, the tension in my neck also begins to subside. Annoyance with the military is useless anyway; in southern California it's like tilting at windmills, only less productive.

The sidewinder, after one last glance in my direction, finally decides to continue with her day by heading up the slight incline behind the smoke tree. With quick, deft movements, she slips sideways up the hot sand, etching her eccentric trail. Sand grains slowly slide down to rest in the lowest part of each track as she moves along, body touching the hot ground at two points only and undulating back and forth in between them. Considering how long I've been waiting here to watch this very thing happen, you'd think I would be able to describe it better. But there are no words precise enough to convey the snake's delicate balance, her swift and steady movements, or the certainty with which she's heading up that hill. Clearly she knows where she is going. Sam and I just watch.

Since I don't know where we're going—or, more accurately, since we don't have anywhere to go this afternoon—I continue to sit in the wash and watch the snake's tracks change as the sun begins to drop lower in the sky. Sam takes another nap. The longer the shadows get, the more visible the tracks are. That's why tracking at high noon is so difficult—without shadows to throw them into relief, tracks might as well not be there. Trackers have to adjust to the flat light conditions of midday: We sometimes use mirrors to backlight the tracks, after shading them with our caps—a slow, painstaking process that is hard on both eyes and patience.

Tracks in sand, like those the sidewinder just left, are relatively easy for the tracker to see no matter what the light conditions, but tracks on scrub rocks practically disappear in flat light. Even shaded and backlit, they're elusive at best, so sometimes the wisest strategy for noon tracking is simply to sit down and eat lunch. Since a nap afterward is a luxury Sam and I wouldn't have on an actual search, in practice sessions we make the most of the opportunity. Today I roll over into the shade next to my dog and we both doze off, soothed by the heat that surrounds us like a warm oven.

Two hours later. The sidewinder has been gone a long time now, and the sun is leaving the sky, washing it with the brilliant hues of a smog-induced sunset. Bats are already out, fluttering and zinging their way up and down the wash, searching for the insects they live on and we think we could live without. A cool evening breeze slightly lifts the branches of a creosote bush and softly rattles through a dry desert trumpet stem. Nearby the birdcage skeleton of one of last year's evening primroses sits placidly as the wind sends tiny particles of sand and plant matter sweeping through its open railings. Somewhere off to the east a coyote yips and another answers from the mountains, and then another and another and another, until the night is ringed with coyote song. Ears full, eyes tired, Samson and I walk down the wash toward the car.

Bounding a few feet ahead, Sam sniffs around under a creosote bush, but the instant I yell "Samson, *leave!*" he whips around and waits for my next words. His immediate obedience may have just saved his nose: At the base of the bush another sidewinder sits coiled, ready to strike at this offensive blond intruder. Sam gallops happily back to me, entirely unaware of the danger behind him, so I snap on his leash, put him on heel and walk up to the bush. Pointing at the snake, I repeat, "Leave." Sam's face first registers the snake, then the command. Not two seconds later, he is ready to continue down the wash, as uninterested in the motionless snake as if it were a rock. I make him stay to watch the snake leave so he will associate the coiled creature with the moving one, repeating the command "Leave" each time he starts to step toward the sliding, retreating reptile. Suddenly Sam looks up, and I can see that he's figured it out. He now knows snakes are off-limits—he can be counted on to avoid them by himself next time. He will tell me with his eyes that one of those strange things is nearby—as any good search partner would—but he won't go bounding into it and wind up getting bitten. The first snake was my teacher, the second one his. We have learned good lessons today, he and I, sitting in the hot sun and walking home at dusk.

Hannah Nyala lives with her two children and search dog in a small town in America. She is author of Leave No Trace *and* Point Last Seen: A Woman Tracker's Story, *from which this story was excerpted.*

*

What is this wild embrace? This slipping away of heat from air at daybreak, these clothes made of bird cries being peeled from my body?...

Lao Tzu exhorts us to listen to the world "not with ears but with mind, not with mind but with spirit." Some days I hear what sounds like breathing: quick inhalations from the grass, from burnt trees, from streaming clouds, as if desire were finally being answered, and at night in my sleep I can feel black tree branches pressing against me, their long needles combing my hair.

—Gretel Ehrlich, *Islands, the Universe, Home*

Up the Volcano

There was more to this Guatemalan
mountain than met the eye.

THE ROAD UP THE MOUNTAIN TO THE VOLCANO WAS ROCKY AND narrow. Too steep for the ancient van we'd driven from Antigua and had to abandon below on the roadside. I focused on the footsteps of Mario, our guide, placed each of my feet in the frames of his shoe prints. They were as small as mine and made with canvas loafers that must have been painful on that hike.

We'd just begun to climb and already my shirt was soaked and my hair lay heavy on my neck. In the middle of the rainy season we were lucky to have only heat to contend with; rain and mud would have made this climb impossible.

Seven of us were climbing toward the crater of Guatemala's Mt. Pacaya, two hours away, hoping to reach it before it became shrouded in afternoon fog. Mario had brought a friend, Alberto, a dark, narrow man who smelled of cigarettes and breath mints. There was also an Austrian couple, who could have been siblings with their identical, translucent green eyes; a Dutch woman, Sylvie, just out of college and taking a year to travel through South America; and another American woman, Cynthia, who like me hovered around thirty. She spoke the Castillian Spanish she'd learned in Madrid her junior year abroad, said *Grathias* instead of *Gracias*.

Pacaya, outside Guatemala City on the eastern edge of the Cuchumatanes Mountains, is one of the country's four live volcanos, a tiny link in the global Ring of Fire. At 2,550 meters high, Pacaya is small for a volcano; since it became active a quarter century ago its eruptions have done little more than harm crops and livestock.

But Mario told us not to get our hopes up. If we were lucky, we might see a thin stream of smoke churning from the crater. "Pacaya erupts when she's in the mood," he said from behind a handlebar mustache.

I looked around as we climbed, taking in this "land of eternal spring," as Guatemalans call it, its shades of pink and purple bougainvillea burgeoning from every crevice, its velveteen grass carpeting hillsides in the distance. But I knew this country's beauty was deceptive. Underlying the still serenity of its landscape, behind the gentle round faces of its indigenous people, Guatemala has been a place of fear for decades. The country's underground civil war left some 100,000 people dead; 40,000 more comprise the *desaparecidos*—people who simply vanished and have never been found.

We came upon a village of squalid shacks, some of cardboard, where children with matted hair stood behind bramble fences. Most merely stared at us, but some waved or shyly smiled with broken teeth. This was San Vicente Pacaya, the village for which the volcano was named. Palmetto trees—called *pacayas* in Quiche, the local dialect—grew all around.

A small girl in an oversized blue dress began to follow us. She wore pink plastic shoes, shiny against the moist earth; a skinny dog slouched after her. Mario asked the girl if she could show us the best path through the jungle. She nodded, then called to her brothers, walking up ahead, to come too. One was a teenager and the other only five or six; each held a machete. I had seen men and boys carrying wood cut with machetes. They tied the wood in heavy bundles to their backs, secured them with a strap across their foreheads.

The girl's name was Bianca. She told me she was twelve, but

she looked about nine. It would catch up with her soon enough; adults there looked ten to fifteen years older than they were. Bianca moved quickly up the narrow jungle path banked by coffee bushes. She was sure-footed, never breathless. Her body and lungs had grown with this climb, which she told me she did almost daily.

Bianca said that Pacaya had erupted just the week before. Her brothers had been working at the top with their machetes; they heard the rumble, saw the crater spewing earth, and ran down to the village, leaving the day's chopping behind.

I thought about what makes a person live near a volcano. Surely it isn't a choice. I'd seen a cemetery that held the dead from the eruption of another Guatemalan volcano, Santa María, at the turn of the century. The villagers who live below Santa María today watch the sun set each night behind a volcano that killed 6,000 people.

Two kilometers from the crater, Bianca pointed to a tree with blackened leaves. Though lava rarely comes down as far as the village, she said, this *arena* does. It was a sandlike ash, pulverized earth and rocks that looked like black, crushed glass. Under a microscope, I've heard, you can see the jagged edges of each piece. A pilot from Guatemala City told me that, during an eruption, planes have to fly high above so the sharp particles won't clog the engines with their tiny teeth.

The men ahead set a too-rapid pace. I had thought I was strong, but falling behind the others and breathing hard, I wasn't sure I'd make it. Up ahead, I glimpsed the turquoise bandanna and blond hair of the Austrian man, but he flitted out of sight again behind large-leafed bushes.

At least I wouldn't get lost; I could hear Mario's footsteps behind me. Falling behind would be dangerous, Mario said to my back; there were thieves in this jungle. I peered ahead through low-hanging vines. Papaya, banana, and pacaya trees loomed. I had heard that robbers stopped at least one group a week here. They held hikers at knifepoint and gunpoint, then made off with cameras, money, boots. A few years back, some tourists were killed on another volcano nearby.

From behind, Mario told me something else: that the Pacaya crater we were climbing to had been used by army death squads, a place where they had once dumped victims' bodies—human rights activists, peasant leaders, students—the *desaparecidos*. It was during the late 1970s, before the mountain became a tourist attraction, he said.

At that point Mario climbed past me and up to the front of the group, where three children were blazing our trail through the jungle. I felt stunned by Mario's words. I wasn't sure I wanted to go forward, but going back alone would be dangerous.

I tripped over rocks and tree roots, my legs shaking on the steep stairs of clay. At last I caught up with the other climbers at a clearing, where they had stopped to look down over green and brown patches of farmland below. Cynthia and Sylvie sat on the ground, emptying clay from hiking shoes and socks. The Austrian couple mopped their foreheads with identical turquoise bandannas. Alberto leaned against a tree and lit up a hand-rolled cigarette. I reached into my knapsack.

"Not too much. You will cramp," Mario said, before I even could pull out my water bottle.

As I unscrewed the cap, I saw the small, round eyes of Bianca's tiny brother watching me. He leaned against his bare machete, his pants falling down despite the knotted piece of rope around his waist. I took a sip and handed him the bottle, and I tried to forget about the wetness I'd seen coming from his nose—one sign, I knew, of the Tuberculosis that is widespread here. He held the bottle with two hands and drank, his eyes fixed on mine. I gave their dog water from my cupped hand. Then Bianca drank.

Her teenage brother, mouth pursed, refused. There was something in the way he looked at me, and for a moment I felt that wave of self-consciousness that travelers to poor countries know well. I watched my reflection in his eyes: my knapsack, my hiking shoes, my water bottle.

When we resumed climbing, I was last again, just behind

Cynthia and Sylvie. Sylvie and I began to talk, complaining how neither of us had expected this tough of a hike. At one point, Cynthia called back something in her Castillian Spanish, and Sylvie gave a short, nervous laugh.

"What did she say?" I asked.

"That the others are already so far ahead, Cynthia can hardly see them," Sylvie said. "They'd better not forget we're here."

We climbed in silence awhile, trying to pick up speed. Cynthia couldn't see the others at all now, and she began to call out: "Mario! Maaa-ri-oo!"

Suddenly she and Sylvie stopped. "I don't know where the path is," Cynthia said. I looked ahead, and indeed the ground had suddenly changed from clay to rocks covered with vines and lichen; there was no trace of footprints.

"Maaaaaaa-rio!" we shouted. Then I clapped a hand over my mouth and we looked at each other: a shout that could bring Mario could also bring thieves. They'll come back, we reassured one another. Mario's already noticed we're gone and he's on his way.

Fifteen minutes passed. Twenty. We sat down on the incline and began to talk quietly. We comforted ourselves that we still had plenty of daylight left. Sylvie said she had two bananas in her pack. Cynthia had a candy bar. I had a banana too, and we all had at least half a bottle of water.

After forty minutes, we decided to try to find our way back down. We scribbled a note to Mario, saying we'd wait for him on the main road in Bianca's village. Cynthia skewered the note on an eye-level palm frond, and we began to walk.

"*O-ye! Oye! Mis Niñas!*" Mario shouted, calling us his "girls." We shouted back and soon we saw him bounding toward us through jungle vines. We began climbing again, and he turned around and shook his finger at us, his mustache bobbing. "Stay close by," he said.

We caught up to the others, who were resting nearby, and Bianca and her brothers grinned at the bumbling gringas who'd gotten lost in the jungle that was their backyard. We began to climb again, making two short stops, anticipating the top. Finally we came to flat ground, where we stopped and stared in silence.

It was an alien place. The earth was burned black but for a few bold patches of young, light-green moss. The remains of trees, deformed stalks charred white and glowing in sunlight, littered the ground. Below, a valley of black, dried lava covered the landscape. A steep slope towered above; Pacaya's crater was just on the other side.

Here Bianca and her brothers left us. We thanked them and awkwardly placed folded bills in their hands. They walked away, playfully shoving each other, machete blades gleaming, their skinny dog yelping along behind.

We began climbing the peak next to Pacaya; a view of the crater awaited us on the other side. Soon we gave up climbing upright and began to *gatear*, to crawl like cats. Pacaya rumbled, first a purr, then a growl. The earth trembled where I clutched it. Mario's friend Alberto gave a cry and went flat on his belly. The Austrian woman began crawling backward down the slope, her husband following close behind.

"Is Pacaya erupting?" I asked Mario.

He shrugged, palms open toward heaven. *"Quién sabe?"*

The wind blew in gusts, gently one minute then suddenly whipping me back the next. I kept close to the ground. The air there, near the summit, was frigid, but the rocks I touched were hot. Steam rose from them, sulfur that smelled acrid. This wasn't dangerous, but the gas rising nearer the crater, like gas from the lava, I'd heard, can kill.

> "This," Miguel says in Spanish, pointing ahead, "is the most dangerous part of the journey. The sun will be setting soon and it is very windy. The sand hits your face and can pierce your eyeballs. Even when the volcano is not active, it is still angry and the surrounding wind carries the anger."
>
> ◆
>
> —Lea Aschkenas, "Between the Volcanos"

Cynthia and Sylvie had already reached the top and, I suspected, found a place from where they could see the crater. The
Austrian couple, discouraged by the pelting wind, said they'd meet
us later near the path below. Alberto and I stopped halfway up and
rested for a moment, listening to the thunderlike rumbling. When
we began crawling again, I tried to anchor myself with the rocks,
but they were deceitful—light and porous, yanking up when I
grabbed them. The wind chill grew ferocious, and I pulled my
jacket sleeves over my palms like mitts.

Pacaya rumbled louder. I thought of one large tombstone I'd
seen in that cemetery near the volcano Santa María. The tomb
held twenty-two people whom no one had been able to identify.
I reminded myself what Bianca had said: Pacaya's lava is slow; one
can usually run from it.

Alberto and I reached the top, just behind Mario. Still I couldn't
see the crater; another peak hid it. Exhausted from the climb, I sat
down for a moment in a little pit that blocked the wind.

"If there were no opening over there," Mario said, pointing in
the direction of the rumbling, "it would have to come out here."
He pointed to where I sat. It was a dormant crater, shallow now
with dried earth from its last eruption years before. I felt a sudden,
sharp heat stab my thighs and I flinched, imagining the ground
bursting beneath me.

We began to move toward the rumbling. I yelled to Mario, "Is
it safe? How far back will we need to stand?"

"*Quién sabe?*" he said.

We ran down a gentle slope and up another. The rumbling was
continuous now, booming. Then I saw it: the volcano crater rose in the
air from an adjacent peak. It was erupting, the mountain exploding.

We walked to where Sylvie and Cynthia stood, and to my
horror, Mario urged us to move closer until we were about 300
meters from the crater. The peak coughed gobs of fiery earth from
an opening about 200 meters wide. I reminded myself that people
climbed Pacaya all the time; Bianca's brothers were right near the
crater when it erupted last week. Still, I was sure we stood at the
very last line of safety. Any closer and the fire would spray us.

Flaming forked tongues danced in the air, black rocks popping around them. Then nothing. Then a staccato rumble and the earth uncorked again, bubbling up rocks and fire, red and orange, almost fluorescent. The volcano overwhelmed everything around it—ground, sky, the air we breathed. Below, two trails of lava drooled from a wound at the base of Pacaya: red, yellow, black—thick and slow, just as Bianca had said. The inside of that mountain was nothing but gurgling liquid, a rolling river of fire.

The crater shot off again, 150 meters high. Then the rumbling again, and darkness covered the sky—smoke and an umbrella of ash, black and burning. The ash, Mario said, would rain on villages below and ride with the wind to other towns.

I thought of what I knew about volcanic eruptions, about weak continental plates submitting beneath thicker ones, and heat from the friction melting the plates into molten rock, compressed gasses squeezing the magma until it bubbles like liquid fire through the earth's thin crust.

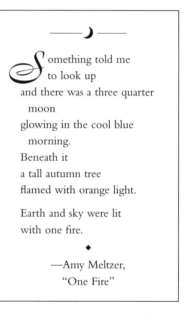

Something told me
to look up
and there was a three quarter
  moon
glowing in the cool blue
  morning.
Beneath it
a tall autumn tree
flamed with orange light.

Earth and sky were lit
with one fire.

♦

—Amy Meltzer,
"One Fire"

But as I watched it happen before my eyes, I thought the ancient Mayans had understood it better. Volcanos are alive; they have heartbeats. They are gods, furiously spewing their admonitions at mortals.

For an hour we watched as Pacaya shot higher and faster. Finally, mist and smoke began to billowed around it, and I felt the terror of the unseen. I imagined fire rocks hurtling at us through the cloudy curtain. The mist soon covered the crater, and we feared it enough to head back down.

I would later learn that, of Pacaya's eruptions in the past half-dozen years, this was the biggest. The newspapers would talk of "a gray mantle" covering the village of San Vicente Pacaya, referring to the massive heaps of ash. Photographs showed villagers holding up clothes that had been hung on lines to dry but that were completely blackened. The ash rained all the way to Atitlan, five kilometers away.

Two villages in the skirts of the volcano, on the other side from San Vicente Pacaya, would be most damaged, and 1,500 people would evacuate. Cows and horses couldn't graze: inches of ash covered the pasture. Small livestock, bean crops, bananas, and coffee were lost. The lava river, as high as eight meters in some places, would flow down a full kilometer. Volunteer fire squads would stay on alert for days to put out fires the lava ignited.

Coming down, we found a well-worn, less treacherous path than the one we'd suffered climbing up. Indeed, the slope we'd climbed was one no one ever took. Another guide I met weeks later in Antigua told me this. Our group's trip was talked about all over town: how the hikers nearly collapsed climbing up the side of that volcano, when a gentler, less windy path lay just 50 meters on the other side. How Mario almost lost three *gringas* in the jungle. It turned out this was Mario's first time up Pacaya since his childhood.

We practically skied down that new path. The dirt was loose, so black it seemed clean. It poured into my shoes and socks, weighing them down as I propelled forward.

It wasn't until then, nearing the bottom and lightheaded with fatigue, that I let myself think about the other victims of Guatemala's eruptions: of those whose bodies had been dumped into that crater by forces of human energy. That the physical danger of the volcano could hardly match the deeper terrors that Bianca and her brothers had faced their whole lives.

Lucy McCauley is editor of this book, as well as Travelers' Tales: Spain.

✳

We started off with great, if unformed, expectations. In a few hours Kevan and I would be viewing the sunrise from the top of the world—or as close as we could get in Southern Sumatra. The only way to the top of Mount Merapi, an active volcano some 2,900 meters high, is to go on foot. Surely this would be some kind of epic adventure.

A minivan dropped us off at the foot of Mount Merapi, which cut a faint outline in the dark sky. It was 11:30 p.m. Our two guides got out with us—we never learned their names—and we set off. We soon learned that the only gear they came with were cigarettes and matches. We complained about their oversight, but when I remembered the SAS Survival Guide we had placed in our backpack, I felt embarrassed.

An hour into the climb we stopped to wait out a downpour. A group of schoolboys, whom we had passed earlier, joined us. They sat with us around a fire, playing Nirvana songs on a guitar and plying us with questions—Do you believe in God? I was in no mood for philosophy. The climb had already become tedious, and I just wanted to get to the top. We resumed the climb when the rain became a steady drizzle. Because there was little to see but the dark, muddy path in front of us, the physical act of climbing took on an exaggerated focus. I felt acutely every twist of an ankle on a slippery rock, every drop of rain through my cheap anorak, every yawn. Most of all, I felt the montonony. As fatigue set in, I imagined I was climbing a long staircase to bed.

When we emerged from the tree line in the pre-dawn light, we saw a rocky lunarscape rise before us. At last! But then we saw the mist, ahead of us obscuring the crater, and another bank below us—and then the realization that we would see no sunrise. The thin ribbon that kept my spirits up snapped. I threw a vertiginious tantrum, halting suddenly and refusing to move. Kevan and one of the guides finished the climb without me. I clutched a rock and waited—intermittently sobbing and directing a bitter stare at my guide, who sat silently smoking.

On the way down, we passed the schoolboys. They were excited and didn't seemed bothered by the mist that now enveloped us. As we said goodbye, one of them shouted, "Don't forget me, Cathy."

Life never hung in the balance. But sometimes adventures come in modest packages.

—Catherine Olofson, "A Modest Adventure"

* * *

On Flying

She soars with eagles
and navigates by rainbows.

THE LAST THING I EXPECTED WHEN I BEGAN TO FLY WAS THAT I would begin a romance not with the sky, but with the earth.

I was captive to the great cliché of roaring into the vast blue yonder. I thought of it as the great escape—that magical moment when lift counteracts gravity and the little single-engine plane leaps upward into release from the ground. Surely, I thought, this was the essence of flight.

But flying resists cliché. Takeoff is certainly very impressive: short, sharp, and powerful. Yet it's somehow too quick to hold the imagination. It's a practical business of getting into the air. Oddly businesslike and abrupt. Instead, to my surprise, I was to become utterly enticed by the process of landing. Long and gentle, at minimum power, landing becomes a sensuous toying with the very idea of coming back to earth.

I talk to the plane on final approach. Softly, but out loud: "Come on now, down you come, easy now, nice and smooth, yes, just a bit more, beautiful, that's it…"

My voice paces both me and the plane, for this drawn-out tension of the long glide in cannot be hurried. It's a matter of simultaneously controlling it and letting it happen. And then, just as you cross the threshold of the runway, of gently lifting the nose to let the plane skim over the ground, the wheels a mere foot or two in the air.

You hold it right there as though you could go on forever like this—as though the last thing you want is to touch down. And you tease the ground this way until the attraction between plane and ground becomes so strong that you can't hold it off any longer. The plane seems to land itself, to decide to stop flying and sink that final foot or two to earth. You sense the sink out of the corners of your eyes, bring the yoke back just a touch, and finally allow plane and ground to meet.

The perfect landing has a sweet inevitability, so smooth it seems utterly natural. There is just the merest squeak of the wheels on the tarmac, and sometimes not even that, so that you check to make sure you really are on the ground. Sometimes achieved, it is far more often not, and all the more treasured for that.

This is the high point. The rest is bringing your mind down to earth: the loss of speed in the rollout on the runway, the slow taxi, shutting down the engine. And in that moment of absolute stillness as the prop shudders to a stop, the earth reasserts itself in its dailiness, and you are suddenly aware of a certain sorrow at having lost lift, at being destined to move again in two dimensions instead of three. Yet together with this sorrow comes a poignant sweetness that has to do with being human, the antithesis of the fundamentally super-human act of flying.

I am convinced that flying is a supremely unnatural activity for man or woman. Lift is produced when slightly warped wings divide the air flow, creating higher pressure below and lower pressure above. This is a law of physics, and the laws of physics are natural laws, but still, I feel that humans were not made to fly. And this sense of transgression is part of my entrancement.

Every time I go out to a plane, there is a touch of fear—a haunting sense that more than any other time, I am on my own. This eases as I go through the checklist, do the engine run-up, announce my presence on the radios. To my relief, it disappears entirely the moment my wheels leave the ground. Yet some part of me welcomes it as a reminder never to take flight for granted.

I watch birds—eagles soaring and circling, gulls swooping and diving—and imagine moving through the air with that same ease and assurance. And then I remind myself that birds too can stall: make a false move, turn too sharply, and plummet down to earth, out of control. That even for birds, flight is not automatic, but demands continuous control, fine sensing of lift and gravity thrust and drag. Even birds can make bad landings.

Sometimes I fly with them. An eagle soars along with me in a mountain valley. Gulls tumble in my slipstream as I take off from a coastal airport. Or as I taxi down a tiny country strip, a flock of young swallows flies alongside the plane, taking it for some huge mother bird.

> *We* swung over the hills and over the town and back again, and I saw how a man can be master of a craft, and how a craft can be master of an element. I saw the alchemy of perspective reduce my world, and all my other life, to grains in a cup. I learned to watch, to put my trust in other hands than mine. And I learned to wander. I learned what every dreaming child needs to know—that no horizon is so far that you cannot get above it or beyond it.
>
> ◆
>
> —Beryl Markham,
> *West with the Night*

This is a world far removed from the sophistication of airline flight. It's a world of aging, sometimes even ancient, single-prop machines that you fly by the seat of your pants—by the feel of the air and the controls—not by the numbers on electronic displays. It's easy to take flight for granted in an airliner; cocooned so high above the earth that you hardly even notice it, you have no sense of motion. Flight becomes merely a kind of vacuum between one place and another. But small planes take you into a time warp, back to the days when flying was an adventure, even a privilege, and to fly was to laugh out loud in delight.

These are planes to be flown through mountain valleys instead of high above them. You can hear the wind rushing by as you pull back the power and nose down for a dive, and you know you're flying with air, rather than merely through it. You begin to sense air in the same way as you sense water, a medium with palpable buoyancy and density.

I think of porpoises playing in water as I do gentle lazy eight maneuvers, tracing invisible looping ribbons that look like a figure eight from the side: climb up to the top of the loop, then just on the verge of stall, let one wing slice down in a moment of near weightlessness, and swoop in a heady earthward rush down the invisible ribbon only to do it all again in the other direction. I can spend an hour cradling the plane back and forth, up and down this way, and think it is only ten minutes.

There is no purpose to this, no end or destination. Like dancing, it's simply movement for the joy of it.

The mountains orient me as I climb and swoop. I fly between two mountain ranges and below me is a sound, dotted with islands like huge lumps of moss. Sunlight streams through clouds in the long shafts a friend calls God's fingers, silvering the water. And above the clouds, a clear blue vastness where I rise to find myself the only human presence.

As pilots must in this part of the world, I become an intimate of the weather. Sometimes low black clouds feather down, long tendrils trailing the earth like fingers trailing in water. They have the exotic name of virga, and I fly alongside them, seduced by such dark beauty. Flying in a clear blue sky is dull by comparison. Such skies are beautiful on the ground, but in the air, they pall easily. Too much sameness, too little sense of detail. Clouds seem to beckon: come up here, fly with us. In a clear blue sky, nothing beckons. And there are no rainbows.

Rainbows go every which way in the air: vertically, like luminous lines of connection between earth and sky; upside down, as though some giant had come along and casually flipped the arcs onto their backs; and sometimes even full circle.

Late one fall day, as I flew home, the lowering sun shone in a golden haze behind me: ahead, the weather closed in, and as I neared home, formed a huge black cloud over the city. I got on the radios, checking to see if I could make it into the city or if I'd have to land at an alternate airport, so I hardly noticed the two vertical rainbows to my left, glowing in the dying light. But rainbows cannot be ignored. The next thing I knew, those two vertical shafts had transformed themselves into a huge double rainbow circle shimmering around my left wing, with the wingtip at its very center.

I stopped checking alternates. How could I turn away from that ethereal circle of color? On we flew, the rainbow and I, away from the light, and for some fifteen minutes it seemed as though it were guiding me through the lowering sky until the rain closed in, the rainbow faded into the gloom, and I dipped down under the deck of that huge black cloud, flew through the rain spattering at the windshield, and snuck safely and gratefully back to earth.

Lesley Hazleton also contributed "No Road? No Problem" in this section.

⋆

Time: 9:55 p.m. Tanks: maybe 1/8 full, maybe not, as the gas indicator kept bouncing from E to 1/4 like a wobbly drunk. Place: altitude 2,500 feet, 5-10 minutes south of the Hopedale Airport in Massachusetts. The runway lights turned off at 10:00 p.m sharp. We had maybe 10-15 minutes of fuel left. I looked below. Needles of light grinned slyly back at me, challenging me to pick out those which marked the route to our roost.

If we had gassed up at the airport instead of hurrying to dinner...if we had taken a taxi back to the airport instead of walking the "short cut," which got us completely lost and put us thirty minutes behind schedule...we wouldn't be here right now, dangling in the air, thin strings of fuel holding us aloft.

Bill had not flown in this area before, but I had for years, which is why I was navigating. My panicked eyes mapped the landscape. Suddenly I sighted the golf course near the airport, just 500 feet to our right. Blue lights marked the landing strip; they would blink out any minute now. I signalled Bill, who pushed the plane into a series of S turns to lose altitude, dropping the Cessna like a wounded bird toward the strip. We fell softly, nose up, flaps down. Just as we were about to touch the ground, the runway lights went out. Time: 10:00 p.m. Tanks: some giddy fumes. The Cessna headlight guided us to our tiedown spot.

We laughed like thieves at large. I caught my breath, looked at Bill—thirty-odd years of flying experience between us—and said, "Couldn't we have called the tower and asked them to leave on the lights for us?"

—Leila Dunbar, "Lights Out"

PART THREE

GOING YOUR OWN WAY

Preying

*A Sicilian tuna slaughter conjures a drama
of sex, death, and betrayal.*

FAVIGNANA APPEARS LOW ON THE HORIZON, A MILKY PROFILE
against the afternoon sky. As the hydrofoil we've taken from the
westernmost point of Sicily draws nearer, the tiny Egadi island
grows in splendor, the crags of its mountains transforming into
three dimensions, its little town popping into view, sand-colored
walls and roofs crowded together like barnacles under bright sun.
The sea below reveals splotches of aqua as we approach shore.

Tomorrow these waters will turn red when a crew of fishermen
carry out *la mattanza,* the tuna slaughter, a ritual the Arabs brought
to Sicily more than a thousand years ago. The men will trap the
fish in an elaborate series of nets, working to the rhythm of a
chant, a prayer to Christ and the Virgin Mary. Then they will spear
their prey one by one.

Vincenzo and his girlfriend Valeria, people I met on a trip to
Sicily last year, have brought me here to witness this event, the second of several *mattanzas* that will take place this spring. I have felt
compelled to see the spectacle since reading about it last year. I
want to know its rawness, to catch a glimpse of something ancient
in action, something that speaks of my ancestry, of origins, of the
way things were long ago when it was simply man and nature. I

want to see, to smell, to taste the terrible mystery: that life necessitates death. I want to understand what it must have been like when killing for food was a holy act, carried out in a spirit of devotion and thanks.

And this: I want to know brute male strength and masculine essence. So lonely in America, so tired of men who are afraid of their essential selves, I am like a panther in heat, craving.

> Vincenzo is leonine: wild beard and a mass of thick, curly blond hair. He is tall, broad. He has a deep understanding of myth, of the power of the gods and goddesses who dwelt here with the Greek colonizers 2,500 years ago. He keeps speaking of Uranus, master of the heavens, and the Titans, the fierce race of giants, and somehow they are all merging

> *I travel for this, to unbalance my heart, to leave behind the litany of predictables in my life.*
>
> ◆
>
> —Rohini Talalla,
> "Dune: A Day in the
> Namib-Nauklauft Reserve"

in my mind, Uranus, Titans, Vincenzo. I have not known a man so intelligent and so animal at the same time. Sometimes I find my breath is low and shallow, that I am obsessed with one thought: touching him.

I would not have dared think it, had he not taken me aside one day, out of Valeria's earshot, and joked that I should come live with him. But now I can't get it out of my mind, even though I know there is Valeria. Even though I know there is his estranged wife, his little son. Even though I know there are all the other women he's offhandedly mentioned to me.

We stay overnight in a little hotel in Favignana. At six the next morning Vincenzo opens the door to my room. He sits on my bed and wakes me with tender words, fingering a lock of my hair. I thank him chastely.

By six-thirty the three of us join a crew of some twenty fishermen out on the docks. We board one of a half-dozen long, wooden boats loosely tied together with rope. More than 100 years old, their heavy planks are gray and dry, the thick tar covering them flaking off. A tugboat leads our rustic armada out to the nets that lie a couple of miles offshore.

The fishermen laid the nets a month ago, in April. All that can be seen from above is an enormous rectangle of rope and buoys that remains stationary in the water. Nets drop from the ropes vertically to the sea bottom to form a long corridor, one end of which is open to admit the fish. More nets, placed crosswise along the length of this corridor, will be raised and lowered as the fishermen force the tuna through the chamber. Eventually they will corner the fish in the far end, an area they call *la camera della morte,* the chamber of death, the place where they will carry out the bludgeoning.

When we reach the trap, the fishermen maneuver three boats around the chamber of death so that we and several hundred other spectators from all over the world will be able to witness the *mattanza* up close. For now, all that's visible below the surface of the water is a net that hangs shallowly like a huge hammock.

The other boats position themselves far off, at the entrance to the corridor. One is a dingy that carries the three head fisherman who are still addressed by the Arabic title *raìs.* These honored chiefs will deliver all of the orders for driving the fish into the trap once a school has been spotted.

It is 7:30 a.m. The sun is hot, the breeze cool. And now the wait begins. Sighting tuna could take several hours. But the fishermen are patient.

Last year, out of the blue, Vincenzo sent me a post card. "What are you waiting for to write?" was all it said. I barely knew him, having met him just once. But I wrote back. Regards to Valeria, I added at the end. "He takes his time seducing someone," Valeria will tell me later. "It took him five months to get me," she'll say, ticking them off on her fingers.

As the morning draws on, the once-attentive crowd begins to dissemble into chatter. A Japanese video crew roves from boat to boat. Italian families open up their lunches of bread and cheese.

People sprawl where they can, taking in the sun. Death is still far off.

Vincenzo is taking photos. His shorts reveal the legs of a Roman centurion. His sandaled feet move confidently from beam to beam as he positions himself for new angles. I talk with tourists from Milan, continually seeking him from the corner of my eye.

After several hours a thrill runs through the crowd—the signal has been given that a school of tuna has been enclosed inside the nets. Now the fishermen, men ranging from 20 to 60, line up on the long edge of the boat at the entrance to the corridor. Silhouetted against the sky, each in his own particular attitude, they look archetypal, primordial.

They begin to sing in Sicilian, pulling up the nets by hand to the rhythm of the chant. Their hefty voices filter through the wind:

Aimola! Aimola!
Let us all go
Jesus Christ with all the saints
Lord, the Savior
Who created the moon and the sun
Who created all humans
The holy Virgin who has given birth
She made a son just like a god

Their boat approaches the chamber of death slowly as they close off the corridor, the tuna trapped inside. Still the waters are calm. From our end, we can see nothing yet. "In ten minutes it will become chaos," Vincenzo says. "You're going to have to put your love of animals aside for now, and accept that this is for survival," he advises me. "The fish don't feel anything; they're just operating on reflex."

I am gripped by a strange mixture of excitement and dread. Suddenly someone behind me cries out: "I see one!" And soon I, too, can see black forms darting below. The fishermen's cries become even more passionate:

It's emerging!
A body is emerging!

Saint Christopher, great and mighty
He who carried Christ on himself
He was the son of Mary
Mary Magdalene
You were pregnant in grace
Of grace you were crowned
Immaculate one!

The tuna are swimming in fast-motion school formation now. Their panic is obvious. One or two tails begin to flip above the surface, and soon the chamber is a mass of approaching white spray as the tuna thrash about, searching for an escape route.

I suddenly fear I might vomit or scream. I think of the story in Anaïs Nin's *Little Birds* where a man anonymously takes a woman from behind during a public lynching, sex the only antidote to death. I long to reach out for Vincenzo.

I find that I am not alone in my absurd desire. The Sicilians intuitively understand the link, it seems, between extremes: the fishermen begin another chant, this time a love song.

Oh Lina, Lina!
What beautiful eyes has this young lady
What a beautiful mouth has this young lady
What beautiful legs has this young lady
What beautiful breasts has this young lady
And to whom shall we give this young lady?
Let us give her to the *raìs!*

The approaching boat eventually meets our vessels, squaring off the chamber of death. The fishermen pick up long poles with thick iron hooks on the end. Reaching over the side of the boat, they begin to hack at the frantically churning waters below. Each time metal meets firm, iridescent flesh, a loud thwock rings out. Bright red blood runs down from the wound, clouding the water below, as the men strain to haul the squirming tuna up and over the side of the boat. Sometimes several men work to lift one fish; Vincenzo has told me a tuna can weigh as much as 300 pounds.

I watch one of the fishermen, Carlo, who looks old and young at the same time, his face leathery, worn, but his head a mass of incongruous blond California ringlets; his stomach protruding but his arms and legs compact and firm. Vincenzo told me Carlo has five wives, that several of his many sons are among the crew. Barefoot, barechested, wearing a bikini, he looks like a kind of Tarzan of the sea. Despite the contortion of his face each time he wrangles with a tuna, his bulging biceps prevail to slither the glistening mass up and over.

> ——— ☽ ———
>
> he human desire for wildness is strong and deep, because we feel so distant from that source and its unconscious movements in our bodies and minds.
>
> ◆
>
> —Alison Hawthorne Deming, "The Edges of the Civilized World," *Orion*

As the vigorous heaving and hoeing continues, another crew shovels over each incoming tuna with ice. The occasional flip of a tail reveals a fish is still alive. I can't help but think of firing squads, mass graves, people piling up on top of one another, stunned but still conscious, the bullets not yet having done their trick.

Twenty minutes later, only a few stragglers of the some 150 tuna in the school remain. One of Carlo's young sons jumps into the net. Moving with stealth like a native in the jungle, he metes out swift blows to passing fish with his hook, rendering them motionless, dragging them to the side of the boat.

Finally the last tuna, the last survivor of his tribe, is caught. The once-bloody waters now clear again, several fishermen plunge in, diving like youths at a pool party.

The crowd roars with applause and cheers. I clap, too. Yes, these men have done well. They have been strong and brave. A warmth infuses in my loins. Still, I am not sure whether what I have seen has been the natural order of things or merely obscene.

Late that afternoon, we return to Valeria's apartment in

Palermo. We lie about together on her small couch, our bodies still swaying from the sea. Vincenzo takes Valeria's hand. Then mine. We all pretend to drowse, but slowly his finger begins caressing my inner wrist. I am heavy with desire, as though it has always been so, as though I had been born this way. Valeria's back is to us, but she knows. Vincenzo's pelvis is insistent against her hip. I long for her to say yes. I pray she will say no. Eventually she turns around and begins to unbuckle his belt, the clink of metal the only sound in the room.

Vincenzo's hands and mouth seek me, only me. I keep pushing him toward Valeria, but I can see that she is merely an afterthought for him. Eyes closed, he writhes like a serpent in his own private ecstasy. How can he be so selfish, so inconsiderate of both of us? I wonder. I suddenly feel like a concubine. My desire dries up like a puddle of water under the August sun. I move away.

We become still, the sound of afternoon traffic below an idle accompaniment to the silence. The pit in my stomach grows. Valeria says something to Vincenzo tersely in Italian; I grasp one phrase: *come tutte le altre,* just like with all the other women. This time the perfidy has been right in front of her nose, confirming all of her haunted imaginings on days Vincenzo has been out of town, she seems to be saying. And I realize with horror: the look on her face during this episode on the couch has been not desire, but resignation.

Valeria rises suddenly and begins washing dishes in the kitchen. I go to her, apologizing. "You're not the first and you won't be the last," she says, just a hint of curtness showing through her Sicilian hospitality. "Maybe this will help me to finally leave him."

I return to the couch. "We've played with fire," I say to Vincenzo, buttoning up my dress.

"Yes, I think maybe something has died today," he says, going into the kitchen. He tries to soothe Valeria, but she yells at him in Sicilian.

Vincenzo returns. We sit far apart, observing Valeria as she moves about the apartment, waiting for her verdict like contrite children. She changes her clothes, smoothing her mood as she smoothes her dress over her hips. Vincenzo suggests we go out together for some air and she agrees. I wonder how many times she has acquiesced like this.

The next day Vincenzo leaves for work but Valeria stays, saying she doesn't feel well. "I'm searching for something," I tell her, trying to explain my behavior.

"You think you're safe at first; it's a game, almost a joke, but then...," she says. "He tires of them so easily. He'll be on the phone in my bedroom for an hour. Just a colleague, he tells me, but I know it's simply one more he's become bored with. Out of sight, out of mind."

"Do you love him, Valeria?" I ask.

"Yes, more than life itself," she replies somberly. "I used to have friends over all the time. I used to be so optimistic. Now I've become all black."

I think of the tuna. How after swimming and swimming to escape they lie motionless in the corners of the net, still alive but exhausted, all but given up.

I feel chilled, clammy. I vow to myself that I will have nothing more to do with Vincenzo.

I leave for a town in the center of Sicily where other friends await me. Vincenzo finds the number and calls me once, twice, three times. *"Amore mio,"* my love, he croons in deep bass tones, "you need my wildness and I need yours."

"Yes," I finally say, "yes I will meet you when I return to Palermo." What could be the harm? I tell myself. Just an innocent night out with a friend. But by ten that evening my fingers are reaching over to the driver's seat, diving into his thick curls. We merge into kisses, searing and true. I revel in the sheer mass of his body. He is savage and tender.

"We could never be together, you would hurt me," I tell him, easing back to my side of the car. "Yes, I probably would," he says sympathetically. His sincerity and concern strike me; yet I know he would take me down all the same. Were I to succumb to his siren song, he would simply pull away the moment he knew he had me, stealing my happiness and freedom to feed his own rapaciousness, leaving me just another addicted wreck accusing and begging on the other end of the phone line. How like a fisherman he is, I think, ensnaring women in his perilous nets with a love song.

I return to America churning with images of land and sea, of love, death, and betrayal. I had wanted to experience the Sicily of my heritage more deeply this time, to see if there were a shadow lurking beneath the loving kindness of the culture that so feeds me. Now I know. I sense that I must move to Sicily for a time, that the wildness is calling me. But I understand now that the beauty of the wild exacts its price, and as I stand poised to enter this new world, I am afraid. Vincenzo's kisses burn in my memory with an intensity I had not expected. When I return, he will be there waiting. And I know I will need wisdom and strength to swim away.

Marguerite Rigoglioso is a writer and college instructor in Northern California. She has published articles and first-person stories on numerous topics in anthologies, magazines, and academic journals, and her first book on the ancient oracular site of Enna and Lake Pergusa in Sicily awaits publication. Marguerite is a Ph.D. student in religion and humanities at the California Institute of Integral Studies, where she earned her M.A. in women's spirituality.

*

Not far along the path, I suddenly stopped. I knew with blinding certainty that I was not alone. I shared this overgrown field with a presence I could feel but not see. Heaviness hung around me, a sense of intrusion was real, but on whose part? And then I saw it. A thick darkness, obscured by vegetation. Slowly, my gaze moved upwards where my eyes met those of a stag whose head loomed over mine. His round black eyes penetrated me, his breath whistled softly through his muzzle. The rich brown fur on his antlers glistened as sunlight broke through the heavy canopy of tree limbs. He was absolutely motionless. So was I.

My mind raced wildly and self-talk throbbed in my head, threatening to unravel me. "Stand still! Wait!" the internal voice commanded.

"Don't take your eyes off him! Don't move!" Was I a threat to him? Was his doe nearby?

Cautiously, slowly, my back to the wall, I slid a fraction of an inch to my left. I had moved. He hadn't. Our eye contact was unbroken. Another minuscule move, then another. The stag still didn't move, hadn't twitched, stamped a foot, or shifted his weight. Eternity was a reality in this neglected meadow.

—Noel C. Horn, "A Walk on the Wild Side"

✦ ✦ ✦

Rescue in the Exotic Animal Market

A guesthouse room becomes a sanctuary
for some endangered furry friends.

THERE WAS A DRAGON FESTIVAL BLOCKING HAM NGHI BOULE-vard, so all traffic was rerouted along the Saigon river—right past the exotic animal market.

The detour changed my life.

I remembered the market from when I first arrived in Vietnam, three months earlier. It catered to the Vietnamese belief in the medicinal value of animal parts—tiger bone for strength, pickled snake for impotence. I'd wandered inside and watched in horror as a newborn kitten was fed to a half-grown civet, and a young clouded leopard slowly strangled from the rusty wire around its neck. I wanted to stuff some of the smug stall owners into their own cages. Instead, I played the coward and fled.

Since then I'd hitchhiked the length of the country and learned that almost everything in Vietnam could be either bribed or forged, and that few things were truly illegal if approached with the right frame of mind. I had also learned by purest happenstance of an endangered monkey breeding center run by a morose German called Tilo Nadler. He was fighting a losing battle against the animal trade and expected to see the extinction of many of Vietnam's endemic species within a few years.

Suddenly, on the sweltering pavement outside the corrugated market shed, I knew what I had to do. I would buy as many animals as I could and bring them to Tilo, to increase his carefully cultivated gene pool of captive animals that would one day be used to repopulate the wilds.

My traveling companion was not impressed with my new idea. Jochen and I had, upon little more than a nodding acquaintance and the discovery that our visas were due to run out on the same day, agreed to share a motorbike to Saigon. Smuggling endangered animals wasn't part of the bargain. Jochen argued, rightly, that purchasing endangered animals would encourage the black market business. I pointed out that Saigon's animal trade was already a superhighway to China that wasn't about to slow down until there were no animals left. We weren't encouraging the trade as much as we were depriving one more wealthy Chinese gentleman of a placebo tonic for his unfortunate arthritis.

Jochen agreed to accompany me inside the market but repeated his objection to my crackpot scheme. I didn't try to change his mind.

The market was as dark and dirty as I remembered it. I trolled for gibbons, ducking behind hide-filled counters and muttering discretely to perspiring proprietors, and eventually a tiny infant appeared. It was snowy white and soft as a merino lamb, with large round eyes and implausibly long arms and legs. Jochen put aside his camera to come and see. The gibbon extended a tentative arm and wrapped his tiny hand around Jochen's equally cautious finger. In a moment they were snuggled in a corner, the infant clinging to his shirt with all its might while Jochen stroked its head and murmured gentle German endearments.

I wandered over. "Does this mean you'll help me put them on the train?" I asked.

"I'm going with you," he said softly. "We'll take as many as we can."

I scoured the market for more gibbons, without success. I returned to the stall where Jochen had finally torn himself away from the clinging baby. Too late. The owner had noted the entire interaction with an appraising eye.

"How much?" I asked. Two hundred was the going rate.

"Two thousand dollars." She smiled sweetly. "Cash."

I banished Jochen to the stall with tiger hides and snakeskin belts, a safer place for his soft heart, and negotiated in earnest. The price dropped in painful fits and starts, and lodged at $260. She had other buyers, she said, five Chinese businessmen who were happy to pay what she asked. I conferred with Jochen and we agreed to play it safe and check our visa status one more time before buying the infant. Besides, if we called her bluff on the Chinamen nonsense then she would have to lower her prices.

We left with heavy hearts.

The next morning Jochen and I were both up early and prowling the streets around the visa office long before it opened its doors. We were eventually ushered into the office of a Mr. Tuan, who demanded everything from our return air tickets to official forms stamped by every hotel we'd been in since we arrived in Vietnam. Six hours later we returned with passable forgeries, and lubricated the deal with a bottle of Black Label scotch. "Your visas will be ready this afternoon," he said and shut his office door firmly in our faces. We raced back to the market.

The infant gibbon was nowhere to be seen. Its former owner shrugged and wiggled her hand. "The Chinamen came back," she said, and waited for the disappointment to sink in. "But I have another..."

It was indeed a different baby, younger than the first. It sat in the middle of its steel cage, its long arms wrapped around itself, sucking mightily on the wrinkled skin just above its elbow. It whistled in terror when the proprietor tried to drag it out, its eyes widening and its arms clinging more tightly to its own body. It made no effort to grab hold of Jochen's shirt and I noticed a bloody spot on each arm where it had chewed off its fur in psychotic distress.

I left Jochen to cruise the market, and this time met with more success. Four gibbons were expected in the city that afternoon, and if not sold would be China-bound by freighter the following morning. I returned to find Jochen trying to coax the downy infant into sucking on the end of a banana, and began the tedious process of negotiating. The implicit competition from the incoming gibbons brought down the price, and soon we were offered the bargain-basement deal of $180 for one of the last remaining Vietnamese gibbons in the world.

"We should wait until we have our visas," Jochen insisted as he rocked the frightened infant. I went through the motions of arguing with him, knowing that a determined infantry platoon couldn't pry him away from his tiny charge. Turnover in the marketplace was so quick, I pointed out, that if we waited another day then this one would probably be sold. Jochen agreed.

"In that case," I said, "I'll be back." I dashed off and returned a few minutes later with my own arms full of three young leopard kittens and a two-month-old clouded leopard cub. Leopards eat gibbons, Jochen pointed out. We reluctantly purchased two of the hateful steel cages. Then we looked at our small mountain of cages and squirmy animals and wondered how on earth we were going to get them back to our guesthouse.

Jochen slalomed expertly through rush-hour traffic while I balanced precariously on the back of his bike, trying to look nonchalant with four restless leopards stuffed inside my jacket and a

> *C*ruelty is surely the very worst of human sins. To fight cruelty, in any shape or form—whether it be towards other human beings or non-human beings—brings us into direct conflict with that unfortunate streak of *inhumanity* that lurks in all of us. If only we could overcome cruelty with compassion we should be well on the way to creating a new and boundless ethic.
>
> ◆
>
> —Jane Goodall, *Through a Window: My Thirty Years with the Chimpanzees of Gombe*

gibbon under one arm. I gritted my teeth against the casually gripping claws, and tried to savor a unique moment that might never come again. A cat fight erupted under my breasts.

We smuggled them up the guesthouse stairs and into my room, and the leopards quickly disappeared under the bureau. Jochen left for the post office to call Tilo and ask just what a baby gibbon might be expected to eat. I stayed behind to turn an old sock into a protective covering for its swollen arms. Jochen returned with a tin of baby formula, an armful of bananas, and instructions to administer both by eyedropper every two hours, day and night. We fed the animals until their bellies were round and tight and they gurgled with contentment. We made them comfortable, the monkey lying among a half dozen soft toys and the leopards curled up like hairballs under the bed, and snuck away to visit Mr. Tuan and retrieve our passports.

The visa office was closed, but we rattled on the chain until an office boy stuck his head out the door and squinted into the sunlight. He approached, flourishing our passports, and handed them to us through the narrow bars. "No visa," he said loudly. "Reject."

"You're kidding," I said, flipping through the pages.

"That's not possible," Jochen managed.

"Reject! Reject!" the young man shouted and waved his hands about.

Our old visas were due to run out in 24 hours. Neither Thailand nor Laos would accept us on such short notice. I tried pointing this out.

"One day! You leave! Good-bye!" He walked away, still windmilling his arms. We stood behind the gate and stared at his retreating back. The door closed firmly behind him.

We wandered blindly into a small cafe and sat in silence over several cups of coffee. "It's not possible," Jochen said again. Vietnamese ingenuity had exceeded the orderly limits of his mind. I wasn't much better off. Our gloomy, circular thoughts were temporarily derailed by Jochen's budding maternal instincts, when an internal alarm reminded him it was time for the gibbon to be fed. We hurried back to the guesthouse.

The leopards were still tucked into the darkest corner of the room, sleeping off their first good meal of milk in weeks. The gibbon had shredded everything within reach and returned to her favorite pastime, chewing wrinkly holes in her arms. With great difficulty I convinced Jochen to put the smallest leopard, barely the size of a fluffy softball, together in one cage with her. I had seen a similar pairing in the animal market, and the mismatched orphans had been a comfort to each other.

Not so these two. Sabine, as Jochen had christened the baby gibbon, seemed determined to take revenge on the kitten for the predatory habits of his entire species. She chased the kitten around, rapping him on the nose and tweaking his ears and tail. When this didn't make enough of an impression she pushed him against one wall with her back and leaned with all her insubstantial weight, trying to squish him through the bars. This time I was the one who objected, though Jochen seemed quite pleased with the arrangement. The kitten went back under the bed and Sabine was given a knotted rag to torment.

We climbed wearily back onto the motorbike to make a run on the Cambodian embassy for an entry visa. They pointed out, pleasantly enough, that my exit stamp required me to leave from Saigon airport and all flights were booked for at least a week.

Time was running out. We raced over to the nearest Vietnamese tourist agency to change my exit stamp. The wait was endless and the chairs were hard, and the woman who eventually took my passport laughed at the idea of restamping my visa in less than a week. I asked for the heavy-duty, no-holds-barred, extortionately priced rush service advertised on the wall. Five days, she said.

We hurried back to the visa extension office, to appeal to their previously untapped altruism in the hopes that they might give us a five-day extension.

The office boy slouched out to see who was pleading at the gate. "Closed now!" he said through the bars.

"But it's only two o'clock," we argued.

"Closed!" he shouted, cranking up the volume once again. We begged.

"Passports," he said and held out a hand. We fled.

It was time to feed the gibbon. As we motored home we passed a Western woman in a long skirt, stiffly upright on a one-speed bike. Jochen throttled back and cruised along beside her.

"Excuse me," I said. "Do you like cats?"

She seemed taken aback. I explained our predicament, playing down the mischievous claws and midnight feedings, while Jochen swerved around pedestrians and ice cream carts to keep pace. "Would you be willing," I concluded, "to take care of a few very tiny leopards for a week while we arrange for a new visa in Cambodia?"

"Certainment pas!" she said, her body stiffening alarmingly on the already unstable bicycle. "I work for the French Embassy. Such a thing would be illegal!"

"So is the animal black market," I pointed out, "which nevertheless is advertised in your tourist guidebook." But the Embassy was no longer listening; head held high, skirt swishing, she pedaled off in a straight, matronly line. We returned home to our unwanted orphans.

I left Jochen to pre-chew a quarter pound of meat and mash some bananas into monkey food, and took off for Saigon's backpacker district. Somehow I had to find a generous spirit willing to take charge of our menagerie until we returned from Cambodia and could transport them to Tilo's sanctuary.

Kim Cafe was overcrowded, the chatter of a dozen languages mingling with smoke and unwashed bodies under the harsh fluorescent lights. Everyone, it seemed, was discussing tours and travel plans, and the few conversations I dropped in on weren't promising; a Danish nutritionist on her way to Dalat by minibus the following morning giving detailed advice to a pair of shaggy Australians, who planned to take a slow boat down the Mekong. Two French couples in a tight huddle at the end of a crowded table, exhaling clouds of smoke and wanting only to be left alone. I stood and tapped my glass with a spoon. No one paid the slightest attention. I sent a brief prayer of forgiveness to the gods of the jungle and pulled the smallest leopard kitten out of my pocket. All conversation stopped. Even the French couples lent a covert ear.

They heard me out in utter silence, every eye fixed on the ball of fur nestled in the palm of my hand. Then, like an auction, people raised their hands, calling out dates and places, and soon were passing the leopard kitten from lap to lap and organizing its social calendar for the next few weeks. A brawny German, utterly captivated by the tiny animal nestled in the crook of his bulging biceps, and immediately canceled his intended visit to the famous Cu Chi tunnels, or "Ze dirty veasel holes in ze ground," as they had suddenly become. An English carpenter was returning from a Mekong tour in three days, and would be happy to host the little dustmops for the weekend. If his guesthouse owner didn't approve, she could jolly well find a new boarder. Two unkempt Canadians promised the orphans a permanent home in their awesome new digs, available a week hence.

I sat off to one side and watched a miracle gradually unfold. People who would haggle for hours over a 50-cent discount, who had scrimped and saved for years to see Vietnam, were fighting for the opportunity to give it all up on behalf of a sleepy ball of fur.

"It's not so surprising," a voice said in my ear. "This is their opportunity to do something extraordinary. That's worth a few tourist traps." He was American, scraping by teaching private English classes while he looked for permanent work. "Will you be buying more?" he asked, and handed me a hundred dollar bill.

That night, I lay in a room momentarily silent, the gibbon fast asleep, its long arms wrapped around a pillow twice as large as itself. The two youngest kittens were quiet after hours of entertaining antics. Unlike their older brethren, they actively courted human contact lying in wait until I came out of the shower and playing Tarzan with my bath towel until I gave up trying to hold it in place. For the first time in my life the monsters under the bed were real, and when I put my bare feet down a playful set of claws wrapped around my ankle. As I drifted off to sleep I felt a feather-soft tail across my face and four tiny paws kneading a depression on my pillow.

I floated up through layered dreams to the rapid pitter-patter of rats running across the roof beams, and awoke to find that they had turned into leopards, dancing on the carpet. I watched their shadowy forms slither around my pack and burst into a pool of moonlight, where they pranced and sparred. I fell asleep to the cottony thud of velvet paws and dreamed of jungle nights, of braided vines and dark green leaves, and mottled shapes that flowed from space to space.

The next morning—a wild, worried rush to the airport, standby on an empty flight—I found myself sitting next to two sleek businessmen from another planet. They chatted loudly about the stock market, the NBA results, and their favorite ski resorts in Aspen. I looked out the window at the earth-brown Mekong flowing smoothly towards the sea, and tried to remember why I had been so afraid when I first flew over this strange and complicated land.

I heard the man beside me say, "It's an opportunity, there's no doubt about that, but it won't be easy." And I thought, you have no idea.

Karin Muller is a writer, filmmaker, and photographer. Her books include Along the Inca Road *and* Hitchhiking Vietnam, *from which this story was excerpted. She also produced TV specials of the same titles, the former for National Geographic and the latter for PBS.*

✳

Poverty rarely brings out the most generous human impulses, especially when it comes to environmental matters. Ask a hungry West African about the evils of deforestation, or an unemployed Oregon logger about the endangered spotted owl, and you'll get just about the same answer: I can't afford to think about that right now. Environmentalists must make a case, again and again, for the possibility that we can't afford *not* to think about it.

—Barbara Kingsolver, *High Tide in Tucson: Essays from Now or Never*

LYNNE COX

✦ ✦ ✦

Swimming Titicaca

From Bolivia to Peru,
doing the crawl.

I COULDN'T BREATHE. MY LUNGS AND CHEST WERE FULLY expanded, but on Lake Titicaca, at an altitude of 12,500 feet, no oxygen was flowing in. Stop swimming. Don't panic. The air will return, I told myself. But I felt like I was pinned to the ocean floor waiting for a series of pounding waves to pass. My lungs burned and spasmed. My fingers were tingling and my head was spinning. I rolled over on the water's surface and floated like a dying fish, my mouth wide open, gasping for air.

I thought I had prepared for this swim back in Breckenridge, Colorado. There, in early spring and at an altitude of 7,000 feet, the mountain lakes were still frozen. I tied a Stretz Cordz—a bungie cord-like device—to a pine tree, placed my hands into the cord's handholds, and pulled them back and forth like I was swimming. After one week I gradually built up to tree-swimming for two hours. The next week, I moved up the mountain to a tall pine at 9,000 feet. Skiers who saw me standing on the edge of the slope, bent over, facing the tree, and rapidly pulling the cord, quickly veered away.

For more than twenty years, I had trained to be the first person on record to swim across the Andes's Lake Titicaca, the world's highest navigable body of water. At age fifteen and sixteen, I broke the men's and women's world records for swimming across the English Channel. Years later, I swam across Lake Tahoe and the frigid waters of the Bering Strait.

"Are you okay?" My crew—Barry Binder, Deborah Ford, and Pete Kelley—was shouting to me from the Bolivian Navy's escort boat nearby.

Thankfully the oxygen was flowing deep into my lungs now and I could lift my head and speak, "The water's fifty-six. It feels colder than I thought it would be. I think I took the swim out too fast to try to get warm," I 'said, huffing between sentences.

In addition to the physical challenge, this swim across Lake Titicaca, from Copacabana on the banks of Bolivia to Chimbo on the shore of Peru, was meant to be a gesture of good will between Bolivia, Peru, and the

———)———

I have swum for almost as long as I have walked, at first because I had an aptitude, later because it soothed my soul, kept me sane. Swimming lessons began the summer I was three years old. Eighty percent of the newborn human body is water, and infants have a well-documented "swimming reflex." I doubt that the one has anything to do with the other, except that perhaps, on some metaphysical level, water and swimming are in our blood.

◆

—Sally Friedman,
Swimming the Channel: A Memoir of Love, Loss and Healing

United States—coordinated by U.S. Assistant Secretary of State Robert S. Gelbard, the Peruvian ambassador to Bolivia, and the Bolivian Ministry of Defense. The Bolivian Navy was supporting these efforts by providing boat support as well as Captain Able Coa and a local Aymaran fisherman to navigate for us.

I was still struggling to regulate my breath. I had swum only six strokes off the Bolivian shore and had already nearly crashed and burned. It was sobering; I had never experienced anything like this before. It nearly psyched me out. But I remembered what Dr.

Robert Schoene, a pulmonary specialist who had climbed many of the world's highest mountains, had told me about the effects of altitude: once you reach the 9,000 foot mark, the effects become exponential and intensify with each additional thousand feet.

To Dr. Schoene's knowledge, no one had done any research on the effects of swimming at altitude combined with the effects of swimming in cold water. No one knew what would happen. That's what made this swim exciting—trying to figure it out, trying to adapt and find how to move on the outer side of the edge.

Rolling back onto my stomach, I started swimming again. On this extreme swim across Lake Titicaca, I was going to have to make a choice: to breathe or maintain a core temperature. At that point, breathing seemed more important. So I cut my speed from two knots down to one. Quickly the fifty-six degree water numbed my skin. But I was thankful for that.

During my workouts in the lake I had gotten sunburned and something had been biting me. My body was covered with quarter-sized pink spots that itched worse than mosquito bites. No one, not even the doctors in La Paz knew what organism was causing them. Few people ever swim in Lake Titicaca. Those who have wore wet suits. There were also a few cows that occasionally waded in as far as their knees, but none seemed to have furry polka dots.

One of my crew members had recommended applying *violeta,* a purple juice from a South American jungle fruit. The juice was a folk remedy supposed to relieve itching. It didn't help, but it did stain my skin purple so that now my body was covered with pink and purple polka dots. When one local woman in Copacabana saw me, she crossed herself and hurried away. For the most part though, the local people were intrigued with what we were doing. In the large and beautiful cathedral in Copacabana, they had prayed for good weather for us. And on the calm morning of the swim, the villagers awoke early and came to see us off. We could hear their shouts of support from behind us echoing across this lake that averaged 45 miles wide and 110 miles long.

The cold quickly penetrated my muscles and I knew that if I

didn't start swimming faster and create more heat, I was going to go into hypothermia. Adjusting, I decided to breathe every two strokes instead of every three to pick up my pace and get enough oxygen. Gradually, I began enjoying the swim. Looking down through Lake Titicaca's crystal clear, dark blue waters, I saw a colony of perhaps fifty giant, prehistoric-looking frogs. Nearly two feet long, the frogs were various shades of khaki and rested peacefully between the algae-covered rocks on the lake's bottom. There was something eerie about them, frozen in place and unmoving when I passed over.

Quickly I moved across the lake until I was three miles from Peru. There the wind suddenly began blowing down from the Andes, picking up speed as it crossed the treeless *altiplano*, whipping the lake into a cauldron of white, breaking waves.

The waves lifted me and I yo-yoed across the bumpy water's surface. With each arm stroke, I tried to grab new water. But it felt like I was swimming in a cold-water jacuzzi. All I got was bubbles and silver foam. There was nothing in my hands to push against. I could feel that my speed had dropped to less than one knot. I'd been swimming for 20 minutes and had gone only about 20 yards; I should have swum a mile by then. I dug down deeper into the lake, lowering my body position in the water. Now I was moving through the waves instead of over them. This saved energy and I began to make progress again.

But I wasn't able to breathe much in this new position. The waves were crashing and washing over my head. I decided to try a different strategy, to try breathing later into my stroke, under my arm pit, and use my arm to shield my face from the breaking waves.

By then I'd been swimming half an hour of what would be about a three hour and forty minute swim. Breathing to the side away from the boat was working, but every time I turned my head toward the boat, I got a mouthful of water: I choked, spit up water, and gasped for air. It didn't take me long to realize that I could breathe only on the side away from the boat.

Now I was swimming blind. I couldn't use the sight of the boat to stay on course. So I had to tune into my senses and feel the hum of the boat's engines through the water to judge my distance from it. And I had to listen hard for the shouts of the crew to tell when I was veering too far away or about to slam into the side of the boat.

I continued on this way over the next few hours.

Finally, the crew started shouting. I looked up. They were pointing to a tiny old Peruvian church on a hill above the village of Chimbo.

We were less than a mile from shore, and I felt like I'd swum twenty-five. The wind was increasing to thirty knots. And now the waves were nearly two feet and churning up deeper, colder water. My muscles tightened in the cold.

Deborah Ford watched me from the boat for signs of hypothermia: purple lips, fingers separating, shivering, or a blue cast to my shoulders. She didn't see any signs but she noticed that I was rapidly falling off pace "Do you want something to drink?" she shouted above the howling wind and crashing waves.

"Yes," I shouted and nodded. I had eaten *quinoa,* an Andean type of protein-packed oatmeal for breakfast, but my energy levels were waning quicker than I had expected. And with the altitude and cold, I was dehydrated, which increased my chances of going into hypothermia. Rolling over onto my back, I drank some Gatorade. The break helped and the drink immediately boosted my blood sugar so that I put my head down for the final sprint into shore. The waves were crashing over my head now and I couldn't see anything but the side of the boat. But I could hear the crew cheering me on in English and Spanish.

Suddenly I looked down and saw the lake bottom rising up. I stepped down and felt the soft Peruvian sand between my feet. In three hours and forty-eight minutes, I had swum the ten miles across the lake.

Deborah jumped into the thigh-high water with me and wrapped a towel around my shoulders while the boat found a place to land. Villagers from Chimbo had heard about the swim over the radio and they were hurrying down from the hillsides to greet us, their flocks of sheep trailing behind them.

At first the villagers were shy, but as we talked to them through an interpreter they warmed up. One old woman touched me on the shoulder and then a group of woman took turns hugging me and welcoming all of us to Peru. Then the village men greeted us. They started cheering and then we cheered, together: "Viva Peru! Viva Bolivia! Viva USA!" Together we celebrated the first official crossing of Lake Titicaca.

Lynne Cox also contributed "The Pelican" in Part One.

✳

So what is wild? What is wilderness? What are dreams but an internal wilderness and what is desire but a wildness of the soul?

—Louise Erdrich, *The Blue Jay's Dance: A Birth Year*

LOUISE ERDRICH

Skunk Dreams

*Wild creatures and forest provide a cure
for "horizon sickness."*

WHEN I WAS FOURTEEN, I SLEPT ALONE ON A NORTH DAKOTA football field under the cold stars on an early spring night. May is unpredictable in the Red River Valley, and I happened to hit a night when frost formed in the grass. A skunk trailed a plume of steam across the 40-yard line near moonrise. I tucked the top of my sleeping bag over my head and was just dozing off when the skunk walked onto me with simple authority.

Its ripe odor must have dissipated in the frozen earth of its winterlong hibernation, because it didn't smell all that bad, or perhaps it was just that I took shallow breaths in numb surprise. I felt him—her, whatever—pause on the side of my hip and turn around twice before evidently deciding I was a good place to sleep. At the back of my knees, on the quilting of my sleeping bag, it trod out a spot for itself and then, with a serene little groan, curled up and lay perfectly still. That made two of us. I was wildly awake, trying to forget the sharpness and number of skunk teeth, trying not to think of the high percentage of skunks with rabies, or the reason that on camping trips my father always kept a hatchet underneath his pillow.

Inside the bag, I felt as if I might smother. Carefully, making only the slightest of rustles, I drew the bag away from my face and took a deep breath of the night air, enriched with skunk, but clear and watery and cold. It wasn't so bad, and the skunk didn't stir at all, so I watched the moon—caught that night in an envelope of silk, a mist—pass over my sleeping field of teenage guts and glory. The grass in spring that has lain beneath the snow harbors a sere dust both old and fresh. I smelled that newness beneath the rank tone of my bag-mate—the stiff fragrance of damp earth and the thick pungency of newly manured fields a mile or two away— along with my sleeping bag's smell, slightly mildewed, forever smoky. The skunk settled even closer and began to breathe rapidly; its feet jerked a little like a dog's. I sank against the earth, and fell asleep too.

Of what easily tipped cans, what molten sludge, what dogs in yards on chains, what leftover macaroni casseroles, what cellar holes, crawl spaces, burrows taken from meek woodchucks, of what miracles of garbage did my skunk dream? Or did it, since we can't be sure, dream the plot of *Moby Dick*, how to properly age parmesan, or how to restore the brick-walled, tumbledown creamery that was its home? We don't know about the dreams of any other biota, and even much about our own. If

—— ☽ ——

J missed my chance. I should have gone for the throat. I should have lunged for that streak of white under the weasel's chin and held on, held on through mud and into the wild rose, held on for a dearer life. We could live under the wild rose wild as weasels, mute and uncomprehending. I could very calmly go wild.

◆

—Annie Dillard, *Teaching a Stone to Talk: Expeditions and Encounters*

dreams are an actual dimension, as some assert, then the usual rules of life by which we abide do not apply. In that place, skunks may certainly dream themselves into the vests of stockbrokers. Perhaps that night the skunk and I dreamed each other's thoughts or are still dreaming them. To paraphrase the problem of the

Chinese sage, I may be a woman who has dreamed herself a skunk, or a skunk still dreaming that she is a woman....

Skunks don't mind each other's vile perfume. Obviously, they find each other more than tolerable. And even I, who have been in the presence of a direct skunk hit, wouldn't classify their weapon as mere smell. It is more on the order of a reality-enhancing experience. It's not so pleasant as standing in a grove of old-growth red cedars, or on a lyrical moonshed plain, or watching trout rise to the shadow of your hand on the placid surface of an Alpine lake. When the skunk lets go, you're surrounded by skunk presence: in-habited, owned, involved with something you can only describe as powerfully *there*.

I woke at dawn, stunned into that sprayed state of being. The dog that had approached me was rolling in the grass, half-addled, sprayed too. The skunk was gone. I abandoned my sleeping bag and started home. Up Eighth Street, past the tiny blue and pink houses, past my grade school, past all the addresses where I had baby-sat, I walked in my own strange wind. The streets were wide and empty; I met no one—not a dog, not a squirrel, not even an early robin. Perhaps they had all scattered before me, blocks away. I had gone out to sleep on the football field because I was afflicted with a sadness I had to dramatize. Mood swings had begun, hor-mones, feverish and brutal. They were nothing to me now. My emotions had seemed vast, dark, and sickeningly private. But they were minor, mere wisps, compared to skunk.

I have found that my best dreams come to me in cheap motels. One such dream about an especially haunting place occurred in a rattling room in Saint Thomas, North Dakota. There, in the Potato Capital of the World, I was to spend a week-long residency as a poet-in-the-schools. I was supporting myself, at the time, by teach-ing poetry to children, convicts, rehabilitation patients, high-school hoods, and recovering alcoholics. What a marvelous job it was, and what opportunities I had to dream, since I paid my own lodging and lived low, sometimes taking rooms for less than ten dollars a night in motels that had already been closed by local health departments.

The images that assailed me in Saint Thomas came about because the bedspread was so thin and worn—a mere brown tissuey curtain—that I had to sleep beneath my faux fur Salvation Army coat, wearing all of my clothing, even a scarf. Cold often brings on the most spectacular of my dreams, as if my brain has been incited to fevered activity. On that particular frigid fall night, the cold somehow seemed to snap boundaries, shift my time continuum, and perhaps even allow me to visit my own life in a future moment. After waking once, transferring the contents of my entire suitcase onto my person, and shivering to sleep again, I dreamed of a vast, dark, fenced place. The fencing was chain-link in places, chicken wire, sagging X wire, barbed wire on top, jerry-built with tipped-out poles and uncertain corners nailed to log posts and growing trees. And yet it was quite impermeable and solid, as time-tested, broken-looking things so often are.

Behind it, trees ran for miles—large trees, grown trees, big pines the likes of which do not exist in the Great Plains. In my dream I walked up to the fence, looked within, and saw tawny, humpbacked elk move among the great trunks and slashing green arms. Suave, imponderable, magnificently dumb, they lurched and floated through the dim-complexioned air. One turned, however, before they all vanished, and from either side of that flimsy-looking barrier there passed between us a look, a communion, a long and measureless regard that left me, on waking, with a sensation of penetrating sorrow.

I didn't think about my dream for many years, until after I moved to New Hampshire. I had become urbanized and sedentary since the days when I slept with skunks, and I had turned inward. For several years I spent my days leaning above a strange desk, a green door on stilts, which was so high that to sit at it I bought a barstool upholstered in brown leatherette. Besides, the entire Northeast seemed like the inside of a house to me, the sky small and oddly lit, as if by an electric bulb. The sun did not pop over the great trees for hours—and then went down so soon. I was suspicious of Eastern land: the undramatic loveliness, the small scale, the lack of sky to watch, the way the weather sneaked up without enough warning.

The woods themselves seemed bogus at first—every inch of the ground turned over more than once, and even in the second growth of old pines so much human evidence. Rock walls ran everywhere, grown through and tumbled, as if the dead still had claims they imposed. The unkillable and fiercely contorted trees of old orchards, those revenants, spooked me when I walked in the woods. The blasted limbs spread a white lace cold as fire in the spring, and the odor of the blossoms was furiously spectral, sweet. When I stood beneath the canopies that hummed and shook with bees, I heard voices, other voices, and I did not understand what they were saying, where they had come from, what drove them into this earth.

Then, as often happens to sparring adversaries in 1940s movies, I fell in love.

After a few years of living in the country, the impulse to simply *get outside* hit me, strengthened, and became again a habit of thought, a reason for storytelling, an uneasy impatience with walls and roads. At first, when I had that urge, I had to get into a car and drive fifteen hundred miles before I was back in a place that I defined as *out*. The West, or the edge of it anyway, the great level patchwork of chemically treated fields and tortured grazing land, was the outside I had internalized. In the rich Red River Valley, where the valuable cropland is practically measured in inches, environmental areas are defined and proudly pointed out as stretches of roadway where the ditches are not mowed. Deer and pheasants survive in shelter belts—rows of Russian olive, plum, sometimes evergreen—planted at the edges of fields. The former tall-grass prairie has now become a collection of mechanized gardens tended by an array of air-conditioned farm implements and bearing an increasing amount of pesticide and herbicide in each black teaspoon of dirt. Nevertheless, no amount of reality changed the fact that I still *thought* of eastern North Dakota as wild.

In time, though, *out* became outside my door in New England.
By walking across the road and sitting in my little writing house—
a place surrounded by trees, thick plumes of grass, jets of ferns, and
banks of touch-me-not—or just by looking out a screen door or
window, I started to notice what there was to see. In time, the
smothering woods that had always seemed part of Northeastern
civilization—more an inside than an outside, more like a friendly
garden—revealed themselves as forceful and complex. The growth
of plants, the lush celebratory springs made a grasslands person
drunk. The world turned dazzling green, the hills rode like comfortable and flowing animals. Everywhere there was the sound of
water moving.

And yet, even though I finally grew closer to these woods, on
some days I still wanted to tear them from before my eyes.

I wanted to *see*. Where I grew up, our house looked out on the
western horizon. I could see horizon when I played. I could see it
when I walked to school. It was always there, a line beyond everything, a simple line of changing shades and colors that ringed the
town, a vast place. That was it. Down at the end of every grid of
streets: vastness. Out the windows of the high school: vastness. From
the drive-in theater where I went parking in a purple Duster: vast
distance. That is why, on lovely New England days when everything should have been all right—a spring day, for instance, when
the earth had risen through the air in patches and the sky lowered,
dim and warm—I fell sick with longing for the horizon. I wanted
the clean line, the simple line, the clouds marching over it in feathered masses. I suffered from horizon sickness. But it sounds crazy for
a grown woman to throw herself at the sky, and the thing is, I
wanted to get well. And so to compensate for horizon sickness, for
the great longing that seemed both romantically German and prag-
matically Chippewa in origin, I found solace in trees.

Trees are a changing landscape of sound—and the sound I grew
attached to, possible only near large deciduous forests, was the
great hushed roar of thousands and millions of leaves brushing and
touching one another. Windy days were like sitting just out of sight
of an ocean, the great magnetic ocean of wind. All around me, I

watched the trees tossing, their heads bending. At times the movement seemed passionate, as though they were flung together in an eager embrace, caressing each other, branch to branch. If there is a vegetative soul, an animating power that all things share, there must be great rejoicing out there on windy days, ecstasy, for trees move so slowly on calm days. At least it seems that way to us. On days of high wind they move so freely it must give them a cellular pleasure close to terror.

> ——— ☽ ———
>
> *T*he desire to merge slowly and imperceptibly is the deeper impulse; adrenaline merely initiates the motion. I have been propelled into the company of maples, irresistibly pulled by the desire to meet. Now, in the actual presence of the tree, I soften with the tenderness of the dance between two beings. I recognize this consummation of yearning, this fulfillment of desire.
>
> ◆
>
> —Stephanie Kaza, *The Attentive Heart: Conversations with Trees*

Unused to walking in the woods, I did not realize that trees dropped branches—often large ones—or that there was any possible danger in going out on windy days, drawn by the natural drama. There was a white pine I loved, a tree of the size foresters call *overgrown*, a waste, a thing made of long-since harvestable material. The tree was so big that three people couldn't reach around it. Standing at the bottom, craning back, fingers clenched in grooves of bark, I held on as the crown of the tree roared and beat the air a hundred feet above. The movement was frantic, the soft-needled branches long and supple. I thought of a woman tossing, anchored in passion: calm one instant, full-throated the next, hair vast and dark, shedding the piercing, fresh oil of broken needles. I went to visit her often, and walked onward, farther, though it was not so far at all, and then one day I reached the fence.

Chain-link in places, chicken wire, sagging X wire, barbed wire on top, jerry-built with tipped-out poles and uncertain corners nailed to log posts and growing trees, still it seemed impermeable and solid. Behind it, there were trees for miles: large trees, grown trees, big pines. I walked up to the fence, looked within, and could see elk moving. Suave, imponderable, magnificently dumb, they lurched and floated through the dim air.

I was on the edge of a game park, a rich man's huge wilderness, probably the largest parcel of protected land in western New Hampshire, certainly the largest privately owned piece I knew about. At 40 square miles—25,000 acres—it was bigger than my mother's home reservation. And it had the oddest fence around it that I'd ever seen, the longest and the tackiest. Though partially electrified, the side closest to our house was so piddling that an elk could easily have tossed it apart. Certainly a half-ton wild boar, the condensed and living version of a tank, could have strolled right through. But then animals, much like most humans, don't charge through fences unless they have sound reasons. As I soon found out, because I naturally grew fascinated with the place, there were many more animals trying to get into the park than out, and they couldn't have cared less about ending up in a hunter's stew pot.

These were not wild animals, the elk—since they were grained at feeding stations, how could they be? They were not domesticated either, however, for beyond the no-hunt boundaries they fled and vanished. They were game. Since there is no sport in shooting feedlot steers, these animals—still harboring wild traits and therefore more challenging to kill—were maintained to provide blood pleasure for the members of the Blue Mountain Forest Association.

As I walked away from the fence that day, I was of two minds about the place—and I am still. Shooting animals inside fences, no matter how big the area they have to hide in, seems abominable and silly. And yet, I was glad for that wilderness. Though secretly managed and off limits to me, it was the source of flocks of evening grosbeaks and pine siskins, of wild turkey, ravens, and grouse, of Eastern coyote, oxygen-rich air, foxes, goldfinches, skunk, and bears that tunneled in and out.

I had dreamed of this place in Saint Thomas, or it had dreamed me. There was affinity here, beyond any explanation I could offer, so I didn't try. I continued to visit the tracts of big trees, and on deep nights—windy nights, especially when it stormed—I liked to fall asleep imagining details. I saw the great crowns touching, heard the raving sound of wind and thriving, knocking cries as the blackest of ravens flung themselves across acres upon indifferent acres of tossing, old-growth pine. I could fall asleep picturing how, below that dark air, taproots thrust into a deeper blankness, drinking the powerful rain.

Or was it so only in my dreams? The park, known locally as Corbin's Park, after its founder Austin Corbin, is knit together of land and farmsteads he bought in the late nineteenth century from 275 individuals. Among the first animals released there, before the place became a hunting club, were thirty buffalo, remnants of the vast Western herds. Their presence piqued the interest of Ernest Harold Bayne, a conservation-minded local journalist, who attempted to break a pair of buffalo calves to the yoke. He exhibited them at county fairs and even knit mittens out of buffalo wool, hoping to convince the skeptical of their usefulness. His work inspired sympathy, if not a trend for buffalo yarn, and collective zeal for the salvation of the buffalo grew until by 1915 the American Bison Society, of which Bayne was secretary, helped form government reserves that eventually more than doubled the herds that remained.

The buffalo dream seems to have been the park's most noble hour. Since that time it has been the haunt of wealthy hunting enthusiasts. The owner of Ruger Arms currently inhabits the stunning, butter-yellow original Corbin mansion and would like to buy the whole park for his exclusive use, or so local gossip has it.

For some months I walked the boundary admiring the tangled landscape, at least all that I could see. After my first apprehension, I ignored the fence. I walked along it as if it simply did not exist, as if I really were part of that place which lay just beyond my reach.

The British psychotherapist Adam Phillips has examined obstacles from several different angles, attempting to define their emotional use. "It is impossible to imagine desire without obstacles," he writes, "and wherever we find something to be an obstacle we are at the same time desiring something. It is part of the fascination of the Oedipus story in particular, and perhaps narrative in general, that we and the heroes and heroines of our fictions never know whether obstacles create desire or desire creates obstacles." He goes on to characterize the Unconscious, our dream world, as a place without obstacles: "A good question to ask of a dream is: What are the obstacles that have been removed to make this extraordinary scene possible?"

My dream, however, was about obstacles still in place. The fence was the main component, the defining characteristic of the forbidden territory that I watched but could not enter or experience. The obstacles that we overcome define us. We are composed of hurdles we set up to pace our headlong needs, to control our desires, or against which to measure our growth. "Without obstacles," Phillips writes, "the notion of development is inconceivable. There would be nothing to master."

Walking along the boundary of the park no longer satisfied me. The precariousness and deceptive stability of that fence began to rankle. Longing filled me. I wanted to brush against the old pine bark and pass beyond the ridge, to see specifically what was there: what Blue Mountain, what empty views, what lavender hillside, what old cellar holes, what unlikely animals. I was filled with poacher's lust, except I wanted only to smell the air. The linked web restraining me began to grate, and I started to look for weak spots, holes, places where the rough wire sagged. From the moment I began to see the fence as permeable, it became something to overcome. I returned time after time—partly to see if I could spot anyone on the other side, partly because I knew I must trespass.

Then, one clear, midwinter morning, in the middle of a half-hearted thaw, I walked along the fence until I came to a place that looked shaky—and was. I went through. There were no trails that I could see, and I knew I needed to stay away from any perimeter roads or snowmobile paths, as well as from the feeding stations where the animals congregated. I wanted to see the animals, but only from a distance. Of course, as I walked on, leaving a trail easily backtracked, I encountered no animals at all. Still, the terrain was beautiful, the columns of pine tall and satisfyingly heavy, the patches of oak and elderly maple from an occasional farmstead knotted and patient. I was satisfied and, sometime in the early afternoon, I decided to turn back and head toward the fence again. Skirting a low, boggy area that teemed with wild turkey tracks, I was just heading toward the edge of a deadfall of trashed dead branches and brush, when I stared too hard into the sun, and stumbled.

In a half crouch, I looked straight into the face of a boar, massive as a boulder. Cornfed, razor-tusked, alert, sensitive ears pricked, it edged slightly backward into the covering shadows. Two ice picks of light gleamed from its shrouded, tiny eyes, impossible to read. Beyond the rock of its shoulder, I saw more; a sow and three cinnamon-brown farrows crossing a small field of glare snow, lit by dazzling sun. The young skittered along, lumps of muscled fat on tiny hooves. They reminded me of snowsuited toddlers on new skates. When they were out of sight the boar melted through the brush after them, leaving not a snapped twig or crushed leaf in his wake.

I almost didn't breathe in the silence, letting the fact of that presence settle before I retraced my own tracks.

Since then, I've been to the game park via front gates, driven down the avenues of tough old trees, and seen herds of wild pigs and elk meandering past the residence of the gamekeeper. A no-hunting zone exists around the house, where the animals are almost tame. But I've been told by privileged hunters that just beyond that invisible boundary they vanish, becoming suddenly and preternaturally elusive.

There is something in me that resists the notion of fair use of this land if the only alternative is to have it cut up, sold off in lots, condominiumized. Yet the dumb fervor of the place depresses me—the wilderness locked up and managed but not for its sake; the animals imported and cultivated to give pleasure through their deaths. All animals, that is, except for skunks.

Not worth hunting, inedible except to old trappers like my uncle Ben Gourneau, who boiled his skunk with onions in three changes of water, skunks pass in and out of Corbin's Park without hindrance, without concern. They live off the corn in the feeding cribs (or the mice it draws), off the garbage of my rural neighbors, off bugs and frogs and grubs. They nudge their way onto our back porch for catfood, and even when disturbed they do not, ever, hurry. It's easy to get near a skunk, even to capture one. When skunks become a nuisance, people either shoot them or catch them in crates, cardboard boxes, Hav-A-Hart traps, plastic garbage barrels.

Natives of the upper Connecticut River valley have neatly solved the problem of what to do with such catches. They hoist their trapped mustelid into the back of a pickup truck and cart the animal across the river to the neighboring state—New Hampshire to Vermont, Vermont to New Hampshire—before releasing it. The skunk population is estimated as about even on both sides.

We should take comfort from the skunk, an arrogant creature so pleased with its own devices that it never runs from harm, just turns its back in total confidence. If I were an animal, I'd choose to be a skunk: live fearlessly, eat anything, gestate my young in just two months, and fall into a state of dreaming topor when the cold bit hard. Wherever I went, I'd leave my sloppy tracks. I wouldn't walk so much as putter, destinationless, in a serene belligerence—past hunters, past death overhead, past death all around.

Louise Erdrich grew up in North Dakota and is of Chippewa and German-American descent. She is an award-winning writer whose books include Love Medicine, The Beet Queen, Tracks, The Blue Jay's Dance, *and several books of poetry.*

✳

"Women are best at dreaming. They have the facility to abandon themselves, the facility to let go…. Women are peerless dreamers," Esperanza assured me. "Women are extremely practical. In order to sustain a dream, one must be practical, because the dream must pertain to practical aspects of oneself. My teacher's favorite dream was to dream of herself as a hawk.

—Florinda Donner, *Being-in-Dreaming*

KYLE E. MCHUGH

Feeling the Green

There are infinite ways to see the colors
and textures of Irish farm life.

WHILE WORKING FOR A MEMBER OF PARLIAMENT IN BELFAST, Northern Ireland one spring, I was invited to spend the weekend on a farm near the shore. I don't know if it actually was considered the shore or the mountains, since it was located in the indescribable geographic space at the base of the Mountains of Mourne, where you can practically touch the ocean with one hand and the mountains with the other. I do not remember the name of the town, except that it had some mellifluous Gaelic name that brings to mind a bird or a song.

I was visiting a family named Kennedy, whose son worked for the same Member of Parliament as I. He had six brothers and sisters, some of whom still lived at home with his parents. He said that they would welcome my visit, and, like everyone I had met in Northern Ireland, his hospitality was genuine. The people of this country had a feeling about their homeland that I had never encountered in America. They were so deeply devoted to their country that they could not imagine why anyone would want to travel, leaving their country or even their own home town. The fact that I had wanted to cross an entire ocean was beyond their comprehension. As I met more of the people and saw more of the countryside, I understood why.

As we drove the two hours from Belfast to his parents home, Kevin Kennedy described the passing landscape. Since I am blind, he took extra care to tell me about the farms that appeared every so often, the colors of the cows and the sheep and the Mountains of Mourne as we approached them.

When we arrived at the Kennedy farm, I stepped from the tiny car and was surrounded by an openness that felt endless. Someone had told me that in Ireland you could find every shade of green that God had created. The air even smelled green with its moist, pungent mixture of fresh grass and even fresher cow manure.

Kevin's family home opened appropriately into the kitchen. This was the primary activity center of the home where meals were prepared and eaten, clothes were sewn and washed, neighbors were entertained, and a kettle of water boiled ever-ready on the back of the stove.

Kevin's father greeted me as if I were a long-lost child, embracing me with a hug that swallowed my entire body and took my breath away. I pictured him a clone of Scarlet O'Hara's father, with a ruddy complexion and a shock of white hair. In reality, he was rather tall with sparkling blue eyes and large, calloused hands.

After determining that I wasn't hungry after my "arduous journey from Belfast," Mr. Kennedy asked if I'd like to see his farm. He asked in a way that denoted great pride in his home, the masterpiece that he had created from the piece of land that God had loaned him.

We left the warmth of the kitchen stove and stepped into the acres of farmland in back of the house. I had the feeling that the air here was always cool, that even the warmth of sunshine could not disturb it. As we walked away from the house, Mr. Kennedy told me the history of his family and how he had come to own this section of his father's farm. He told me about his two older brothers who had died in the war, his sister who had contracted polio and died as a young mother, and his own seven children, all but three of whom lived in nearby towns.

We reached a stone wall that surrounded part of the house and divided the property from the adjacent farm. Mr. Kennedy placed my hand on a low spot on the wall and instructed me to sit. The place where I sat had been worn smooth by years of wind and rain. It felt cool through my thin summer dress but was a perfect companion for the soft, thick soil under my feet. It did not take long before I heard the story behind this wall, a history which Mr. Kennedy related to me with the enthusiasm of a young farmer creating his own legacy.

He had built the wall stone by stone, placing each one carefully to sit for eternity. He described the varying shades of grey in the stone, which ranged from coal black to a gritty, whitish stone that felt like hard sand. He led me to several stones in this section of the wall, placing my hand firmly on their surfaces. One, he explained, came from the land where his mother had been born, in County Cork, and another was from the farm his grandfather had owned. Several had been carried down from the mountains,

> *H*ands—knees seek
>   these cleansed bones
> of Earth.
> Silence rings like a spear
>   upon a shield.
> Somewhere did my ancestors
>   stand this way and watch
>   the receding ice lay bare
>   the rock?
> Something older than I or
>   memory stirs within me in
>   salute to stone.
>
> ◆
>
> —Margaret P. Stark,
> *How Deep the High Journey*

while others were huge boulders that had been smashed by the sea. Touching my fingertips to a particularly smooth and cool section of the wall, he told me that this piece had come from the marble he used to create a headstone for his daughter, who had died at birth.

He pointed to the mountains in the distance, explaining that they kept him safe. As he spoke, I could feel their massive presence like the arms of a protective mother who hovered nearby. The farm was on a small rise that apparently gave a panoramic view in many directions. I imagined seeing this farm from the air, with its short stone wall dividing the fields of one farm from the next like a raised scar on the landscape.

Walking farther down the road, Mr. Kennedy told me about the sheep and cows grazing in the grass next to us. This observation was almost redundant, for the overpowering smell of manure hung thickly in the air. Yet somehow, the smell here was not offensive, but simply a reminder of the cycle of life, nature and basic earthly foundations. I wanted to reach down and grab a handful of the soil and rub it between my palms, become closer to the essence of Mr. Kennedy.

We climbed the hill and returned to the kitchen. Mr. Kennedy removed his heavy boots at the door, thumping them against the back stair to remove the caked-on soil. He seated me at a huge wooden table. Large enough, he told me, to seat eighteen people.

After placing a steaming cup of tea in front of me, he left the room to find his wife. Moments later she bustled in, dropping her armload of clean laundry at the door, and embraced me with a squeeze equal to her husband's. She insisted that I eat something as she pulled plates and paper packages from the cupboards.

Mrs. Kennedy was also rather tall, with leathery skin but a quick and ready smile. As she slathered fresh butter and apricot jam on thick slices of warm bread, she told me about her family. This was her turn to glow with pride. She spoke first about Kevin and how she still couldn't understand why he had chosen to leave the farm and live in a city.

"He's chock full of politics, that one," she said, doing nothing to conceal her delight in his accomplishments.

Jimmy, her youngest, was still in high school and liked listening to American rock music. Jennifer also remained at home, but worked as a waitress and spent time riding her horse whenever she had the chance. After placing the bread in front of me, Mrs. Kennedy sliced pears and apples from the yard to accompany it. The bread had a deep, yeasty smell and the sweet, rich butter snuck into each crevice in the spongy surface. The apricot jam stuck to my lips and fingers and I sucked it off, hoping that I was quiet in the process.

Mrs. Kennedy went on to tell me about three of her daughters who were married and lived on nearby farms. Each had from three to four children, but she was sure that they were just getting started.

Suddenly interrupting herself, Mrs. Kennedy asked me if Kevin had told me about his brother Jack. While I recognized the name, I explained that we hadn't really discussed any of his brothers and sisters in depth.

Jack, she explained, was her middle son. He was born severely retarded and now, as an adult, required complete full-time care. Jack could not feed himself, dress himself, or even use a toilet. He could make a few sounds which Mrs. Kennedy had learned to interpret over the years. Jack was sleeping now but would join us shortly.

Mrs. Kennedy described her children with the same loving tenderness that Mr. Kennedy had used when talking about his farm. Each seemed to exude pride that God had given them a specific task in life and they had dedicated themselves to fulfilling his mandate.

Before Jack joined us at the table, I wondered how Mrs. Kennedy had the energy for all of her tasks. I had been impressed by her ability to maintain a spotless and organized farmhouse, raise seven children, handwash tub-loads of laundry each day, bake bread and rolls and cakes for an army of people, and still have time to attend mass every day at the closest church, which happened to be eight miles away.

After meeting Jack I was dually impressed with Mrs. Kennedy's skills and unwavering patience. As she wheeled Jack to the end of the kitchen, she murmured endearments and soft reassurances to him. She explained to me without embarrassment that it was time to wash Jack, a chore that she undertook three times a day, and would do right here in the kitchen. Removing his clothes and covering him with soft flannel blankets, she proceeded to wash his skin gently with a tub of warm water and a soap that smelled simply like a solid piece of clean.

I sat with Jack and Mrs. Kennedy as she slowly fed him a bowl of soup and a soft paste she had made from lamb and potatoes. Between bites she sliced radishes and carrots, beat butter into boiled potatoes, and occasionally peeked at a ham roasting in the oven. She never tried to rush Jack and treated him with the respect earned by a fully-functional man. I knew that the idea of institutionalizing a child like Jack would have been totally anathema to her, for obviously, he was a part of what God had intended for her life.

Later after dinner, when the rest of the family had gone to bed, Mrs. Kennedy and I sat by the fire and talked for hours. She told me stories about her struggles with Jack, the death of a daughter, her girlish dreams of being a ballerina, and her occasional attempts to write children's stories. She spoke in an uncomplaining voice that reflected an absolute acceptance of her condition. She radiated a peacefulness that stemmed from her desire to continue exactly the life which God had intended for her.

I reflected on the afternoon that I had spent with Mr. Kennedy. He had delighted in showing me his world, one of natural beauty, freedom and possibility. With God's help, he had turned the land into a productive resource, and sheep and cows into essential spokes in his life cycle. He had combined the green of the grass and bushes with the thick black of the land beneath him into a harmonious symphony of perennial beauty.

But Mrs. Kennedy, too, had turned nature into its ultimate consequence. I realized that it was easy to find the accomplishment in her beautiful home and successful children.

But what was there to find in Jack? This man was the ultimate example of simplicity, retaining only the essence of a human being. He had all of the external features we see in ourselves, yet nothing inside to make him a man that would hold a place in the world. Why, I wondered, was the most basic form of humanity so foreign from the beauty of the most basic forms of nature? In many ways, Mrs. Kennedy was proudest of Jack. The two of them had shared the most elementary struggle to maintain life, showing them both that we all have a place in the hand of God. I did not need to see into her eyes to know that she saw in Jack the most basic beauty of life, the same beauty that Mr. Kennedy saw in the earth beneath his feet.

That night, as I crawled beneath the thick down coverlet and freshly ironed linen sheets, I felt an unusual harmony within my heart. This was not my home, my bed, or even my country. And yet, I knew that God had created this haven, secreted between the mountains and the sea, for a people who had found peace in the hollow of His hand.

Kyle E. McHugh was a consultant in international health care who worked in a psychiatric asylum in England, for an M.P. in Northern Ireland, for the homeless in Germany, and who wrote an evaluation of the health care system in Ukraine. She was the first blind woman to receive an M.P.A. from Harvard's Kennedy School of Government. She died in 1999.

✳

Sometimes I wonder how I didn't get into trouble for stealing the gypsy's horse. I had taken the bus to Ballinasloe, near Galway, Ireland, to the famous October horse fair. Unfortunately, the fair was over, and all that was left in the way of horseflesh were the massive piebald carthorses of the "tinkers"—Ireland's itinerant gypsy folk—left to graze untethered on the empty fairgrounds.

Rather than explore the local pubs, I decided to befriend the horses calmly munching in the evening light. One brown-and-white gelding was particularly friendly. I found a discarded rope and fashioned a bridle, waiting until dark to hop bareback on my puzzled but obliging pal and take a spin around the village green. We kept out of the patchy light from the surrounding streets, slipping through the shadows until I had gotten my fill, my "horse fix" satisfied again. Sliding down, I patted his broad neck, lifted the rope over his head, and walked away content, my jeans covered in telltale sweat and horsehair.

—Archer Gilliam, "Irish Horses"

SHARON BALENTINE

Walking Her Sorrow into Life

An expatriate finds comfort in the sierras
of her small Spanish village.

THE FOREIGN WOMAN WALKS OUT OF THE VILLAGE IN THE WARM-cool autumn air. The sky is blue and high, hazy far out over the sea. The wild sierra sends her its scents of rosemary and thyme and pine. She looks up along the flanks of the mountains as she walks, running her eyes over the gray rocky ribs and spines covered with scrub and thorn bushes, and she almost loses her balance, suddenly dizzy from the shift of her eyes from horizontal to vertical. She walks, leaving the village sparkling in the sun below.

Ah, she thinks, good to walk high, let the wind blow my sorrow away. She calls to the wind, blow my sorrow away. Mountain, she says, make me strong. Sky, she says, heal me, heal my heart. My foolish heart that will not listen.

Off the road, dropping down in falling crescendos of terraced fields, are groves of olive trees, custard apple, and grape vines. Some of the high slopes are also planted in steep terraces. Others are wild, sloping and looking, deceptively, as soft as a woman's body, or broken and eroded in scars of gray and rust-colored earth, rock, slashes of stunted pine, mountain madrone, scrub and wild herbs. High overhead, above the ridge where she walks, a large hawk hovers for minutes, wings whiffling in the wind, before dropping like a hurled stone to some hidden point below. Rounding a side of the mountain, she looks back and sees the village again, white and sharp as milk glass and curving naturally up and along its own rocky outcrop.

She sometimes needs this distance, this freedom—to walk away from the village and its tight, narrow streets, the constant sounds of voices and motorbikes, and the eyes and emotion of the people. The warmth, the heat, the closeness of the people—the living web—sometimes become unbearable. So she walks, she walks. She strides along, feeling the strength of her body, still young, though she knows she's on that crest that must drop, eventually, to the sea, the gray and sinewy sea.

She wonders if the ten years or more of grieving over the end of her marriage must now go into a new phase of grieving. What journey is this? Other years, alone here or with her daughters, she had traveled over the past, trying to understand, lay things to rest, open a way for herself. It always seemed to her that here, in this village and on this land, was the only place where she could do this, because here life is real in a way it is not real where she comes from. The people have not placed machines between themselves and life. They do not live life through their machines but touch the world directly, intimately, and it touches them and teaches them.

The village stretches like a white seagull across the flank of the mountain. The mountain is rough, creviced, and behind it rise higher mountains—smoky looking or sharply defined, depending on the light and the clarity of air. The land around and below the village is cultivated in scalloped fields that fall all the way to the white city on the coast and to the gray-blue, deep-blue, or white sea. The color of the sea as seen from the village changes constantly with the light, the seasons, and the weather. It changes also with the wind or lack of wind from Africa, whose coastal mountains can be seen from the highest parts of the village on a clear day like a mirage of mountains floating and shimmering in the air above the far water.

The village has been here for a very long time. It has been taken and retaken by many tribes and groups of people, and it has assimilated and changed all those who came from other lands across the sea, as well as those who came from over the mountains. The earth is rich because it has been bled for and sweated over, worked and reworked. Over the centuries it has been fought for many times. Because of this, it has been loved, desperately. Worked, shaped and reshaped, it has fed and tormented many generations and races of people, yet the people who live here do not say they love it. They just say they know no other, as a man knows no other woman, a woman no other man.

> *P*erhaps I would be better off committing to a place for life rather than to a person. Just hunker down on this island, pour myself into this life and release all the rest that looms over me like a rain-laden sky.
>
> ◆
>
> —Marybeth Holleman,
> "The Wind on My Face,"
> *Solo: On Her Own Adventure*
> edited by Susan Fox Rogers

They call themselves here The People. They have other names too, that refer to distinctive traits and realities, past or present, such as the talent and good fortune they once had for growing juicy apricots. But fortune changes, and there are always new realities. Years ago, a disease appeared that killed all but a few of the apricot trees.

Always, however, they are The People, and they are fond of reminding one another and outsiders that The People are as bad as they are good, as ugly and impossible as they are beautiful, as naïve as they are wise, and as cowardly as they are brave. They say they can't be trusted as often as they can be, lie more often than they tell the truth, and talk too much. But we have to talk, they say, we have to. It is life flowing. Sometimes, however, they are brilliant at keeping secrets. They are noble and strong and ridiculous. They are dangerous. Trust the people, but also, beware of them.

*

He comes up out of the barranco with the goats—80 or more—to the dirt road that embraces the hill and eventually meets the curved road that winds into the village. The females, kids, and two males with asbestos shields tied under their bellies in front of their genitals, trip along in their rhythmical yet uneven motion, stirring up the dust with their light hooves. His two dogs run back and forth, helping to keep the edges of the herd from straying into adjacent fields. But the goats listen more to him than they pay attention to the dogs. The interaction between him and the goats is constant and intimate. He knows them, each one, and they know him.

The flow of goats shifts, changes and moves on like a river—forever the same, forever different, twisting, the individual elements changing position but holding together, keeping a directed form when they are on the path, exactly like a flock of migrating geese in the sky. Off the road, he lets them scatter to feed and forage among harvested fields or among the wild growth that separates fields. He feels the shifting sameness and difference of himself among this eternally varying yet unchanging world. He knows himself to be also a river, of the river. A mote of light or darkness, depending on how the sun and moon strike within and without him, for he is often coming in, back to the village, under the moon, under that one whose creature he is, that goddess.

In summer, he takes the goats out for shorter periods. There is much less to eat, especially during these years of drought, and the August heat is intense. In summer he brings them back well before dusk and gives them extra feed in their bins for the night. He stays with them, talks to them, scolds them, until the sun is behind the western hills. Then he locks the big iron door, mounts his motorbike, and rides into the village. He stops at the kiosk for a cold beer to wash the dust from his throat and to talk a little with Mercedes. He then goes on to a bar where they sell *tapas,* and he eats a little and takes another beer. Finally, he has a cognac and goes home, where his mother will have placed some cold food on the table for him in case he is hungry.

Every day, every season, this is his life.

He can't see her, and then he must see her, like a fool stopping
at that bar where he knows she is having a glass of wine and smoking her cigarettes and sitting so still. He pulls up and parks his
motorbike. He walks very straight, which is his way, looking neither to the right nor to the left, but he sees her skirt and sandalled
foot, and he feels what comes off her, the presence of her. He
walks to the end of the bar farthest from her and looks at Manolo,
who starts the coffee machine and gets the bottle of Soberano
brandy, and sets it on the bar. He sees her from the corner of his
eye, or, rather, he sees the colors of her, the configuration she
makes there at the end of the bar.

When he finishes the brandy he pays and walks out, exactly as
he walked in—straight, looking neither to the right nor the left, at
the same pace he walks in the street, or in the *campo* with his goats.
He feels his face flush as he passes her. From the corner of his eye
he sees her lowered head. She is writing in her notebook. The
spark of her hits him.

He takes this physical sense of her with him out into the fields,
like food or water. He can see her house from far out, if he is up
high enough or close enough in. The uneven windows, the roof
terrace where she might be hanging clothes or standing looking
out at the mountains. She knows when he is bringing the milk in
and sometimes comes up to watch him ride up the curving road
far below her. Loving air and light, she opens both balcony doors
in the morning when she gets up. In the afternoon, when he is
preparing the goats to take them out, she closes one or both of
them against the intense glare and heat of the sun. In the early
evening, as the sun drops to the horizon, she opens first one, then
the other, and she leaves them open until midnight or one in the
morning, when she goes to bed. He knows these things. He almost
always knows where she is.

She has come to the village to stay, and everything is on another
plane. He tells himself that he does not care who she might be
with in that house, but he also knows that she is with no one,

wants to be with no one. He knows that she is waiting for him.
But he will not go to her.

She walks at night. She walks to cool her mind and heart, allow
wind into her heart and open her mind to the ink black sky, which
is as dense as velvet. The people know she walks at night, and it
excites them, or it angers them. They say she is like an animal.
Only a woman who is an animal would walk at night as if unafraid,
uncaring. She walks quickly, in long strides, stopping now and then
to look out at the land and mountains, a more dense black than the
sky. She walks through the village to its very end, then back again
along the darker streets to the other end and up a way along the
road into the mountains.

She feels the night on her skin. She smells it, tastes it. She wants
to wrap herself in the night, and this is how she does it, by walking out into it, getting night in her hair and under her nails. This
is her freedom. Then she returns to her house and stands a while
on her terrace before she goes down, locks the door, washes her
face and hands and teeth, takes off her clothes, puts on a white cotton gown, turns down the bed covers, turns off the light, opens the
balcony door a few inches so night can enter, and lies back on the
pillow, her arms curved up on either side of her head, welcoming
the sweet, dangerous night and whatever it wishes to bring her,
whatever dreams, whatever half-conscious, dark or lit thoughts.
Sleeplessness, that too, if it is what the night wants to bring her.
And she asks the night to bring the spirit of her love to her.

The village wraps around her. She lies in one cell of the many-
celled hive. Her lover lies in another. She thinks of all the people
sleeping in the cells—children, old women, tired old men dreaming of the *campo*, of work, work. She thinks of the other night
creatures out there, of men who can't sleep, wandering along the
road, across the rough fields, *barrancos*, and *bancales*, silently, far from
the lights of the village. The people have always lived in the night,
worked in the night. They traveled through the mountains, hid
out from the Guardia Civil, stole grapes and olives from the high
vineyards and groves, carried food to the guerrillas hiding in the

mountains, spied on each other, met a secret lover, lost themselves in the night, cloaked by the night. They were as alone as anyone can be in a village where no one is ever alone.

The many, many nights of the village overlap one another—the Tartessian night, the Phoenician night. Burial ceremonies and dancing before the fire. The Carthaginian, Greek, Roman night. The intricate Moorish night. The Catholic, pagan night. The foreign and familiar night, the male and female night. The human, animal night, when the mountain pines sigh and tremble in the clear air, when *dama de la noche* releases her scent, welcoming moths.

This is what she remembers: a night at Amparo's bar, talking with Mateo and Eduardo at a table outside. Talk of the past, of the village, as always. Mateo and Eduardo are two of the old ones of the village, and her oldest friends here. But he is on her mind. She wonders when she will see him again. She goes inside to order drinks for all of them and he is there at the other end of the bar, a glass of brandy in front of him. Other men stand between her and him, but he is the one she sees. She orders and waits for the barman to pour the drinks and bring the coffee. As she stands there he turns his face to her and sends her a deep, dark look. He holds her eyes for a long moment and the rest of the bar disappears. No one else is there. Then the barman setting down the coffee breaks the spell. She pays and takes the drinks outside. She continues the conversation with her two friends, watching to see him come out, but she does not see him again. He's gone out by the other door and around the back way.

She has not wanted anyone for a long time. She is not thinking about whether she wants this man or not. Something seems to be happening in her deeper than thought, but she is not even this aware. She's adrift on the sea, letting the swells and wind carry her. Something in her has told her to let go and drift with what comes. When that something speaks to her, she listens, or she cannot help but listen. She is usually a highly conscious woman, critical, reading the signs, but not now. He is not speaking to her there. He is speaking to her from that deeper place in himself. He is calling her.

Then a night comes, another night like all the nights when the full moon rises in summer to shed her grace and mystery on the village. He finds her and says, where do you want to go? And she points to the mountain above the village where the Moorish castle once stood. The moon is full, she says. He turns and says, come, and they walk out of the village side by side and then up along the road into the sierra, taking the turning to the reservoir and *acequia,* up, up along the moonlit road, then along a dirt track that circles the peak on the village side.

———— ☽ ————

*H*e doesn't ask any-more why this is called the Broken Heart Trail. I can tell by the ragged sound of his breathing and the unsteady thump of his soggy boots that he has discovered the reason.

◆

—Mary Sepulveda,
"Table Mountain"

He finds the footpath that goes up to the top, where the castle stood and where a small wall guards the overlook. She walks on ahead of him in her summer skirt. At the wall she stops and looks down at the white village lit and shadowed by moonlight and street lamps. He watches her. She looks up at the moon, then down at the village, then up at the moon again. Suddenly, with a move-ment so quick he later wonders if he really saw it, she drops down behind the wall, presses her forehead to the stone and rises again. He comes up beside her. She turns to him. He covers her left breast with his hand and kisses her on the mouth.

She turns away from him and walks out to an open space under the moon. He is with her, following her movements. She sits down in the scant growth covering the dry summit. He lowers himself beside her. She turns to him and he holds her, kissing her again. He holds her to him and then moves his body, searching under her skirt with his hand, finding her. She makes small, animal sounds and moves against him. He feels his body is her body, lost, turning in the night. His soul seems to be within her, and he sees himself moving darkly above her. Then he feels himself flow out into her and he stops. He watches her face as she turns it slowly from the moon to him. Her eyes are so dark. He sees his own face through her eyes. His grave, shadowed, charged face.

When he rises from her and adjusts his clothes, he can't take his eyes from her. She sits there looking up at him. His heart is pounding as if his whole body is heart, his whole being. When they go to leave, she tries to brush the grass from her hair and clothes. She wants to take the shortcut back down through the old village. He tells her more people will see them that way, but if she wants to go, he will go with her. I will always be in accord with you, he says. She says she will go back down the way they came if he thinks it best. He says her name three times. Never did I think I would be with you, he says. Do you love me then? She says. He does not answer. Do you think of me? She says. He cannot answer.

The next morning, she sees Eduardo and Mateo sitting at a table outside Amparo's bar. She goes up to greet them. They are both acting strangely. Finally Mateo bursts out, Everyone is talking about you. Could you not have told me, your oldest friend in the village, so I would know what to say? She stands there looking at them, feeling her dream hit the rock reality of the village. At the kiosk, Eduardo mutters. I told them it was all lies, he says. I have done nothing bad, she says. She leaves her two old friends and walks home.

The two men sit there in silence a while, thinking. Mateo finally says, she doesn't know how bad this village can be, the talk, the *mala leche*. Eduardo nods. His old owl's face is expressionless.

But that was over a year ago now. And her love has not returned to her; they pass each other in the village without speaking.

So she walks. She climbs a long, steep road, feeling something chemical releasing from her cells. She turns finally down a dirt and gravel road that leads to a village abandoned in the final years of the war. All the whitewashed walls are crumbling back to earth. Prickly pear cacti grow like surreal trees in the rubble of rooms open to the sky. The built-in cupboards and shelves along the inner walls where once women stacked their plates and placed their few ornaments are now ledges open to wind, dust, dew, birds and lizards.

She finds a shady spot on a boulder in the riverbed, sits down, and opens her picnic lunch of boiled eggs, ham, cheese, bread, and fruit and wine. She sits there looking at the land, the crumbling walls of the houses on the hill above the river, the dry stones in the riverbed. At peace, glad in her heart, she tells herself, let come what comes. She wants the spirit of the place, this place, to teach her of loss, leave-taking, new life, grieving, and laying aside, love, death, the new day, and memory of the old forever present. She sits there a long time.

Coming back up the road, she meets a goatherd with his flock of 50 or 60 goats, some of them pregnant, tripping along on feet that sound in the dry road like a small rain falling, the rain that does not come. But this man is not her love. He does not walk as proud and tall beside his animals as he whom she used to watch from her window moving upright among his flock as they flowed like a river along the side of the distant hill before pouring into the road below the village. Her heart is stricken remembering the beauty of that vision.

She had lived with him in her soul so long, nourishing herself on memories of their times together, that the present dry reality has left her bereft. It doesn't want to rain, she thinks, no. She is a tree that can live long without rain. As is he, she thinks. So we live without rain, so used to it now that we perhaps cannot imagine rain, cannot. As if it would hurt, burn, destroy us.

Suddenly she has a sense of intense dislocation, as if the woman walking this road is a mirage, as if she is back where she used to be, imagining or dreaming she walks this road, as if her longing is so intense that she has projected herself here, but she is not really here.

It doesn't matter, she thinks. It doesn't matter anymore. I walk here or dream I walk here. What does it matter? She has dreamed so many dreams of this land and the village that it is composed of layers and layers of dream and waking realities within and without her.

She comes to the crest above the abandoned village and walks along before descending the other side. The sea stretches to the horizon. If the sky were very clear she could see Africa from here, but a haze hangs over the sea to the south and west. She can just make out ripples of white where the wind is blowing the surface of the water into curls. Pine trees fill the gorge that falls below her, and she stands there breathing in the sharp, clean air before beginning her descent to the hard, white, sun- and sea-scoured village of her heart.

Sharon Balentine (a pseudonym) taught literature at the University of Texas at Austin for ten years before moving to Spain permanently in 1995. She is the author of the books of poetry Spellbound *and* Isis, *and has published poetry in* Stone Drum, Aileron, Balcones Review, *and* The Canon.

⋆

I am in Luca, on the western coast of Italy. We are about to catch a ferry to the island of Elba. You befriend me on deck, as the fog horn moans deeply and we spit and sputter slowly away from the dock. My Italian is mediocre at best so you speak slowly. You are the kind of old Italian woman we Americans imagine from across the Atlantic. Wrinkled and dark and warm. You are a widow, dressed in black, reminiscing about your house on the island and your life before your *moglio*, your husband, passed away. I tell you it is my first time to the Italian coast and you exclaim and clap your hands together. This island, you whisper, will never let you go.

—Kate Kane, "To Another Island"

Among Chimpanzees

*The renowned scientist reflects on
her thirty years in Gombe.*

I ROLLED OVER AND LOOKED AT THE TIME—5:44 A.M. LONG YEARS of early rising have led to an ability to wake just before the unpleasant clamour of an alarm clock. Soon I was sitting on the steps of my house looking out over Lake Tanganyika. The waning moon, in her last quarter, was suspended above the horizon, where the mountainous shoreline of Zaire [now the Democratic Republic of Congo] fringed Lake Tanganyika. It was a still night, and the moon's path danced and sparkled towards me across the gently moving water. My breakfast—a banana and a cup of coffee from the thermos flask—was soon finished and, ten minutes later I was climbing the steep slope behind the house, my miniature binoculars and camera stuffed into my pockets along with notebook, pencil stubs, a handful of raisins for my lunch, and plastic bags in which to put everything should it rain. The faint light from the moon, shining on the dew-laden grass, enabled me to find my way without difficulty and presently I arrived at the place where, the evening before, I had watched eighteen chimpanzees settle down for the night. I sat to wait until they woke.

All around, the trees were still shrouded with the last mysteries of the night's dreaming. It was very quiet, utterly peaceful. The only sounds were the occasional chirp of a cricket, and the soft murmur where the lake caressed the shingle, way below. As I sat there I felt the expectant thrill that, for me, always precedes a day with the chimpanzees, a day roaming the forests and mountains of Gombe, a day for new discoveries, new insights.

Then came a sudden burst of song, the duet of a pair of robin chats, hauntingly beautiful. I realized that the intensity of light had changed: dawn had crept upon me unawares. The coming brightness of the sun had all but vanquished the silvery, indefinite illumination of its own radiance reflected by the moon. The chimpanzees still slept.

Five minutes later came a rustling of leaves above. I looked up and saw branches moving against the lightening sky. That was where Goblin, top-ranking male of the community, had made his nest. Then stillness again. He must have turned over, then settled down for a last snooze. Soon after this there was movement from another nest to my right, then from one behind me, further up the slope.

Today, a recent poll reveals, Jane Goodall is the most easily recognizable living scientist in the Western world.

"Her work is almost comparable with Einstein's," says Roger Fouts, whose work with the sign-language-using chimpanzee Washoe has challenged man's claim to uniqueness as a language user, just as did Jane's findings of hunting, warfare, and the use of tools by chimps.

Jane's approach, once ridiculed as amateurish, is now often held up as a standard to which other field ethologists should aspire. Now some respected scientists are beginning to argue that it is the lens of theory and methodology that clouds vision, not the focus of empathy.

◆

—Sy Montgomery, *Walking with the Great Apes: Jane Goodall, Dian Fossey, Biruté Galdikas*

Rustlings of leaves, the cracking of a little twig. The group was waking up. Peering through my binoculars into the tree where Fifi had made a nest for herself and her infant Flossi, I saw the silhouette of her foot. A moment later Fanni, her eight-year-old daughter, climbed up from her nest nearby and sat just above her mother, a small dark shape against the sky. Fifi's other two offspring, adult Freud and adolescent Frodo, had nested further up the slope.

Nine minutes after he had first moved, Goblin abruptly sat up and, almost at once, left his nest and began to leap wildly through the tree, vigorously swaying the branches. Instant pandemonium broke out. The chimpanzees closest to Goblin left their nests and rushed out of his way. Others sat up to watch, tense and ready for flight. The early morning peace was shattered by frenzied grunts and screams as Goblin's subordinates voiced their respect or fear. A few moments later, the arboreal part of his display over, Goblin leapt down and charged past me, slapping and stamping on the wet ground, rearing up and shaking the vegetation, picking up and hurling a rock, an old piece of wood, another rock. Then he sat, hair bristling, some fifteen feet away. He was breathing heavily. My own heart was beating fast. As he swung down, I had stood up and held onto a tree, praying that he would not pound on me as he sometimes does. But, to my relief, he had ignored me, and I sat down again.

With soft, panting grunts Goblin's young brother Gimble climbed down and came to greet the alpha or top-ranking male, touching his face with his lips. Then, as another adult male approached Goblin, Gimble moved hastily out of the way. This was my old friend Evered. As he approached, with loud, submissive grunts, Goblin slowly raised one arm in salutation and Evered rushed forward. The two males embraced, grinning widely in the excitement of this morning reunion so that their teeth flashed white in the semi-darkness. For a few moments they groomed each other and then, calmed, Evered moved away and sat quietly nearby.

The only other adult who climbed down then was Fifi, with Flossi clinging to her belly. She avoided Goblin, but approached Evered, grunting softly, reached out her hand and touched his arm. Then she began to groom him. Flossi climbed into Evered's lap and looked up into his face. He glanced at her, groomed her head in-

tently for a few moments, then turned to reciprocate Fifi's atten-
tions. Flossi moved half-way towards where Goblin sat—but his hair
was still bristling, and she thought better of it and, instead, climbed
a tree near Fifi. Soon she began to play with Fanni, her sister.

Once again peace returned to the morning, though not the silence of dawn. Up in the trees the other chimpanzees of the
group were moving about, getting ready for the new day. Some
began to feed, and I heard the occasional soft thud as skins and
seeds of figs were dropped to the ground. I sat, utterly content to
be back at Gombe after an unusually long time away—almost
three months of lectures, meetings, and lobbying in the USA and
Europe. This would be my first day with the chimps and I planned
to enjoy it to the full, just getting reacquainted with my old
friends, taking pictures, getting my climbing legs back.

It was Evered who led off, thirty minutes later, twice pausing
and looking back to make sure that Goblin was coming too. Fifi
followed, Flossi perched on her back like a small jockey, Fanni
close behind. Now the other chimps climbed down and wandered
after us. Freud and Frodo, adult males Atlas and Beethoven, the
magnificent adolescent Wilkie, and two females, Patti and Kidevu,
with their infants. There were others, but they were travelling
higher up the slope, and I didn't see them then. We headed north,
parallel with the beach below, then plunged down into Kasakela
Valley and, with frequent pauses for feeding, made our way up the
opposite slope. The eastern sky grew bright, but not until 8:30
a.m. did the sun itself finally peep over the peaks of the rift escarpment. By this time we were high above the lake. The chimpanzees stopped and groomed for a while, enjoying the warmth of
the morning sunshine.

About twenty minutes later there was a sudden outbreak of
chimpanzee calls ahead—a mixture of pant-hoots, as we call the
loud distance calls, and screams. I could hear the distinctive voice
of the large, sterile female Gigi among a medley of females and
youngsters. Goblin and Evered stopped grooming and all the
chimps stared towards the sounds. Then, with Goblin now in the
lead, most of the group moved off in that direction.

Fifi, however, stayed behind and continued to groom Fanni while Flossi played by herself, dangling from a low branch near her mother and elder sister. I decided to stay too, delighted that Frodo had moved on with the others for he so often pesters me. He wants me to play, and, because I will not, he becomes aggressive. At twelve years of age he is much stronger than I am, and this behaviour is dangerous. Once he stamped so hard on my head that my neck was nearly broken. And on another occasion he pushed me down a steep slope. I can only hope that, as he matures and leaves childhood behind him, he will grow out of these irritating habits.

> We could hear the gorillas singing as we approached. It is not widely known that gorillas sing, but it is the only word I can find to describe the phenomenon. Just occasionally, on a sunny day, with plentiful food and in a relaxed mood, the group would make these pleasant little noises to each other, tuneful sighs.
>
> ◆
>
> —Rosalind Aveling, "Ndume: A Moment in Time"

I spent the rest of the morning wandering peacefully with Fifi and her daughters, moving from one food tree to the next. The chimps fed on several different kinds of fruit and once on some young shoots. For about forty-five minutes they pulled apart the leaves of low shrubs which had been rolled into tubes held closely by sticky threads, then munched on the caterpillars that wriggled inside. Once we passed another female—Gremlin and her new infant, little Galahad. Fanni and Flossi ran over to greet them, but Fifi barely glanced in their direction.

All the time we were climbing higher and higher. Presently, on an open grassy ridge we came upon another small group of chimps: the adult male Prof, his young brother Pax, and two rather shy females with their infants. They were feeding on the leaves of a massive *mbula* tree. There were a few quiet grunts of greeting as Fifi and her youngsters joined the group, then they also began to feed. Presently the others moved on, Fanni with them. But Fifi made herself a nest and stretched out for a midday siesta. Flossi stayed too, climbing about, swinging, amusing herself near her mother. And then she joined Fifi in her nest, lay close and suckled.

From where I sat, below Fifi, I could look out over the Kasakela Valley. Opposite, to the south, was the Peak. A surge of warm memories flooded through me as I saw it, a rounded shoulder perched above the long grassy ridge that separates Kasakela from the home valley, Kakombe. In the early days of the study at Gombe, in 1960 and 1961, I had spent day after day watching the chimpanzees, through my binoculars, from the superb vantage point. I had taken a little tin trunk up to the Peak, with a kettle, some coffee and sugar, and a blanket. Sometimes, when the chimps had slept nearby, I had stayed up there with them, wrapped in my blanket against the chill of the night air. Gradually I had pieced together something of their daily life, learned about their feeding habits and travel routes, and begun to understand their unique social structure—small groups joining to form larger ones, large groups splitting into smaller ones, single chimpanzees roaming, for a while, on their own.

From the Peak I had seen, for the first time, a chimpanzee eating meat: David Greybeard. I had watched him leap up into a tree clutching the carcass of an infant bushpig, which he shared with a female while the adult pigs charged about below. And only about a hundred yards from the Peak, on a never-to-be-forgotten day in October, 1960, I had watched David Greybeard, along with his close friend Goliath, fishing for termites with stems of grass. Thinking back to that far-off time I re-lived the thrill I had felt when I saw David reach out, pick a wide blade of grass and trim it carefully so that it could more easily be poked into the narrow passage in the termite mound. Not only was he using the grass as a tool—he was, by modifying it to suit a special purpose, actually showing the crude beginnings of tool-*making*. What excited telegrams I had sent off to Louis Leakey, that far-sighted genius who had instigated the research at Gombe. Humans were not, after all, the *only* tool-making animals. Nor were chimpanzees the placid vegetarians that people had supposed.

That was just after my mother, Vanne, had left to return to her other responsibilities in England. During her four-month stay she had made an invaluable contribution to the success of the project: she had set up a clinic—four poles and a thatched roof—where she had provided medicines to the local people, mostly fishermen and their families. Although her remedies had been simple—aspirin, Epson salts, iodine, Band-Aids and so on—her concern and patience had been unlimited, and her cures often worked. Much later we learned that many people had thought that she possessed magic powers for healing. Thus she had secured for me the goodwill of the local human population.

Above me, Fifi stirred, cradling little Flossi more comfortably as she suckled. Then her eyes closed again. The infant nursed for a few more minutes, then the nipple slipped from her mouth as she too slept. I continued to daydream, re-living in my mind some of the more memorable events of the past.

I remembered the day when David Greybeard had first visited my camp by the lakeshore. He had come to feed on the ripe fruits of an oil-nut palm that grew there, spied some bananas on the table outside my tent, and taken them off to eat in the bush. Once he had discovered bananas he had returned for more and gradually other chimpanzees had followed him to my camp.

One of the females who became a regular visitor in 1963 was Fifi's mother, old Flo of the ragged ears and bulbous nose. What an exciting day when, after five years of maternal preoccupation with her infant daughter, Flo had become sexually attractive again. Flaunting her shell-pink sexual swelling she had attracted a whole retinue of suitors. Many of them had never been to camp, but they had followed Flo there, sexual passions overriding natural caution. And, once they had discovered bananas, they had joined the rapidly growing group of regular camp visitors. And so I had become more and more familiar with the whole host of unforgettable chimpanzee characters who are described in my first book, *In the Shadow of Man*.

Fifi, lying so peacefully above me now, was one of the few survivors of those early days. She had been an infant when first I
knew her in 1961. She had weathered the terrible polio epidemic
that had swept through the population—chimpanzee and human
alike—in 1966. Ten of the chimpanzees of the study group had
died or vanished. Another five had been crippled, including her
eldest brother, Faben, who had lost the use of one arm.

At the time of that epidemic the Gombe Stream Research
Centre was in its infancy. The first two research assistants were
helping to collect and type out notes on chimp behavior. Some
twenty-five chimpanzees were regularly visiting camp by then, and
so there had been more than enough work for all of us. After
watching the chimps all day we had often transcribed notes from
our tape recorders until late at night.

My mother Vanne had made two other visits to Gombe during
the sixties. One of those had been when the National Geographic
Society sent Hugo van Lawick to film the study—which, by then,
they were financing. Louis Leakey had wangled Vanne's fare and
expenses, insisting that it would not be right for me to be alone in
the bush with a young man. How different the moral standards of
a quarter of a century ago! Hugo and I had married anyway, and
Vanne's third visit, in 1967 had been to share with me, for a couple of months, the task of raising my son, Grub (his real name is
Hugo Eric Louis) in the bush.

There was a slight movement from Fifi's nest and I saw that she
had turned and was looking down at me. What was she thinking?
How much of the past did she remember? Did she ever think of
her old mother, Flo? Had she followed the desperate struggle of
her brother, Figan, to rise to the top-ranking, alpha position? Had
she even been aware of the grim years when the males of her community, often led by Figan, had waged a sort of primitive war
against their neighbours, assaulting them, one after the other, with
shocking brutality? Had she known about the gruesome cannibal-
istic attacks made by Passion and her adult daughter Pom on newborn infants of the community?

Again my attention was jerked back to the present, this time by the sound of a chimpanzee crying. I smiled. That would be Fanni. She had reached the adventurous age when a young female often moves away from her mother to travel with the adults. Then, suddenly, she wants mother desperately, leaves the group, and sets off to search for her. The crying grew louder and soon Fanni came into sight. Fifi paid no attention, but Flossi jumped out of the nest and scrambled down to embrace her elder sister. And Fanni, finding Fifi where she had left her, stopped her childish crying.

Clearly Fifi had been waiting for Fanni—now she climbed down and set off, and the children followed after, playing as they went. The family moved rapidly down the steep slope to the south. As I scrambled after them, every branch seemed to catch in my hair or my shirt. Frantically I crawled and wriggled through a terrible tangle of undergrowth. Ahead of me the chimpanzees, fluid black shadows, moved effortlessly. The distance between us increased. The vines curled around the buckles of my shoes and the strap of my camera, the thorns caught in the flesh of my arms, my eyes smarted till the tears flowed as I yanked my hair from the snags that reached out from all around. After ten minutes I was drenched in sweat, my shirt was torn, my knees bruised from crawling on the stony ground—and the chimps had vanished. I kept quite still, trying to listen above the pounding of my heart, peering in all directions through the thicket around me. But I heard nothing.

For the next thirty-five minutes I wandered along the rocky bed of the Kasakela Stream, pausing to listen, to scan the branches above me. I passed below a troop of red colobus monkeys, leaping through the tree tops, uttering their strange, high-pitched, twittering calls. I encountered some baboons of D troop, including old Fred with his one blind eye and the double kink in his tail. And then, as I was wondering where to go next, I heard the scream of a young chimp further up the valley. Ten minutes later I had joined Gremlin with little Galahad, Gigi and two of Gombe's youngest and most recent orphans, Mel and Darbee, both of whom had lost their mothers when they were only just over three years old. Gigi, as she so often does these days, was "auntying" them both. They were all feeding in a tall tree above the almost dry stream and I stretched out on the rocks to watch them. During my scramble after Fifi the sun had vanished, and now, as I looked up through the canopy, I could see the sky, grey and heavy with rain. With a growing darkness came the stillness, the hush, that so often precedes hard rain. Only the rumbling of the thunder, moving ever closer, broke this stillness; the thunder and the rustling movements of the chimpanzees....

It must have taken about an hour before the rain began to ease off as the heart of the storm swept away to the south. At 4:30 the chimps climbed down, and moved off through the soaked, dripping vegetation. I followed, walking awkwardly, my wet clothes hindering movement. We travelled along the stream bed then up the other side of the valley, heading south. Presently we arrived on a grassy ridge overlooking the lake. A pale, watery sun had appeared and its light caught the raindrops so that the world seemed hung with diamonds, sparkling on every leaf, every blade of grass. I crouched low to avoid destroying a jewelled spider's web that stretched, exquisite and fragile, across the trail.

The chimpanzees climbed into a low tree to feed on fresh young leaves. I moved to a place where I could stand and watch as they enjoyed their last meal of the day. The scene was breathtaking in its beauty. The leaves were brilliant, a pale, vivid green in the soft sunlight; the wet trunk and branches were like ebony; the black coats of the chimps were shot with flashes of coppery-brown. And behind this vivid tableau was the dramatic backcloth of the indigo-black sky where the lightning still flickered and flashed, and the distant thunder rumbled.

There are many windows through which we can look out into the world, searching for meaning. There are those opened up by science, their panes polished by a succession of brilliant, penetrating minds. Through these we can see ever further, ever more clearly, into areas that once lay beyond human knowledge. Gazing through such a window I have, over the years, learned much about chimpanzee behaviour and their place in the nature of things. And this, in turn, has helped us to understand a little better some aspects of human behaviour, our own place in nature.

But there are other windows; windows that have been unshuttered by the logic of philosophers; windows through which the mystics seek their visions of the truth; windows from which the leaders of the great religions have peered as they searched for purpose not only in the wondrous beauty of the world, but also in its darkness and ugliness. Most of us, when we ponder on the mystery of our existence, peer through but one of these windows onto the world. And even that one is often misted over by the breath of our finite humanity. We clear a tiny peephole and stare through. No wonder we are confused by the tiny fraction of a whole that we see. It is, after all, like trying to comprehend the panorama of the desert or the sea through a rolled-up newspaper.

As I stood quietly in the pale sunshine, so much a part of the rain-washed forests and the creatures that lived there, I saw for a brief moment through another window and with other vision. It is an experience that comes, unbidden, to some of us who spend time alone in nature. The air was filled with a feathered symphony, the evensong of birds. I heard new frequencies in their music and, too, in the singing of insect voices, notes so high and sweet that I was amazed. I was intensely aware of the shape, the colour, of individual leaves, the varied patterns of the veins that made each one unique. Scents were clear, easily identifiable—fermenting, over-ripe fruit; water-logged earth; cold, wet bark; the damp odour of chimpanzee hair and, yes, my own too. And the aromatic scent of young, crushed leaves was almost overpowering. I sensed the presence of a bushbuck, then saw him, quietly browsing upwind, his spiralled horns dark with rain. And I was utterly filled with that peace "which passeth all understanding."

Then came far-off pant-hoots from a group of chimpanzees to the north. The trance-like mood was shattered. Gigi and Gremlin replied, uttering their distinctive pant-hoots. Mel, Darbee and little Galahad joined in the chorus.

I stayed with the chimps until they nested—early, after the rain. And when they had settled down, Galahad cosy beside his mother, Mel and Darbee each in their own small nests close to the big one of auntie Gigi, I left them and walked back along the forest trail to the lakeshore. I passed the D troop baboons again. They were gathered around their sleeping trees, squabbling, playing, grooming together, in the soft light of evening. My walking feet crunched the shingle of the beach, and the sun was a huge red orb above the lake. As it lit the clouds for yet another magnificent display, the water became golden, shot with gleaming ripples of violet and red below the flaming sky.

Later, as I crouched over my little wood fire outside the house, where I had cooked, then eaten, beans and tomatoes and an egg, I was still lost in the wonder of my experience that afternoon. It was, I thought, as though I had looked onto the world through such a window as a chimpanzee might know. I dreamed, by the flickering flames. If only we could, however briefly, see the world through the eyes of a chimpanzee, what a lot we should learn.

A last cup of coffee and then I would go inside, light the hurricane lamp, and write out my notes of the day, the wonderful day. For, since we cannot know with the mind of a chimpanzee we must proceed laboriously, meticulously, as I have for thirty years. We must continue to collect anecdotes and, slowly, compile life histories. We must continue, over the years, to observe, record and interpret. We have, already, learned much. Gradually, as knowledge accumulates, as more and more people work together and pool their information, we are raising the blind of the window through which, one day, we shall be able to see even more clearly into the mind of the chimpanzee.

Jane Goodall was a young secretarial school graduate when Louis Leakey sent her to Tanzania in 1960 to study chimpanzees. She later received a Ph.D. from Cambridge University and has become one of the world's most honored scientists and writers. Her books include In the Shadow of Man *and* Through a Window: My Thirty Years with the Chimpanzees of Gombe, *from which this story was excerpted.*

★

Ever since the 1960s, when reports began trickling back from Tanganyika that a young woman was sitting quietly in the jungle taking notes on chimpanzee behavior, I wanted to be Jane Goodall....

So when an opportunity to study primates on the lush Caribbean island of Grenada came along, I signed on in tribute to my old dream. My 18-year-old son, Jacob, a veteran backpacker and confirmed naturalist, came too. Our job: to help anthropologist Mary Glenn collect data on mona monkeys—winsome cat-size creatures about which almost nothing is known....

During the day we sat outdoors enchanted, watching the monkeys, filling our notebooks with tidbits of behavior as they ate, groomed one another and rested, stretched lazily along a tree limb....

On the trail one afternoon, I heard the sound of falling debris. In slow motion I raised my binoculars and scanned the treetops. I caught a momentary view of a finely chiseled face, festooned with white tufts of spunglass beard.

Just then, I felt the beginnings of light tropical rain on my arms. It had swept up on the wind unannounced. As the rising rhythmic sound of drops on leaves filled my ears, I grew utterly content, enclosed in a dim green twilight. For the moment there was no place else on earth. I knew then the delight Jane Goodall reported in being completely by herself in Africa's forests.

—Jo Broyles Yohay, "Primates 101, on an Island in the Sun,"
Travel & Leisure

REBECCA AALAND

⋆ ⋆ ⋆

The Nature of Birth

The author feels kinship with bears,
mice, and skunks.

I AM LARGE BEYOND BELIEF. I FEEL LIKE A PREGNANT PRAIRIE DOG
that the Mutual of Omaha's *Wild Kingdom* cameras are following
around. I am a sight to behold. Thankfully my body knows what
to do, because I don't.

I am drawn to water. On a trip to the island of Menorca, Spain,
I swim in pools, coves, the open sea. The water is sensual against
my skin, the buoyancy a gift. On the tiny beach at Bini Dali I wear
a bikini in the sun, mistress of more physical form than I thought
possible. I carry this new body along the Roman roads and ancient
footpaths that crisscross the island, past the rough ever-present
stone walls and white farmhouses that hug the earth. I feel deeply
connected to the world around me and attuned to everyday things
that used to escape my notice. Ants. Trees blowing in the wind.
The birds outside my window.

More than any encounter I've had in the animal or mineral
kingdoms during my travels around the world, childbirth has
drawn me closest to nature. As someone who has struggled to gain
some control over my life, to have a career, to find the freedom to
travel alone, in short to create my life rather than follow what I
thought was a stereotype of woman as mother and keeper of the

home, it is a shock to confront the power of nature within me. There are forces I can strive to ignore, but cannot control. No matter how big a city I live in, no matter how big the traffic jams, nature remains.

Part of nature's presence is the proverbial biological clock, ticking and sometimes thundering. In the face of such racket what could I do? My suits and office gave me the illusion that instinct was under wraps, that the nature within was tamed and domesticated. Then one day on the bus commuting to work, suits no longer possible with my belly mimicking a basketball, I realize this is all pretense. For me, this so-familiar office life of the mind suddenly seems foreign, a strange land I have dwelled in too long. I succumb to a wave of confusion, that which I thought I knew no longer relevant, no longer essential. My body is doing something much more profound, and my mind needs to catch up.

More than anything else I find it is my very consciousness, my mind, which separates me from the world. A tremendous gift, this brain, yet it is also the means by which I disconnect from my environment. My regular journeys into the wild have been opportunities to let go and come more into balance, the mind at peace and at one with the body. Pregnancy has made me dwell in my body at all times. In conference rooms my body announces its presence to me. I become aware of how deep the disequilibrium is in my life, the life before this new life started growing inside of me.

I am alone in the house at 5 p.m. when the contractions start. I am relieved and terrified the moment has come. My mind gets put on the back burner and my body takes over. I am hungry. My husband comes home and we eat between contractions. A call to the doctor confirms it is time to go.

To be human and give birth in America generally means giving birth in a hospital, a sterile environment regardless of the amount of wood paneling, surrounded by high-tech equipment, even if hidden in another room. In labor on the hospital bed, I am stripped of socialization. I am physical, in the moment, feeling kin more to bears and mice and skunks than to the other humans in the room. I strain, everything stripped away except the moment. My journey is to the wilds within.

The stretching of my body in preparation for what seems an impossible feat takes me farther and farther from the familiar into an animal world, body and instinct. It is pure and uncomplicated and more difficult than anything I have done before.

I walk, tiny steps, grasping the arm of my husband, my midwife, my friend. In the shower I am eased by the warmth, my body not battling itself quite so hard. I wonder vaguely what has made this so difficult for us humans, looking for an explanation other than Eve and her apple to make sense of the disconnect, thinking of the easier births of puppies.

At 4 a.m. I have been working hard for hours. I am exhausted and panic is setting in. I am back exactly in the place I found myself on a climb years ago, in the Sangre de Cristo mountains in southern Colorado. Hanging from ropes, facing panic and weakness, I no longer had the belief I could go on in the too-thin air. The immediate world receded and I was alone and lost in fear, unable to allow my body to do what it knew how to do. Then beneath the feeling of weakness, strength. My body, stronger than my fear, took over, leading me up to the summit and the glory of the open, impossibly huge sky.

My body knows what to do now, but my mind, fearful in the face of pain, rebels. Have I learned nothing these past nine months? My whole being fights for the strength that comes of balance. I struggle to find the connectedness within myself, and to everything around me. My husband's voice is anxious. My midwife is exhorting me to do the impossible, to keep going. I am lost within, yet intensely present, and acutely aware that I must succeed, for ultimately this is not about me at all. It is in the selflessness of childbirth that I finally find my strength.

My daughter is born at dawn, pale light greeting her through the window at the start of another day of Indian summer. At the moment of birth the sense of being made whole, not rendered asunder. It is the birth of a new universe, the one with my daughter in it. I am no longer the same woman. Having made my peace within, I greet my daughter celebrating the change of all I have known, and begin the difficult task of starting anew.

Rebecca Aaland is a former foreign service officer, an environmental scientist, a writer, and a mother. She resides in San Francisco.

✷

Where other than in our own bodies could we hope to know nature so well?

Women know this when they menstruate, the cycle reminding us monthly that we are controlled, at least in part, by biological forces not subject to will. Women know this who have given birth—an experience that surely should be ranked among any species' most heroic. By the eighth month of pregnancy, any woman with her eyes open knows that she has trekked into a fearsome wilderness from which there is no turning back. In labor she howls like a shot animal, lost to everything but pain, until she speaks her first words as a mother: "I want to protect you from everything."

—Alison Hawthorne Deming, *Temporary Homelands:*
Essays on Nature, Spirit, and Place

Alone with the Rabari

*In India's scorching desert, the author
asks herself, "Why?"*

ONE NIGHT AFTER THE LIGHTING OF THE INCENSE WE VISITED Phagu's brother Pala's camp for *bhajjans* (devotional songs). One man would start the first line of a song, his companions joining in. Then the women would begin, huddling together under their black wool, competing with the men, keening their lungs out, laughing when someone got the words wrong, or felt a little shy. They sang a song about Ratti ben, my ancient namesake, who had lain between the bodies of two slain men—one a Rabari, the other an enemy—to prevent their blood from mixing. They drank tea and sang until the stars swung past midnight. They sang themselves into intoxication.

It was as if they took a spiritual bath in the music, their troubles washed away with songs as old as the subcontinent. And I was struck once again at their intimacy with each other—the bonds among them continually strengthened, like calcium laid down in a bone, by singing, or sharing *prashad,* or sewing each other's mats, or smoking each other's *chillums.* How comforting it must be to pass through life's storms always with the support of the group infusing every action and every thought with one voice extending from the time of one's ancestors down through the generations, saying, "It is all right. We are all here. There is no such thing as alone."

But the ancestors were too far back in time for their voices to reach me and with each day my isolation from my companions grew. They had welcomed me into the warmth of their communion; now I was out in the cold watching them through a window. They would see me peeping at them and turn away as if to say, Why are you looking at us? Go away! What had begun with good will was atrophying for the want of language to nourish it. I had imagined I could understand, through a kind of pre-lingual sign language, quite complex interactions, as if I could just manage to stay afloat on an ocean of incomprehension. The truth was I was going under.

There were more than forty people on the *dang*. Jaivi said disparagingly, "We can remember all our sheep. How come you can't remember our names?" She made me draw a map of the camps, then write the names and the degrees of relationship. They tested me. Who is that boy over there and who is his mother's sister's daughter?

"Samji natti!" ["Doesn't understand!"]

During the day we sheltered from that poisonous sun under a tarpaulin. The wind rushed under it, gusting hot grit into our faces. Hour upon hour of unparalleled boredom as we waited to shift camp. Time stretched out as it does in dreams. I buried myself in Proust, his cool, privileged world. Marcel was waking up, enchanted by the songs of peasants selling their wares beneath his window. He lay in white sheets; soon he would pull the bell for Francoise to bring him his morning coffee. I tiptoed out of the bedroom in Paris and looked up. Pressed against me, the women stitched, blew snot out of their noses, spat and belched. There were a couple of men under the tarp with us, shivering with fever. One crawled out to vomit. Nakki rubbed his legs and arms with raw onion. Baby goats covered in sores drank from our water pots and urinated on our mats. The air was mostly dust. The horizon promised nothing but dust. Where was I? Why was I here?

I tried to write notes but the words ran out, evaporated into the blue above. I heard them talking about me. In that forest between sleep and wakefulness I understood, with immeasurable relief, their words. I tried to fix them in my brain for later, knowing the futility of the exercise. My everyday mind would close over that fertile place like parking lot cement. I was suspended in a vast loneliness as pure and cruel as the sky. The women were talking to me. I wanted to grab my head and shake the cement out of it. They shouted as if to a deaf person or an idiot. They put the pen in my hands, indicating that I write and remember names—uncles, cousins, mother's sisters' husbands—then a jab in the ribs.

"Ratti ben, cha pio." Nakki was standing over me with a cup of tea in her hand. I must not sleep there. Scorpions. It was time to move camp.

I had not slept more than two hours a day for how many days? Ten? Twenty? I had lost all sense of time. I had a soaring temperature and could barely swallow. They taunted me constantly: "If you're ill, you'd better go back to Bhuj...Aren't you tired yet? So tired that you'll have to go back to Bhuj?"

Do they really want me to leave? How must I behave? I do not understand what is going on around me. I hear them talking about me the whole time, turning my presence over like a rock. What are they saying?

I had set up my tent, hoping for sleep but the sheep spent all night jumping on it and two spent the night inside it. They rubbed their noses on it so that globs of anthrax green snot hung off it in the morning. Another night I dragged my swag about fifteen feet outside the flock and fell into unconsciousness. No one saw me as they had gone to an uncle's camp to sing. But I was woken by the women—black ghosts against a background of stars. They ordered me back to my cot. I seethed with rage. Didn't they understand that I could not keep going without sleep? They laughed, pecked at me. Their fingers dug, bony as witches.

"If you sleep out here, Phagu will send you back to Bhuj." How I hated them. The sheep and goats chewed and digested and coughed. They were so full of disease they were barely alive, yet they chewed the country into dust. The great grinding stomach of India, everything feeding off everything else.

When I woke each morning it was to dread. I must face them. I must sit and eat with them. Sometimes they smiled at me or laughed but I could not read their faces. They looked at me sideways and thought their own thoughts. They had no inkling what torture it was to be unable to speak, unable to order the world in any way, exposed and wretched in a place where even the sky was strange. My other life was

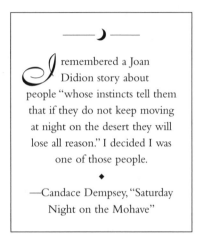

I remembered a Joan Didion story about people "whose instincts tell them that if they do not keep moving at night on the desert they will lose all reason." I decided I was one of those people.

♦

—Candace Dempsey, "Saturday Night on the Mohave"

unimaginable to them and so therefore was the degree of stress—solitary confinement and sleep deprivation combined.

The country was butchered, nothing but rubble and dust. Nothing invited the eye or the soul. The light beat the colour out of everything. Blue became white. Green, a dull grey or dun. Only the women's black withstood the domination of sun, like tiny rents in the sheet of light. The men in white merged with sheep or rocks and became invisible. In the evening the flocks poured out of the ravines. When they arrived in camp, the dust was unendurable. Throughout the night the animals, packed close around me, scraped themselves against my cot. I whipped at them with a rope in fury. I damaged my elbows and hands by punching them.

Sometimes it happened that I could not get water for myself as my companions had not told me we were to break camp early. I had no way of finding out how far I might have to walk without a drink. I was as helpless as an infant. I went by myself to a nearby train siding, nameless to anyone but its occupants. Perhaps there would be a shop. Something cool. Maybe even ice. To step out of the shade was to feel nausea. It was already autumn. How do they survive the summer? How does anything? Just a five-mile walk and at the end of it something cool. Something different. And I could be on my own during that five miles if I could avoid being seen. I approached the siding, pulled an *orni* over my face. A rutted street, dusty trees, a few sick dogs with ribs like piano keys, panting in the shade. A line of track ran one way to nothing and lost itself in nothing in the other direction. Along that line, from one end of north India to the other, I imagined identical clusters of huts, the same cows nosing garbage, the same children in rags and silver, eyes filled with flies. In either direction there was nowhere to go.

There was a shop, the usual shack distributing goods from tins and sacks, even here tricked out to entice with cheap little gee-gaws. No ice, but orange soda the temperature and consistency of blood. I drank four bottles. People began to collect. Hastily I bought sweets—hardened, spun sugar covered in grey dirt—and hurried back to camp.

Sometimes we passed the outskirts of villages, which to me were defined by whether they might have a telephone and if so how I might get there. If I could hear Narendra's voice, if I could express even one fluent thought, I could keep going. I could ring for Koju and the jeep. An interpreter from somewhere. The village might be so close you could see its detail. Why did they refuse to let me go? It would take an hour and a half to walk there, an hour and a half to walk back, and by then it would be nightfall and too dangerous to be out alone. Was that it? Perhaps they knew that particular village had no phone? Or were they keeping me here out of sheer spite? Sometimes Nakki would announce that we were all going to a village the following day and I would go to bed curling around the idea of tomorrow as if it were my child. Then, when it was time to break camp in the morning, we would leave the vicinity of the village altogether and walk in the opposite direction. The desire to talk was like some fantastic hunger; they were my torturers, keeping the food just beyond reach.

Malaria began to fell the shepherds where they stood. My own body was slimy with fever. I must not get ill. I *must* not...One afternoon, at last, the women directed me to get ready; we were heading into town for injections and supplies. Three miles along a path, then on to the road, all the while imagining Narendra's voice—like being alone on a boat at night, tossing in a stormy sea but seeing the steady blink of the port beacon.

The doctor called me into his office and as usual the Rabari trooped in behind me. He laughed and sat them down, ordering tea and water.

"I, too, admire these people. Their lives are very hard."

"You're telling me," I said.

"Now you will go to my home next door and meet my wife. There you will have a hot shower." I turned to check with Nakki. "It's all right," said the doctor. "They will wait out under the shade once I have attended to them."

I do not even remember his name. But to that doctor I owe a portion of my sanity. Nor did I care that I abandoned my friends for the comforts of my class. I scrubbed and scrubbed in that shower and I think I probably sang. Half an hour later we were back in the streets, pushing upstream against the river of souls. I bought of box of sweets to take to the doctor on the way home and as many vegetables as I could carry for the *dang*. Then I told Nakki that I must find an STD booth to ring Jodhpur. Yes, I could go but I must be quick. (This she indicated by snapping her fingers.) They would wait for me here. I hurried off.

It took a long time to find the booth. Everyone I asked seemed to point in a different direction. Then, as usual, someone from the crowd I had gathered, about thirty people by now, took command and led me up narrow alleys and behind bazaars. Ten people crowded into a room the size of a lavatory. Breathing was difficult. Sweat saturated clothes. My head was bursting. The booth *wallah* couldn't get Jodhpur. (Oh please, please.) After ten minutes or so, he handed the phone to me.

"Madam, the line is very bad. You must shout."

I shouted, "Narendra..." and there was his faint, infinitely longed for voice.

"Are you all right? Where are you? Should I come?"

"I can't talk now," I yelled. "Too difficult, Yes, I'm all right..."

"What? I can't hear you."

"*I'm all right...*" But the line had gone dead. I tried to reach Dr. Rama Krishna but could not get through. I put the receiver down and to my shame, in front of thirty people, whose staring faces crammed the doorway and pressed up against the window, I hid my eyes with my hand and cried.

I almost ran back to our meeting place to find that a shepherd had come from the flocks to tell us to wait in town, which we did for four hours. As we did not know when we would be leaving I could not go back to the telephone nor could I deliver the sweets.

Four hours. We sat on the scorching pavement or took turns lying on a narrow wooden plank half shaded by a wall, next to an open latrine whose stench mixed with the smells of rotting garbage, cooking oil and spice. Fifty yards down our gully was the meat market. People sipped tea beside a mound of steaming offal—chickens' heads and feet, goats' stomachs, other less recognizable pieces of anatomy being shovelled into wooden carts by thin, glistening men up to their knees in blood and muck, naked to the waist, the sunlight pounding down on them like a hammer ringing on a metal lid screwed down tight. Heat and light, flies which whirled around the piles of sticky sweets, the teacups, the children's eyes, the running pigs, the women in crisp white sari stepping daintily amidst the shit.

Along came a man carrying a large python. He wore rags; there were weeping sores up and down his legs. He extracted money from passers-by by thrusting the snake into their faces. He saw mine and bounded over. From up close I saw that the snake's lips were stitched together crudely with string and its mouth was bloody and deformed. It had no limbs with which to struggle, no mouth to protest its fate. All its suffering was condensed in its eyes which, in memory, are humanly expressive. From a comfortable distance—let's say twenty feet, that is to say the distance money can buy you—the sight of the man with the snake is marvelous, something to capture in a lens. Up close it is merely terrible.

How one longed for the poor to say, just once, "War on the palaces, peace to the cottages!" Yet whenever a look of fury replaced the self-control on the faces around me, fear would creep up my back and I would repeal the instinct for revolution. Because here would be no vertical eruption—the bottom layer forcing its way to the top—only a lateral one in which everyone turned on everyone else, a war of all against all. Sometimes I thought the conflagration must be imminent and all that was needed to ignite it was just one more crooked official, one more lorry, one more decibel, one more stitched-up snake thrust into one more face by one more hungry man.

The shepherd came to fetch us. I don't remember how many we were, ten perhaps, crammed into a tin rickshaw. At the end of the ride we had a couple of miles still to walk, cross-country. But now there was an altercation. The driver was waving his arms around, demanding more money. It was a matter of five rupees. I took a woman aside and said I would pay. But Nakki's sense of injustice overwhelmed her greed. It went on and on. Ten minutes, twenty minutes. Why didn't I just hand five rupees to the man, twenty, a hundred? I don't know. I did as the group did. We had two sick children with us and one very sick man. I stood at the back of the group and turning saw, for just one moment in the face of the woman next to me, beneath the Indian forbearance, a despair as old as the continent itself. I pushed through the women, handed the man five rupees and we set off across the fields. Nakki muttered to herself about crooks and thieves.

Arjun was weaving from side to side as he walked. Down he went. We picked him up. Another hundred yards, down again, mumbling to himself in delirium. Two women shouldered him for a while, distributing their heavy head bundles among the rest of us. Down again. We waited with him for five minutes as he lay moaning on the ground. Another hundred yards. Another five-minute wait. And thus to the *dang*. It was time to pack up and move, quickly. Arjun was shoved on to the camel with the sick and newborn lambs. We walked twelve miles.

Robyn Davidson is the author of the novel Ancestors *and the nonfiction books* Tracks *and* Desert Places, *from which this story was excerpted.*

★

And what about the bigger questions aroused by travel, such as Who am I? and Where do I belong? I admit that the most excruciating form of those existential questions was brought on in my life through psychedelic mind travel, but I also have felt pretty strange and alienated turning down a side street off Division. In fact, a walk around my own block in Grand Rapids, with my smiles and hellos dismissed by an averted glance, is much more unsettling than the urchins who ran after me in Majorca and Sardinia, begging for pennies or a stick of gum. Which is a worse torture—to feel the guilt of privilege or the snub of exclusion? These are some of the dangers of travels.

—Debby Topliff, "Travel"

PART FOUR

IN THE SHADOWS

✱ ✱ ✱

Lightning Strike

In Wyoming, the author
struggles toward life.

DEEP IN AN OCEAN. I AM SUSPENDED MOTIONLESS. THE WATER IS gray. That's all there is, and before that? My arms are held out straight, cruciate, my head and legs hang limp. Nothing moves. Brown kelp lies flat in mud and fish are buried in liquid clouds of dust. There are no shadows or sounds. Should there be? I don't know if I am alive, but if not, how do I know I am dead? My body is leaden, heavier than gravity. Gravity is done with me. No more sinking and rising or bobbing in currents. There is a terrible feeling of oppression with no oppressor. I try to lodge my mind against some boundary, some reference point, but the continent of the body dissolves...

A single heartbeat stirs gray water. Blue trickles in, just a tiny stream. Then a long silence.

Another heartbeat. This one is louder, as if amplified. Sound takes a shape: it is a snowplow moving grayness aside like a heavy snowdrift. I can't tell if I'm moving, but more blue water flows in. Seaweed begins to undulate, then a whole kelp forest rises from the ocean floor. A fish swims past and looks at me. Another heartbeat drives through dead water, and another, until I am surrounded by blue.

Sun shines above all this. There is no pattern to the way its glint comes free and falls in long knives of light. My two beloved dogs appear. They flank me like tiny rockets, their fur pressed against my ribs. A leather harness holds us all together. The dogs climb toward light, pulling me upward at a slant from the sea.

I have been struck by lightning and I am alive.

Before electricity carved its blue path toward me, before the negative charge shot down from cloud to ground, before "streamers" jumped the positive charge back up from ground to cloud, before air expanded and contracted producing loud pressure pulses I could not hear because I was already dead, I had been walking.

When I started out on foot that August afternoon, the thunderstorm was blowing in fast. On the face of the mountain, a mile ahead, hard westerly gusts and sudden updrafts collided, pulling black clouds apart. Yet the storm looked harmless. When a distant thunderclap scared the dogs, I called them to my side and rubbed their ears: "Don't worry, you're okay as long as you're with me."

I woke in a pool of blood, lying on my stomach some distance from where I should have been, flung at an odd angle to one side of the dirt path. The whole sky had grown dark. Was it evening, and if so, which one? How many minutes or hours had elapsed since I lost consciousness, and where were the dogs? I tried to call out to them but my voice didn't work. The muscles in my throat were paralyzed and I couldn't swallow. Were the dogs dead? Everything was terribly wrong: I had trouble seeing, talking, breathing, and I couldn't move my legs or right arm. Nothing remained in my memory—no sounds, flashes, smells, no warnings of any kind. Had I been shot in the back? Had I suffered a stroke or heart attack? These thoughts were dark pools in sand.

The sky was black. Was this a storm in the middle of the day or was it night with a storm traveling through? When thunder exploded over me, I knew I had been hit by lightning.

The pain in my chest intensified and every muscle in my body ached. I was quite sure I was dying. What was it one should do or think or know? I tried to recall the Buddhist instruction regarding dying—which position to lie in, which direction to face. Did the "Lion's position" taken by the Buddha mean lying on the left or the right? And which sutra to sing? Oh yes, the Heart Sutra...*gaté, gaté, paragaté*...form and formlessness. Paradox and cosmic jokes. Surviving after trying to die "properly" would be truly funny, but the chances of that seemed slim.

Other words drifted in: how the "gateless barrier" was the gate through which one passes to reach enlightenment. Yet if there was no gate, how did one pass through? Above me, high on the hill, was the gate on the ranch that led nowhere, a gate I had mused about often. Now its

> ——) ——
>
> *C*autious as I am, I've been caught above timberline in lightning a handful of terrifying times.... You hope to keep your head in such tight spots. You hope to fend off panic. But if you didn't feel fear, there'd be something wrong with you. These are the moments your body confronts the body of the earth most starkly. You can't ignore it: you'll die sometime, and that time might be now.
>
> ◆
>
> —SueEllen Campbell, *Bringing the Mountain Home*

presence made me smile. Even when I thought I had no aspirations for enlightenment, too much effort in that direction was being expended. How could I learn to slide, yet remain aware?

To be struck by lightning: what a way to get enlightened. That would be the joke if I survived. It seemed important to remember jokes. My thinking did not seem connected to the inert body that was in such terrible pain. Sweep the mind of weeds, I kept telling myself—that's what years of Buddhist practice had taught me...But where were the dogs, the two precious ones I had watched being born and had raised in such intimacy and trust? I wanted them with me. I wanted them to save me again.

It started to rain. Every time a drop hit bare skin there was an explosion of pain. Blood crusted my left eye. I touched my good hand to my heart, which was beating wildly, erratically. My chest was numb, as if it had been sprayed with novocaine. No feeling of peace filled me. Death was a bleakness, a grayness about which it was impossible to be curious or relieved. I loved those dogs and hoped they weren't badly hurt. If I didn't die soon, how many days would pass before we were found, and when would the scavengers come? The sky was dark, or was that the way life flew out of the body, in a long tube with no light at the end? I lay on the cold ground waiting. The mountain was purple, and sage stirred against my face. I knew I had to give up all this, then my own body and all my thinking. Once more I lifted my head to look for the dogs but, unable to see them, I twisted myself until I faced east and tried to let go of all desire.

When my eyes opened again I knew I wasn't dead. Images from World War II movies filled my head: of wounded soldiers dragging themselves across a field, and if I could have laughed—that is, made my face work into a smile and get sounds to discharge from my throat—I would have. God, it would have been good to laugh. Instead, I considered my options; either lie there and wait for someone to find me—how many days or weeks would that take?—or somehow get back to the house. I calmly assessed what might be wrong with me—stroke, cerebral hemorrhage, gunshot wound—but it was bigger than I could understand. The instinct to survive does not rise from particulars; a deep but general misery rollercoasted me into action. I tried to propel myself on my elbows but my right arm didn't work. The wind had swung around and was blowing in from the east. It was still a dry storm with only sputtering rain, but when I raised myself up, lightning fingered the entire sky.

It is not true that lightning never strikes the same place twice. I had entered a shower of sparks and furious brightness and, worried that I might be struck again, watched as lightning touched down all around me. Years before, in the high country, I'd been hit by lightning: an electrical charge had rolled down an open meadow during a fearsome thunderstorm, surged up the legs of my horse, coursed through me, and bounced a big spark off the top of my head. To be struck again—and this time it was a direct hit—what did it mean?

The feeling had begun to come back into my legs and after many awkward attempts, I stood. To walk meant lifting each leg up by the thigh, moving it forward with my hands, setting it down. The earth felt like a peach that had split open in the middle; one side moved up while the other side moved down and my legs were out of rhythm. The ground rolled the way it does during an earthquake and the sky was tattered book pages waving in different directions. Was the ground liquifying under me, or had the molecular composition of my body deliquesced? I struggled to piece together fragments. Then it occurred to me that my brain was torn and that's where the blood had come from.

I walked. Sometimes my limbs held me, sometimes they didn't. I don't know how many times I fell but it didn't matter because I was making slow progress toward home.

Home—the ranch house—was about a quarter of a mile away. I don't remember much about getting there. My concentration went into making my legs work. The storm was strong. All the way across the basin, lightning lifted parts of mountains and sky into yellow refulgence and dropped them again, only to lift others. The inside of my eyelids turned gold and I could see the dark outlines of things through them. At the bottom of the hill I opened the door to my pickup and blew the horn with the idea that someone

> Counting the seconds between a lightning flash and the thunder, I then divide by five, and get a rough idea of how far away it is—seven miles. In one second, sound travels 1,100 feet. If the lightning flash and the thunder arrive at the same time, one doesn't have much of a chance to count.
>
> ◆
>
> —Diane Ackerman,
> *A Natural History of the Senses*

might hear me. No one came. My head had swollen to an indelicate shape. I tried to swallow—I was so thirsty—but the muscles in my throat were still paralyzed and I wondered when I would no longer be able to breathe.

Inside the house, sounds began to come out of me. I was doing crazy things, ripping my hiking boots off because the bottoms of my feet were burning, picking up the phone when I was finally able to scream. One of those times, someone happened to be on the line. I was screaming incoherently for help. My last conscious act was to dial 911.

Dark again. Pressing against sore ribs, my dogs pulled me out of the abyss, pulled and pulled. I smelled straw. My face was on tatami. I opened my eyes, looked up, and saw neighbors. Had they come for my funeral? The phone rang and I heard someone give directions to the ambulance driver, who was lost. A "first responder," an EMT from town who has a reputation with the girls, leaned down and asked if he could "touch me" to see if there were any broken bones. What the hell, I thought. I was going to die anyway. Let him have his feel. But his touch was gentle and professional, and I was grateful.

I slipped back into unconsciousness and when I woke again two EMTs were listening to my heart. I asked them to look for my dogs but they wouldn't leave me. Someone else in the room went outside and found Sam and Yaki curled up on the porch, frightened but alive. Now I could rest. I felt the medics jabbing needles into the top of my hands, trying unsuccessfully to get IVs started, then strapping me onto a backboard and carrying me out the front door of the house, down steps, into lightning and rain, into what was now a full-blown storm.

The ambulance rocked and slid, slamming my bruised body against the metal rails of the gurney. Every muscle was in violent spasm and there was a place on my back near the heart that burned. I heard myself yell in pain. Finally the EMTs rolled up towels and blankets and wedged them against my arms, shoulders, hips, and knees so the jolting of the vehicle wouldn't dislodge me. The ambulance slid down into ditches, struggled out, bumped from one deep rut to another. I asked to be taken to the hospital in Cody, but they said they were afraid my heart might stop again. As it was, the local hospital was thirty-five miles away, ten of them dirt, and the trip took more than an hour.

Our arrival seemed a portent of disaster—and an occasion for comedy. I had been struck by lightning around five in the afternoon. It was now 9:00 p.m. Nothing at the hospital worked. Their one EKG machine was nonfunctional, and jokingly the nurses blamed it on me. "Honey, you've got too much electricity in your body," one of them told me. Needles were jammed into my hand—no one had gotten an IV going yet—and the doctor on call hadn't arrived, though half an hour had elapsed. The EMTs kept assuring me: "Don't worry, we won't leave you here." When another nurse, who was filling out an admission form; asked me how tall I was, I answered: "Too short to be struck by lightning."

"Electrical injury often results in ventricular fibrillation and injury to the medullary centers of the brain. Immediately after electric shock patients are usually comatose, apneic, and in circulatory collapse...."

When the doctor on call—the only doctor in town—waddled into what they called the emergency room, my aura, he said, was yellow and gray—a soul in transition. I knew that he had gone to medical school but had never completed a residency and had been barred from ER or ICU work in the hospitals of Florida, where he had lived previously. Yet I was lucky. Florida has many lightning victims, and unlike the doctors I would see later, he at least recognized the symptoms of a lightning strike. The tally sheet read this way: I had suffered a hit by lightning which caused ventricular fibrillation—cardiac arrest—though luckily my heart started beating again. Violent contractions of muscles when one is hit often causes the body to fly through the air: I was flung far and hit hard on my left side, which may have caused my heart to start again, but along with that fortuitous side effect, I sustained a concussion, broken ribs, a possible broken jaw, and lacerations above the eye. The paralysis below my waist and up through the chest and throat—

called kerauno-paralysis—is common in lightning strikes and almost always temporary, but my right arm continued to be almost useless. Fernlike burns—arborescent erythema—covered my entire body. These occur when the electrical charge follows tracings of moisture on the skin—rain or sweat—thus the spidery red lines.

"Rapid institution of fluid and electrolyte therapy is essential with guidelines being the patient's urine output, hematocrit, osmolality, central venous pressure, and arterial blood gases...."

The nurses loaded me onto a gurney. As they wheeled me down the hall to my room, a front wheel fell off and I was slammed into the wall. Once I was in bed, the deep muscle aches continued, as did the chest pains. Later, friends came to visit. Neither doctor nor nurse had cleaned the cuts on my head, so Laura, who had herded sheep and cowboyed on all the ranches where I had lived and whose wounds I had cleaned when my saddle horse dragged her across a high mountain pasture, wiped blood and dirt from my face, arms, and hands with a cool towel and spooned yogurt into my mouth.

I was the only patient in the hospital. During the night, sheet lightning inlaid the walls with cool gold. I felt like an ancient, mummified child who had been found on a rock ledge near our ranch: bound tightly, unable to move, my dead face tipped backwards toward the moon.

In the morning, my regular doctor, Ben, called from Massachusetts, where he was vacationing, with this advice: "Get yourself out of that hospital and go somewhere else, anywhere." I was too weak to sign myself out, but Julie, the young woman who had a summer job on our ranch, retrieved me in the afternoon. She helped me get dressed in the cutoffs and torn t-shirt I had been wearing, but there were no shoes, so, barefoot, I staggered into Ben's office, where a physician's assistant kindly cleansed the gashes in my head. Then I was taken home.

Another thunderstorm slammed against the mountains as I limped up the path to the house. Sam and Yaki took one look at me and ran. These dogs lived with me, slept with me, understood every word I said, and I was too sick to find them, console them— even if they would have let me.

The next day my husband, who had just come down from the mountains where he worked in the summer, took me to another hospital. I passed out in the admissions office, was loaded onto a gurney, and taken for a CAT scan. No one bothered to find out why I had lost consciousness. Later, in the emergency unit, the doctor argued that I might not have been struck by lightning at all, as if I had imagined the incident. "Maybe a meteor hit me," I said, a suggestion he pondered seriously. After a blood panel and a brief neurolgical exam, which I failed—I couldn't follow his finger with my eyes or walk a straight line—he promptly released me.

> *"Patients should be monitored electrocardiographically for at least 24 hours for significant arrhythmias which often have delayed onset...."*

It was difficult to know what was worse: being in a hospital where nothing worked and nobody cared, or being alone on an isolated ranch hundreds of miles from decent medical care.

In the morning I staggered into the kitchen. My husband, from whom I had been separated for three months, had left at 4:00 a.m. to buy cattle in another part of the state and would not be back for a month. Alone again, it was impossible to do much for myself. In the past I'd been bucked off, stiff and sore plenty of times but this felt different: I had no sense of equilibrium. My head hurt, every muscle in my body ached as if I had a triple dose of the flu, and my left eye was swollen shut and turning black and blue. Something moved in the middle of the kitchen floor. I was having difficulty seeing, but then I did see: a rattlesnake lay coiled in front of the stove. I reeled around and dove back into bed. Enough tests of character. I closed my eyes and half-slept. Later, when Julie came to the house, she found the snake and cut off its head with a shovel.

My only consolation was that the dogs came back. I had chest pains and all day Sam lay with his head against my heart. I cleaned a deep cut over Yaki's eye. It was half an inch deep but already healing. I couldn't tell if the dogs were sick or well, I was too miserable to know anything except that Death resided in the room: not as a human figure but as a dark fog rolling in, threatening to cover me; but the dogs stayed close and while my promise to keep them safe during a thunderstorm had proven fraudulent, their promise to keep me alive held good.

When you are sad, dogs come to give you things.

—Emma Strother, age 4

Gretel Ehrlich's essays have appeared in such publications as The New York Times, Harper's, *and* The Atlantic Monthly. *Her books include* The Solace of Open Spaces; Islands, the Universe, Home; *and* A Match to the Heart, *from which this story was excerpted.*

I have thought of the hospital as a place in nature, a peculiarly desperate invention of our species born of our love of life and our passionate resistance to death. And I have begun to think of death, too, as a place in nature—"Yes," the Tohono O'ohdam elder said to my Yaqui friend, "it's a place in the desert right over there." Death is our home—where we all go at the end. I mean this quite literally—space and time being one—that the end of time each of us must experience is the one place we all share in common, and therefore a place we must not defile.

—Alison Hawthorne Deming, *Temporary Homelands: Essays on Nature, Spirit and Place*

JOANNA GREENFIELD

Hyena

*She just wanted to work
with animals.*

SPOTTED HYENAS ARE THE SHARKS OF THE SAVANNA, SUPER-predators and astounding recyclers of garbage. They hunt in large, giggling groups, running alongside their prey and eating chunks of its flesh until it slows down through loss of blood, or shock, or sheer hopelessness, and then the hyenas grab for the stomach and pull the animal to a halt with its own entrails or let it stumble into the loops and whorls of its own body. They eat the prey whole and cough back, like owls, the indigestible parts, such as hair and hooves....

I once saw a family of hyenas playing on an elephant skull. They rolled on their backs, biting gently at each other's legs. Two cubs squeezed under and then out of the elephant's mandible. A female turned on her side, paws in the air, and broke off a piece of the skull as if eating a biscuit in bed. Hyenas almost never kill humans—only now and then taking a piece from the cheek of a sleeping man, and that probably because some villagers used to put out their dead for hyenas, flies, and any vultures in the area. As the man jumps up—perhaps he is a messenger between vil-lages or someone searching for a bride—the hyena instantly, peaceably, retreats.

Africa is like no other place on earth, and there is no better place to watch animals. They roam sun-dazed on the savanna by the million, sniffing up the scent of dried grass, swishing their tails, eyes often half closed. Sometimes they ignore human beings, sometimes they stare, but always there is something to look at: impalas dancing together in a mock fight, giraffes slow-swinging across the horizon. In the distance, vervet monkeys hop through branches. An ostrich runs with tail rampant, all the while flapping its wings in agitation, like a maiden aunt caught in a shower. A baboon nurses its toe. A lion quietly chuffs to itself.

I had wanted to go to Africa since my childhood, in Connecticut. Before I was born, my eyes lost their attachment to each other, the instinctive knowledge of how to swivel together, how to analyze data in tandem. The vision of one eye is only slightly cloudy, but it withdraws from cooperation with the other. My eyes do not work like two halves of a whole, and I have no perception of depth, so human faces blend into their background and are unreadable. The unreadable is frightening. When I was a child, friendly voices could dig deep and sharp without warning: without depth perception, there is no warning. I had to learn about emotions, which are subtle and often masked, from animals, who signal theirs so much more clearly, with mane and tail and the position of the body. Human beings were a hazard.

There was only one thing that my eyes took in with ease. As the school bus crossed the marshes on a small cement bridge, we could see down the river to the horizon, and up the river toward a bend of trees. In the swamp that ran alongside it grew cattails and rushes, as naturally gold as they were tall. They were semi-translucent. Each blade glowed separately in the morning sun as if lit within. Together in their bending, high-feathered swamp, they bowed under the weightlessness of light. Sometimes there was mist rising from the water, and altogether it was the only masterpiece I ever saw in my suburban town. I don't know why I needed to see those rushes so badly, or how I knew Africa would be the same, but it was.

I had never wanted to work anywhere except in Africa, but after I graduated from college a wildlife-reserve director from

Israel told me that he needed someone to set up a breeding site for endangered animals and I decided to go. When I got there, I was told that the project had been postponed and was asked if I'd mind taking a job as a volunteer at another reserve, cleaning enclosures. The reserve was dedicated to Biblical animals, many of them predators from the Israeli wild—hyenas, wolves, foxes, and one un-mated leopard—attackers of kibbutz livestock. It was something to do, with animals, so I trudged off every day in the hundred-and-fourteen-degree heat with half a sandwich and a water canteen. I was being groomed for the job I'd initially been offered, but for the moment I sifted maggots for the lizards and snakes, and cleaned the fox, cat, hyena, wolf, and leopard corrals.

As the days got hotter, my fellow-workers and I carried gallon jugs of water in our wheelbarrows, poured it over our heads, and drank the rest until our stomachs were too full for food. It became a steady rhythm: sift dung, pour, drink, sift. We worked in pairs among the larger animals for safety, but toward the end of the month I was allowed to feed a young hyena and clean his cage. Efa had been taken from his parents as a cub because his mother re-jected him. Also, he was a cross between a North African and an Israeli striped hyena, and nobody wanted him to confuse the gene pool further by mating. He was a beautiful animal. A mane trick-led down sloped shoulders like a froth of leftover baby hair; he looked strangely helpless, as if weighed down by the tangled strands, and his back rounded to a dispirited slump. Even though he had a hyena's posture, he was like a German shepherd, a little dirty, but graceful, and so strong he didn't seem to have any mus-cles. His stripes twisted a bit at the ends and shimmered over the coat like feathers at rest. With his bat face and massed shoulders, he would have been at home in the sky, poised in a great leap, or swooping for prey. But here he was given aged meat, and he often left even that to rot before he ate it.

He had been, they said, an adorable cub, crying *"Maaaaa!"* to Shlomi, the gentlest of the workers and the one who reared him, and he followed Shlomi everywhere. Then he grew too big to run loose, and he started biting at people, so they put him in a corral—

a square of desert surrounded by an electrified fence with a large water basin perched in the center.

Efa was bored and lonely. He flipped the basin over every day, attacking it as if it were prey. When we fed him in the morning, there was nowhere to put his water. He knocked over everything, so we had no choice: we had to put him in a holding cage outside his corral while we built a concrete pool that he couldn't move. This was worse. Locked in a cage, he rebelled. He refused to eat, and every box we gave him for shade was torn to pieces. After a few days, I walked by and saw him standing defiant in the cage, his shade box in splinters and his water overturned again. *"Maaaaaaa! Mmaaaa!"* he croaked at me. I made a note to return and water him when I'd finished with the others....

Efa was in a frenzy of *"Mmmaaaaaaaaa"s* when I returned to his cage. He crouched like a baby, begging for something. I filled a water tray and unlatched the door that opened into a corridor running between the cage and the corral, then I closed it. If only I'd just squirted the hose into the cage, but instead I unlatched the cage door and bent over to put the dish down, talking to him. The mind, I found, is strange. It shut off during the attack, while my body continued to act, without thought or even sight. I don't remember him sinking his teeth into my arm, though I heard a little grating noise as his teeth chewed into the bone.

Everything was black and slow and exploding in my stomach. Vision returned gradually, like an ancient black-and-white television pulling dots and flashes to the center for a picture. I saw at a remove the hyena inside my right arm, and my other arm banging him on the head. My body, in the absence of a mind, had decided that this was the best thing to do. And scream. Scream in a thin angry hysteria that didn't sound like me. Where was everyone? My mind was so calm and remote that I frightened myself, but my stomach twisted. I hit harder, remembering the others he'd nipped. He'd always let go.

Efa blinked and surged back, jerking me forward. I stumbled out of my sandals into the sand, thinking, with fresh anxiety, I'll burn my feet. I tried to kick him between the legs, but it was awk-

ward, and he was pulling me down by the arm, down and back
into the cage. When I came back from Africa the first time, I took
a class in self-defense so I'd feel safer with all the soldiers, guerrilla
warriors, and policemen when I returned. I remembered the move
I'd vowed to use on any attacker: a stab and grab at the jugular, to
snap it inside the skin. But the hyena has callused skin on its throat,
thick and rough, like eczema. I lost hope and felt the slowness of
this death to be the worst insult. Hyenas don't kill fast, and I could
end up in the sand watching my entrails get pulled through a cut
in my stomach and eaten like spaghetti, with tugs and jerks. I
started to get mad, an unfamiliar feeling creeping in to add an acid
burn to the chill of my stomach. Another removal from myself. I
never let myself get mad. I want peace. I tried to pinch his nostrils
so he'd let go of my arm to breathe, but he shook his head, pulling
me deeper into the cage.

I think it was then that he took out the first piece from my arm
and swallowed it without breathing, because a terror of movement
settled in me at that moment and lasted for months. He moved up
the arm, and all the time those black, blank eyes evaluated me, like
a shark's, calm and almost friendly. By this time, my right arm was
a mangled mess of flesh, pushed-out globs of fat, and flashes of
bone two inches long, but my slow TV mind, watching, saw it as
whole, just trapped in the hyena's mouth, in a tug-of-war like the
one I used to play with my dogs—only it was my arm now instead
of a sock. It didn't hurt. It never did.

The hyena looked up at me with those indescribable eyes and
surged back again, nearly pulling me into his face. I remembered
self-defense class and the first lesson: "Poke the cockroach in the
eyes." All the women had squealed, except me. "Ooooh, I could
never do that." Ha, I'd thought. Anyone who wants to kill me has
no right to live. I'd poke him in the eyes.

I looked at those eyes with my fingers poised to jab. It was for
my family and my friends that I stuck my fingers in his eyes. I just
wanted to stop watching myself get eaten, either be dead and at
peace or be gone, but other lives were connected to mine. I'm not
sure if I did more than touch them gently before he let go and

whipped past me to cower against the door to the outside, the Negev desert.

Events like this teach you yourself. We all think we know what we would do, hero or coward, strong or weak. I expected strength, and the memory of my tin-whistle scream curdles my blood, but I am proud of the stupid thing I did next. He cowered and whimpered and essentially apologized, still with those blank unmoving eyes, and I stood still for a second. My arm felt light and shrunken, as if half of it were gone, but I didn't look. From the corridor, I had a choice of two doors: the one through which I'd entered, leading back to the desert, and the one opening onto the corral. I didn't think I could bend over him and unlatch the door to the desert. He'd just reach up and clamp onto my stomach. And I didn't want to open the door to the corral, or he'd drag me in and be able to attack the men if they ever came to help me. My body, still in control, made the good hand grab the bad elbow, and I beat him with my own arm, as if I had ripped it free to use as a club. "No!" I shouted. "No, no!" *Lo lo lo*, in Hebrew. I might even have said "Bad boy," but I hope not. It was the beating that damaged my hand permanently. I must have hit him hard enough to crush a ligament, because there is a lump on my hand to this day, five years later, but he didn't even blink. He came around behind me and grabbed my right leg, and again there was no pain—just the feeling that he and I were playing tug-of-war with my body—but I was afraid to pull too hard on the leg. He pulled the leg up, stretching me out in a line from the door, where I clung with the good hand to the mesh, like a dancer at the barre. It felt almost good, as if the whole thing were nearer to being over. In three moves I didn't feel, he took out most of the calf.

I opened the door to the desert and he ran out, with a quick shove that staggered me. I couldn't move the right leg, just crutched myself along on it into the Negev. He waited for me. The cold in my stomach was stabbing my breath away. The hyena and I were bonded now. Even if someone did come to help, there was still something left to finish between us. I was marked—his. I saw, in color, that he was going to knock me over, and I thought, in black-and-white, No, don't, you'll hurt my leg, I should keep it still.

A workman stood by a shed up-hill, leaning on a tool in the sand. He watched me walk toward the office, with the hyena ahead and looking back at me. He was the only spectator I noticed, though I was told later, in the hospital, that some tourists, there to see the animals, were screaming for help, and three—or was it five?—soldiers had had their machine guns aimed at us throughout the whole thing. Israeli soldiers carry their arms everywhere when they're in uniform; but they must have been afraid to shoot. I don't know. Stories get told afterward. I didn't see anyone except the workman, looking on impassively, and the leopard, pacing inside her fence, roaring a little....

As I walked, the black-and-white faded, and color washed back in. I saw the blood for the first time. It was in my hair, had soaked into my clothes all the way to the skin, and was drying in a trickle from arm and legs. Each step left a cold puddle of blood around the right foot. I held up the arm and fumbled for the pressure point. The hyena trotted ahead of me as if he were afraid to be alone in the

---

*O*ne evening around midnight, I woke to hear the lions sounding differently, louder and very clear. Then silence. Twenty minutes later, the deep "huh, huh" sounded again, this time close enough for me to detect a lower rumbling and more defined breaths. I was terrified, alone in my tent on the edge of camp. The lions had definitely chosen a route that passed through our camp. I could barely breathe. I just lay in the silence with my eyes wide open and body stiff, waiting for a giant paw to slash across the side of my canvas wall. Thirty agonizing minutes later, the grunts sounded again—in the distance, far behind us. I sighed deeply, letting out the shock, then I began to cry.

◆

—Thalassa Wild Skinner, "In Africa"

desert but was all right with me. Every now and then, he looked back, as if thinking about finishing me off—once again a predator, calm and competent, silver, and splashed with blood. But then men ran up shouting, and I stopped, and snapped, sorry even then for sounding like a bitch, "Get Efa and bring around the van."

Shlomi ran up and grabbed my good left arm, hustling me forward. Not so fast, I wanted to say, but I didn't. Every step felt more wrong, and I dragged back against moving until he almost shoved me forward.

In the van, blood sloshed around my feet and I tried to find the pressure point of the groin but gave up. I held up the arm instead, and pretended I knew what I was doing. Shlomi stopped to open the reserve gate, and then again to close it: as he got back in, I lost feeling in my right leg.

We drove for what seemed like a long time, then turned into a kibbutz and roared past lines of women planting pineapples, past a cement yard, and then he was running me into a clinic past gasping women. And I wanted to apologize. I never cut in line. Shlomi pulled me forward while I stiffened up. Damn it. I wanted to be carried, I've done enough by myself, I remember thinking. But I made it to the examining table and Shlomi yelled for a doctor in Hebrew. A woman came in and told him there was no doctor—only nurses. They stopped telling me what was happening. Hands shaking, she yanked me forward and stuck my arm under a faucet. Hey. She turned on the water and it fell onto the bone and a minor nerve, full force. That was a sensation I wish I couldn't remember. No pain, but a tremendous feeling of wrongness. My insides were out.

She tried to get my leg into the sink, pulling at the ankle, and the shrivelled arm twitched in the air for balance. I tensed, so she couldn't; I wished later that I'd let her, because it was weeks before the dried blood and dirt peeled off. She told me to get on a stretcher, and then she poured hydrogen peroxide into the trenches in my leg. It foamed with a roar that spat froth in the air. That felt wrong, too. Shlomi grabbed the sink for support. I told him it didn't hurt. He wasn't listening. I was starting to feel better. Someone was making the decisions.

"Don't worry, Shlomi. I never wanted to dance ballet."

"No, I don't know, the leg is very bad."

Like all Israelis, he could make a statement of fact sound like an accusation. I knew it was bad, I just didn't see the need to dwell on it when I was so very surprised to be alive. The nurse picked up a towel and started wiping off the blood and dirt with brisk, scratchy strokes, and I cramped in the stomach again, worrying about infection. And what were we waiting for? We waited awhile, and then she gave me anti-shock injections.

"I'm not in shock," I said, and meant it. I thought I was thinking more clearly than she was. Shlomi told me that we were waiting for an ambulance. He was gray, with sick, inturned eyes, the way I must have looked while the attack was happening. But I was over it, and he was just beginning. He and the nurse did not share my pleasure. In fact, they seemed taken aback at my jokes, so I stopped talking.

I had a new terror, but it was peaceful compared with the other, so I lay back. Fly home, microsurgery, I can spare the leg if something has to go, but I have to have the hand for graduate school. Helicopters, international flights, nerve damage.

The ambulance came. The nurse and Shlomi looked as bloodless as I felt. They pushed me around, telling me to get onto the gurney, and I tried to make them go so I could just roll onto it instead of jumping down from the table. They did, and wheeled me out in state through a crowd of horrified kibbutzniks. They showed no excitement over it; pain is too real to Israelis.

I am sure Efa crawled out to greet me with no intention to kill. He had cried to me like an infant in distress, hunched over and rounded. His ruff lay flat and soft and his tail hung down. He attacked me, I think, in a moment of thirst-induced delirium and loneliness. If he had wanted to eat or to attack, he could have taken my arm in a snap: one sharp jab and jerk, and the wrist would have been gone before I even noticed. If he had wanted to kill me, he could have leaped for my stomach as soon as he had pulled me down by the arm.

Cheetahs often catch hold of their prey's nose and run alongside it. As the victim stumbles and falls, or staggers, or tries to run, the cheetah holds tight, closing mouth and nostrils in one stapled hold, or—with larger prey—biting into the throat to cut off air. Leopards like to leap down from trees for a quick crack of the back. Lions improvise. Each has its own specialty. Some leap up from behind, like a terrestrial leopard; some try a daring front leap, risking hooves and horns to bite into neck or face.

Hyenas are far more efficient. They catch hold of flesh, not with small nips and throwing of weight but by smoothly and quickly transferring chunks of it from toothold to stomach. Like human infants nursing, they seem to swallow without pausing for breath, as if food and air travelled in separate channels. They are the only predators adapted to eating bone. Their dung is white with it.

I heard a story of a young boy in Nairobi who was watching over a herd of goats and fell asleep leaning on his stick. A hyena appeared and opened the boy's stomach with one quick rip. For the hyena it might have been play, this trying on of assault. But he won, as he was bound to do. I was told that someone took the boy to a doctor and he died a while later. He could have lived; we don't need all our intestines, and the hyena had probably left enough behind. But maybe they didn't have the right antibiotics or sterile dressings. I would have liked to ask him what he saw in the hyena's eyes.

In the ambulance, the driver chatted for a bit, then said, "Don't close your eyes. If you feel faint, tell me and I'll stop right away."

To do what, watch me? I didn't tell him that I'd been exhausted for months—I'd got parasites in Africa—and always shut my eyes when I had the chance. I closed them now, and he asked me questions with an anxiety that warmed my heart. I love to be taken care of. It was good to be strapped down and bandaged, all decisions out of my hands after the hard ones, the life-and-death ones. It was also, I learned, a good thing to have the wounds hidden. Once they were open to the air, my stomach clenched with pain that made life temporarily not worth living. The arm, I finally noticed, was curled up on itself, like paper shrivelling inward in a fire, but heavy instead of too light.

We arrived at the hospital with a screech and a yank and a curse. The doors were stuck, but the driver pushed, and ran me in. Then he left with a wave of farewell. I waited and waited. A doctor came in and plowed my arm in search of a vein with blood, going deep under the muscle, to attach a saline drip. My nails were white, like things soaked in formaldehyde, and I was freezing. Bled white, I was. Nothing left to fill a test tube.

I asked the doctor to talk with the reserve's veterinarian before he did anything. Hyena bites are violently infectious. The animals' mouths are full of bacteria from rotten meat. He shrugged. But when Shlomi told him to wait for the vet he did. The vet told him to clean the holes out and leave them open for now, because the infection could kill me.

"The infection will probably take the leg anyway," the doctor told me. "The chances are fifty-fifty that we'll have to amputate."

I looked down once at the leg before they began cutting out the dirtier shreds of flesh and paring the whole surface of the wound. The holes were impossibly wide, more than twice the size of the hyena's face. I know now that skin and muscle are stretched over bone like canvas over a canoe. One thinks of skin as irrevocably bonded to flesh, and all as one entity. But skin is attached to flesh only with the lightest of bonds, and, once it has been ripped, the body gives way naturally, pulling the flesh back to its scaffolding of bone. The invisible woman, I thought, as the chill took me; I can see right through my leg.

I couldn't see all of it because of my bad eyesight, and the leg was still covered with blood-stuck sand, but it was strange the way the leg went down normally, then cut in to the bone, along the bone, and then out again to a normal ankle, except for a small gash on the side with fat poking out. I couldn't yet see the other hole. It was lower down, starting halfway past the one I could see, and continuing around the back of the leg to the other side, so almost the whole leg was girdled around. I still don't know how blood got to that stranded wall of flesh.

The doctor worked on the leg for an hour, clipping pieces of flesh out of the wounds with little scissor snips, as if my leg were a piece of cloth that he was carefully tailoring with dull tools. I asked for a larger dose of anesthetic, not because I felt any pain— I never felt any, really—but because I could feel the scissors scissoring away the flesh and I couldn't breathe. Between bouts of cutting, I kept joking, happy it was over, or might be over, and people crowded into the room to watch. No sterilization? Who cares? I was alive. They pumped saline into me so fast that my arm swelled and I had to go to the bathroom. For the first time, I realized how my life had changed. There is, after all, no simple dichotomy: intact and alive versus torn and dead.

They sent some of the people out and stuck a bedpan under the sheet. With one wrist locked to the I.V. and the other paralyzed, I couldn't wipe. Warrior to newborn babe in an hour. Someone brought me my sandals. They were dirty and covered with dried blood, like small dead animals.

> *I*'m often afraid in cities and almost never in wild places. Freeways and sirens and the local newscasts make me uneasy, not weather or wild animals....
>
> Still, once in a while fear catches me, too, shrinks my chest muscles and chops my breath, distorts my vision like a surrealist movie.
>
> ◆
>
> —SueEllen Campbell, *Bringing the Mountain Home*

I had expected the hyena bite in Africa, not in Israel. I had expected the price I paid for Africa to be high. The need that had driven me since I was eight years old had made me willing to risk anything, even death, to be in Africa watching animals. Anyone who works with animals expects to get hurt. You are a guest in their life—any intrusion is a threat to them. It is their separateness that makes them worthy of respect.

After the hospital, I went back to America for physical therapy and treatment of the parasites, which burned a path in my stomach for the next six months. Before I left, people from the reserve asked me to stand near Efa's cage. They wanted to know if his animosity was specific to me. He looked at me, again with those friendly blank eyes, and then rose up against the wire with a crash so loud that I thought he was breaking through. For one second, I saw his face coming toward me, mouth open, and I hopped back. They told me they were going to send him to a zoo where the keepers wouldn't have to go into the cage, but I heard later that a veterinarian came and put Efa to sleep. ("Forever asleep," the workers said.) Shlomi was there.

Back in America, too ill for school, I read about animals on my own. Then I went to graduate school, but I found the statistical and analytical approach to animals too reductive. So I gave it up. But I couldn't not return to Africa. Five years after the hyena bite, I went back. Without a joy, or any scientific purpose, I backpacked between Tanzania and Kenya, seeing the savanna in short bursts of safaris and hired cars and *matatu* buses.

Africa smells of nothing but dust, and that dust lingers with sweetness in the nose and like powder on the skin. It comes from everywhere, even the greenest grass, and it fingers into clothing like minuscule parasites. Shirts blossom red or brown, sometimes yellow, with dust; when clapped they puff into a cloud of color, like a dandelion blown adrift. With the wind in my face and the dust drifting over me, I have never felt so clean.

In spite of its color, the dust is translucent. African sunsets are famous. People say the dust rises into the atmosphere and reflects the sun's light. I think the particles rise, with their own separate colors, and the sun shines through them, heat through translucent splendor.

I believe that, even if you pass through quickly, there are landscapes that are particularly yours. Thousands of explorers returned home with shards of Africa embedded in their lungs. Breathe deeply enough, and you become part of that world, filled to the brim and clogged with its clays and dust.

In the Kenyan highlands, the nights are always cool, and there are so many stars that a book can be read by their light if there's no moon. Eyes sparkle in the light. At night, they reflect it back in

small round circles. Snakes are tiny pinpricks in the grass, hares in
a field sparkle like fireflies as they turn their heads to look at the
car. Mice eyes are like snakes', but closer together. As we drive by,
antelope flash one eye and then the other at us, white orbs of light
in gray shadows. If you sit in the open mouth of your tent before
the fire, the eyes of the hyenas shine green and gold, low down to
the ground, and they look at you. People in Africa usually put their
garbage pits too close to their camps, so we ate our dinner next to
baboons screaming over a cabbage leaf, or hyenas snarling over
bones. I hadn't told anyone here about the hyena bite. I liked to
watch the hyenas rushing in and out of the pit, squabbling and
rolling over each other, but still very friendly, trotting away flank
to flank and stopping to look at me. An animal trainer told me that
once you've been bitten badly enough to limp, even if the limp is
almost imperceptible the animals will know, and from then on you
are prey, not master.

Driving away from my tent camp in Africa, I came upon a den
of hyenas. The first one stood like a statue on the great pan of
rock, the kind I loved to play on as a child, full of towers and caves
and little ledges, with the rock smooth underfoot. It was a silvery
animal, very serious, like a young sentinel, and it wasn't until we
saw the mother that we realized it was a hyena. Three generations
lived in the den. Babies rolled in balls under the mother's feet and
she pricked her ears at us and stepped clear, to watch with the sentinel. Water pooled in a curve before her, rocking with flashes of
light in the wind, decadent somehow against the dried grasses. We
moved and she made a noise and they disappeared—the babies
first, then the mother, then another adult, who had been sleeping
in the grass. The sentinel walked to the shaded side of the rock and
stared at us from there.

I had almost died, eaten alive, and I was glad to be alive. The
scars had healed. Three long dents ran around the arm and the leg,
blurred with spider tracks of canine punctures. The one war
wound, the bump that grew where I hit the hyena, still hurt, but I
was back in Africa.

Joanna Greenfield is a graduate of the Columbia Creative Writing Program. This story originally appeared in The New Yorker.

✱

Suddenly, I was startled from my reverie by a sinister growl to my right. I glanced to the side of the road and spotted a large black bear not more than ten feet from where my dog, Bounder, and I were standing. The bear had taken note of two intruders and sounded his warning.

Knowing from past lore that one should not try to outrun a bear, I froze on the spot in a cold chill (actually, the action was involuntary). Motionless, speechless, I realized in a flash of the mind's eye that this achingly beautiful Sunday morning could be the last day of my life. How ironic that such a magnificent day should come to such a terrible end. My baby was asleep safely in a crib, my husband was fishing at a nearby lake, and my hostess didn't even know I was missing.

There was simply no way out; my number was up and I was paralyzed with fear. At that moment, Bounder barked loudly and lunged at the bear. The bear reared on its hind legs and growled with menacing intent. I remained glued to the road. The two adversaries advanced and retreated in turn, snarling and thrusting. When Bounder started to chase the bear into the underbrush at the side of the road, I began to put one foot in front of the other, almost imperceptibly, taking baby steps until I judged that my distance from the bear was great enough to attempt running. Then I took off like a bat out of hell; pure adrenaline carried me all the way back to the cabin.

—Heather McCoy, "Close Encounter: Ursus Major"

Looking for Footprints

Sometimes the beast in the woods is human.

I CROSS THE STREAM AND ENTER THE WOODS, WALKING QUICKLY. My large German Shepard is bounding ahead, seeking out terrific smells, maybe something to eat. I watch her move, not with pleasure, but for cues. When her ears go forward, I look to see what she is noticing. I hope it is a squirrel or a deer.

As I walk, my eyes are glued to the narrow, rocky trail, a spur to the Appalachian Trail. I notice a flower in bloom, and am surprised I even see it, not because it is late in the season and everything seems to be dying, but because I'm not paying attention to things like flowers or mushrooms, leaves or vistas. I'm looking for footprints. I want to know that I'm out here alone. And if not, I want to know how big his feet are.

Since the deaths of Julie Williams and Lollie Winans on the Appalachian Trail in May 1996, I haven't moved happily in the woods, especially on sections of the Appalachian Trail, which runs near my home in the Berkshires. It's as if what happened there in Virginia will ride its way north, following those white blazes, into Massachusetts. Or rather he will walk north into my back yard.

When I teach writing I always send my students out on a walk, asking them to sit and write, to hear, taste, and see the outdoors.

They think this is fun; I think this is learning. But the college where I taught this summer reminded me that in the last year there had been two rapes on campus, or rather in the woods surrounding the campus. So I kept my students caged in the room until finally I gave in, not from pressure from them, but from myself. I decided we would take a group walk. They learned about poison ivy, picked up pine cones and other wood treasures as we walked deep into the woods, to an area that students have named the Enchanted Forest. I could feel the enchantment in the calm that came with the light as it filtered through the leaves.

In the woods we began looking for a shrine, a memorial for someone's rabbit, that I had heard about. Our class fanned out, scanning for the four-by-four box, and I immediately thought: this is what they do when they go looking for bodies in the woods, when they looked for that crazy boy Mckandless in Alaska, Daniel in the Adirondacks, Rebecca on Knob Hill, no doubt for Julie and Lollie just last spring. I wonder again: Did they die because they loved the outdoors or because they loved each other?

I call out to my students: let's stick together, keep in sight of each other.

——— ☽ ———

*B*ehind naming, beneath words, is something else. An existence named unnamed and unnameable. We give the grass a name, and earth a name. We say grass and earth are separate. We know this because we can pull the grass free of the earth and see its separate roots— but when the grass is free, it dies. We say the inarticulate have no souls. We say the cow's eye has no existence outside ourselves, that the red wing of the blackbird has no thought, the roe of the salmon no feeling, because we cannot name these. Yet for our own lives we grieve all that cannot be spoken, that there is no name for, repeating for ourselves the names of things which surround what cannot be named.

◆

—Susan Griffin, *Woman and Nature: The Roaring Inside Her*

⋆

I am deep in the woods, at mid-point in the four hour loop I am hiking. It feels remote, far from roads, a phone, help. Usually getting away feels safer than a city street or driving my car, but not today. Not anymore. When I see the footprints, I get a burst of adrenalin so strong my legs buckle. I'm shaking as I walk, and I feel this split between mind and body, wish I could transport my body away, home, out of the woods.

I keep my eye on the footprints, watch where they've gone, make sure they don't lead behind a bush where they will be waiting. I rehearse what I will say: my husband is right behind me, if you see him, tell him I have the sandwiches. Both the husband and the sandwiches are fictions. And I realize that they are fictions that make me more of a girl. Do I think that denying that I am a tough dyke who can walk all day without eating is safer?

I wonder if my strong reaction to the deaths of these women is because the closer it gets to home, the more I care? Does that make me a NIMBY (Not In My Back Yard) sort of activist? Or is it because Julie and Lollie were me: women who loved the outdoors and each other? Or is it because there have just been too many deaths that I have heard about, that there are now enough women killed on trails in this country that it's not a freak event, it's what could happen? Whatever the reason, the fear is so deep in my bones my reactions go beyond reason.

When I reach the summit of Alander Mountain I don't even hesitate, though in the past I have stopped to drink water, give the dog a treat, eat some nuts or dried fruit. On this clear early fall day, the views are long: I can see far across the Berkshires, then over west to the Catskills on the other side of the Hudson River. I breathe a little more freely because I'm nearing home, but I keep moving.

I try to remember if I ever felt completely safe in the outdoors, and realize perhaps this is just a fantasy I have. As a child I often slept out in the Indiana Dunes with my sister and our friends, our grandparents' house sitting lit and tall on a hill above the blow out, a safe retreat in case of bad weather. We spent most of our nights playing cut the pie or flashlight tag. This kept away our fear of spirits, and of the older local kids. We had heard they came and raided campers, took food, ice chests, sleeping bags. And what else?

But from those early campouts I have always wanted, craved sleeping and being outside. And the places I have been happiest are in the mountains, when my legs feel a slow subtle burn, when my shoulders are tender and I smell—of sweat, yes, but also of sun and dirt and sky and pine sap and burned oatmeal. I often do not want to wash when I come back from the mountains. I want to cup my hands to my nose and breath in deeply of that stink of place. This is my *querencia,* my home. It is not me going to the mountains or the mountains themselves but when the mountains are in me, on me, perhaps like a lover. Other lovers have come and gone, but I don't want to lose this one.

As my students continued their search, we took to the ravines, the hillsides, sure we would find the shrine. Julius and Ishmael disappeared over into the valley, we were all smacking through spider webs and stumbling into holes. Tatiana found a box turtle and we all gathered to look, to hold it and hope it would emerge to look at us, and us to see its inquisitive eyes. But it was too scared and I understood, I would want a secure shell like that if I lived in the woods. I would want a hard shell and maybe a gun too. The other day I dreamed of owning a gun.

In the fall I moderated a panel at the Pacific Northwest Bookfest entitled "Solo: On Her Own Adventure." This is also the title of an anthology I have edited and published on women's outdoor solo adventures and travel. This little book has struck a chord in women—they write me letters, email, and telephone me telling me how important these stories are, how these stories have given them the courage to go do what they need to do. On their own. My readers are more brave than I am.

How strange, I think, that at the time this book is published I am not likely to go solo myself. I'm a fraud, perhaps, encouraging women to do what I am now too afraid to do. But I once did go solo, and I need to get back to that place. And I worry that I can't.

Soon my class drew together, walked as a group down a path, perhaps a deer path. The woods were hiding what we were looking for, and we were not persistent or curious enough to continue our search. I thought: we would not have found those bodies. Is this what happens to searchers? Do they get discouraged, tired, distracted. But also: what they are searching for they do and do not want to find. Just as the woods are and are not home. The woods are and are not safe.

My sister and I spent hours at a place called Duck Pond, a pond that never froze over in the winter because the water that fed it flowed directly from the sewage plant. This wasn't clean nature but there was a tree and a rope swing and a small, silty-bottomed stream to swing over—and definitely not fall into. This was part of the game, the fun. One day a man came to the other side of that stream, the side we leapt for, sailing through the air. He pulled down his pants and showed us how his penis worked: how it grew large and hard when he touched it. When we finally were brave enough to tell our father about this, he said: you cannot go there anymore. It was the only place that was forbidden. Penis-man, I called him, and I hated him, not for what he'd done but for how he'd taken away our playground.

After the Bookfest panel, a woman came up to me and asked: "Why don't you carry a gun?"

My fear had shone through clearly in all I had said. And to her the solution was obvious.

"I've thought of it," I said. "I'm just afraid that a gun will invite violence into my life, that carrying a gun into the woods will change my experience forever."

Her question makes me realize I'm the one who has to change, do something different, because it doesn't seem that the world is becoming a more gentle place.

*

I run the last quarter mile back to my truck, climb in and lock the door. I sit in the dirt parking lot, looking into the woods through the windshield. I see the leaves, a dozen shades of orange and yellow, and regret that during my walk I did not savor the colors that will be gone in less than a week.

Those footprints were never matched with a person. In fact, I did not see anyone in the four hours I was in the woods. But still, the fear is there. I breathe more slowly and accept that being afraid is not a character flaw; I'm not weak or silly. I'm being realistic, and that is even harder to admit. But I can't live with this kind of fear, can't let it ruin days of hiking.

I decide to come back tomorrow, maybe even the day after. I'm going to walk every day until I can sit on the summit of Alander mountain and enjoy the view.

Susan Fox Rogers has edited several outdoor anthologies including
Solo: On Her Own Adventure *and* Another Wilderness: Notes from the New Outdoorswoman. *She hikes with her oversized German Shepard, Babka.*

*

In the wilderness, I feel not as though I am escaping the "real world" but that I am entering it. There is an essential part of myself that gets lost in my indoor life—a part as necessary and tangible as an arm or an eye—and I go to the wilderness to get it back. In some moments, it is a place of sanctuary; in other moments, it is the most violent place I know....

When one human enters the forest and kills another, it is not evidence that something is wrong with the forest. It is evidence of how one person has lost the sense of himself or herself as a member of the human species, as a creature, as an animal who is here to breathe and eat, to sleep and bear children, to raise them and to die naturally, to walk on the earth and wonder at it; to share it with other living things.

The brutal killing of Julianne Williams and Lollie Winans is, as the director of the National Park Service said, an occasion not for panic but for sorrow. It is an occasion to wonder when we started calling the techno-virtual-mega-machine we have created in our cities the "real world." It is an occasion not to stay away from wild places but to rethink our relationship to them, to begin to learn again the lessons they have to teach.

—Pam Houston, "The Bear in the Woods, the Bear in Us,"
The New York Times

JOY NICHOLSON

✦ ✦ ✦

Beyond the Ruins

In Mexico, a tourist learns
the hard truth.

WE HAD BEEN WALKING STEADILY UPHILL FOR AN HOUR. THE interior of the jungle was dim, but every so often the thick tree-tops would part, revealing a startling glimpse of noonday sun. Silvery, spotted birds peered through moving vines, spider monkeys shrieked, laughing, from high in the trees. Wet, muddy fruits hung low in the heat, buzzing with wasps. Some of the fruits had fallen to the forest floor where they lay half hidden and slippery on the mossy path. As we continued to climb, sweat poured from my face. I felt insects crawling on my arms and legs, but when I looked, nothing was there. The guide was far ahead.

"Hey," I called, trying to sound nonchalant, secretly furious.

The guide turned quickly, watching me chop at the air, waving away a cloud of mosquitoes. As he surveyed my ungraceful movements, he shrugged, walking even faster. Frustration bubbled up, hot, uncontrollable. I glared at the back of his shirt.

The picture had been very clear in my mind. For months I had been planning my trip to see the ancient ruins of Palenque. I'd spend a whole day alone, walking leisurely among the romantic rubble of the mysterious Mayan city. But upon my arrival I had

245

been jostled, elbowed, and poked by roaming bunches of fellow tourists. The heat had been so intense, the tourists so numerous, that I had sat down, depressed, in the shade of a pyramid. Though I knew I was being ridiculous, I couldn't stop myself from trying to will the others away. The longer I rested, the more shimmery and lightheaded I'd begun to feel. When the guide approached, I shook my head.

"No, no," I said, before he had a chance to speak.

He was tall for a Maya, about five-foot-seven, in his mid-thirties, very dark skinned, wearing a traditional white shirt. His teeth were very small when he smiled, rounded like a baby's. His head was oblong, large, and covered by a closely woven hat. He was dressed exactly as the other guides in the vicinity. He ignored my rebuff.

"Americana?" he asked, grinning, exposing his babyish teeth. His smile touched me, and I found myself talking to him, confiding how disappointed I was in the crowds. His English was quite good, he was patient with my terrible Spanish. As we talked, I began to feel bad for him. He didn't have any customers because the large tour groups always arranged for their own, prepaid guides.

"Come on a tour," he pleaded. "It won't cost much."

Briefly I considered his offer, but looking out at the hordes of people clomping from one structure to the next, I decided against it. I explained guiltily that I might come back when there were fewer people—but it was out of the question now.

His expression was peculiar, a mixture of regret and sympathy. He looked out at the crowd, squinting.

"You like to go on a jungle tour? See the real forest? Not only the ruins?"

His sales approach couldn't have been better: it was *exactly* my intention to get off the safe, well-worn path, to see things others don't see.

He named a good price, and we set off.

The trail began at the base of a low, lush mountain. From the beginning, the walk was much more challenging than I'd expected. We headed east, up a side trail that led into the thick jungle. As I groped along the rock formations and jumped across swampy pools, I began to feel uneasy. As soon as we left the other tourists behind, the man didn't seem to act like a guide at all. He neither offered me a hand in difficult spots, nor turned to see if I were keeping up. Instead, he steadily increased his pace, eyes straight ahead.

I forged on, determined. His inattention was even flattering—I was now a true explorer, pushing past the safe boundaries of regular, easy travel. The guide believed I was different from the soft, frightened tourists we'd left behind. I walked through hundreds of filmy spider webs, my arms scraped against low branches inhabited by stinging ants. My confidence ebbed. Anger made me walk faster. At one point I cried out, twisting my ankle. He looked back at me briefly. I dogged him, cursing under my breath. When I finally demanded that we slow down, he immediately complied. But it was easy to see it irritated him.

> ——— ☽ ———
>
> *T*he tight trail wound up and down between precariously balanced giant piles of sandstone boulders. The rocks were decorated with low flowering scrub and yucca and prickly pear that found roothold in the gaps. Earth Woman architecture—a natural cathedral with its roof open to the sky.
>
> Suddenly, at mile three, the East/West Stronghold Divide, rain and hail lashed down onto the rocks and me. Thunder boomed above the rush of wind. I was dressed in hiking shorts, t-shirt, windbreaker, and hat. Turn back? Not this time.
>
> ◆
>
> —Marcia Fairbanks, "The Stronghold"

The farther we got into the forest, the more his mood seemed to darken. He began speaking, telling me he was a biologist, forced to take a job as a guide in order to make a living. He didn't like being a guide—people always wanted to see the same things, old buildings, Maya ruins.

"They always want to hear about the sacrifices—always how many heads, how much blood." He shook his head, disgusted. The path had narrowed considerably. Mounds of hewn rocks were covered by thick vines. When I asked about them, he explained wearily that they were unreconstructed ruins.

"Ruinas, ruinas, ruinas," he said angrily.

After we reached a fork in the path, his mood seemed to switch back. He slowed his pace. Sometimes his face would light up—he'd point out flashes between the leaves—puff-throated lizards, jewel-colored birds, an indolent iguana with expressionless amber eyes. We rested for awhile on a flat stone that had once been part of a river—now diverted—he said crisply. Thinking about the river made him quiet and dark again. As we trudged farther along, he asked a few questions. When I told him I lived in Los Angeles, he nodded, his eyes hard and shiny, like polished stones. I took his expression to be one of envy. Here I was, younger than he, traveling freely in his country. He'd never make enough money to do the same in mine.

We walked without talking for a long time. A rushing water sound filled the air, a distant waterfall. He lifted his head and smiled.

"You like it?"

"I like it," I said, swatting. My shoes had soaked through with gooey, gray mud. Something had bitten my ankle, my clothes stank of sweat and swamp. I was anxious to get to the secret, watery place I imagined we were going.

"How much farther?" I ventured.

He looked at me, his face grim. "Why do Americans come here?" he said. " You don't see anything. Just like ants, coming and coming and coming in your buses with your *aire acondicionado.*" He wheeled, walking fast again. I struggled behind, truly shocked by his words.

"What do you come to see? Here is the forest, but you only look at the mosquitoes." He didn't want an answer. Instead he continued to walk, his face an impassive mask. Creepers and vines hung low; he pushed them back roughly.

"Maybe we go back to your bus now."

We moved along in a dreamlike march—the trail forked again. Sunlight poked in at crazy angles, mist rose and dispersed into the covering branches. I avoided his eyes, looked out into the moving leaves. My legs ached, my breath was ragged, shallow.

I began to hate him. Fucker, fucker, I murmured.

He stopped, the peculiar sympathetic/sad expression returning to his face. "We go back?" he asked.

I looked at him defiantly. "No."

The walk had become a test. It had wholly ceased to be enjoyable—rather it was something to be gotten through. As I mechanically lifted my legs, I remembered all the times I'd competed with my brother to get to the top of the cliffs by our house. Whoever was breathing harder at the top, lost. My brother would put his hand against my mouth, measuring, gleeful, always winning. As the procession of memories came, weakness and rage flooded through me.

"Let's go then," I said curtly to the guide. I knew I was being absurd, but the realization only made me more angry. His face was kinder now. Suddenly he took an orange out of his pack, tossed it to me. I sucked on the sweet flesh, nearly in tears. Several times I thought he would say something, but he did not.

Looking back, I know the guide was lost in his own memories. But at the time, I assumed he was trying to shame me, win, break me down. When he walked beside me, I pointedly ignored him, concentrating on keeping my breathing quiet, light. The trail had leveled off. After another half hour he turned in at a smaller trail, waved for me to follow. Inwardly I groaned, but I kept a small, tight smile fixed on my face.

We stopped at the edge of a promontory. As I looked out, he stared with some satisfaction at my horrified expression. Bald, harsh mountain peaks jutted out in every direction, trees had been sliced, chopped, and hacked into merciless bundles. Beyond lay a wasteland of similarly plundered mountaintops. Mounds of trash littered the hillside, thrown by careless workers,—Coca-Cola, Clorox, Dial soap, Nescafe. Here and there a lone stump protruded against the sky, contrasting with still-uncut lush patches.

Now he was eager to talk—his words came out in a passionate, garbled mix of Spanish and English. As he spoke, he bent near, seeming to regard me as an ally. When he was a boy, the forest had been healthy. But a slew of foreign lumber companies had come to Chiapas a few years ago, offering sums of cash to the peasants in exchange for the rights to cut the trees. The uneducated peasants didn't understand it would take 20,000 years for the forest to grow back. Now the forest animals were dying, the birds disappearing. He told me bitterly that there would soon be only a single ring of trees around the ruins, for the benefit of the tourists. He suddenly turned on me again.

"They think only of the tourists," he spat out. "Very nice for you to have our trees."

I told him that I didn't have his trees; I was a single person, not a country. He made a small hissing sound.

"Yes, yes! Your USA!" He pronounced it Oooo Essay Ahhh.

We listened to the wind rustling the trees overhead. A confused mass of limbs slapped against one another, dropping dew onto our heads. Neither of us spoke. After a while, we got up and started walking back.

"I don't know why you come here," he said a few times. I realized his words were not meant for only me, but for all foreigners; moneymen, corporations. I felt suddenly sick, as if someone had punched me in the stomach.

At the tourist kiosk he kept walking. I did not see him after that.

Joy Nicholson is the author of the novel The Tribes of Palos Verdes.

★

We point out our wildest lands—the Amazon rain forests, the Arctic tundra—to inspire humans with the mighty grace of what we haven't yet wrecked. Those places have a power that speaks for itself, that seems to throw its own grandeur as a curse on the defiler. Fell the giant trees, flood the majestic canyons, and you will have hell and posterity to pay.

—Barbara Kingsolver, *High Tide in Tucson: Essays from Now or Never*

EVELYN C. WHITE

Nature, Fear, and Race

An African-American tries to make
peace with the wilderness.

FOR ME, THE FEAR IS LIKE A HEARTBEAT, ALWAYS PRESENT, WHILE
at the same time, intangible, elusive, and difficult to define. So per-
vasive, so much a part of me, that I hardly knew it was there.

In fact, I wasn't fully aware of my troubled feelings about nature until I was invited to teach at a women's writing workshop
held each summer on the McKenzie River in the foothills of
Oregon's Cascade Mountains. I was invited to Flight of the Mind
by a Seattle writer and her friend, a poet who had moved from her
native England to Oregon many years before. Both committed
feminists, they asked me to teach because they believe, as I do, that
language and literature transcend the manmade boundaries that
are too often placed upon them. I welcomed and appreciated their
interest in me and my work.

Once I got there, I did not welcome the steady stream of in-
vitations to explore the great outdoors. It seemed like the minute
I finished my teaching duties, I'd be faced with a student or fellow faculty member clamoring for me to trek to the lava beds,
soak in the hot springs, or hike into the mountains that loomed
over the site like white-capped security guards. I claimed fatigue,
a backlog of classwork, concern about "proper" student/teacher

relations; whatever the excuse, I always declined to join the expeditions into the woods. When I wasn't teaching, eating in the dining hall, or attending our evening readings, I stayed holed up in my riverfront cabin with all the doors locked and window-shades drawn. While the river's roar gave me a certain comfort and my heart warmed when I gazed at the sun-dappled trees out of a classroom window, I didn't want to get closer. I was certain that if I ventured outside to admire a meadow or to feel the cool ripples in a stream, I'd be taunted, attacked, raped, maybe even murdered because of the color of my skin.

I believe the fear I experience in the outdoors is shared by many African-American women and that it limits the way we move through the world and colors the decisions we make about our lives. For instance, for several years now, I've been thinking about moving out of the city to a wooded, vineyard-laden area in Northern California. It is there, among the birds, creeks, and trees that I long to settle down and make a home.

Each house-hunting trip I've made to the countryside has been fraught with two emotions: elation at the prospect of living closer to nature and a sense of absolute doom about what might befall me in the backwoods. My genetic memory of ancestors hunted down and preyed upon in rural settings counters my fervent hopes of finding peace in the wilderness. Instead of the solace and comfort I seek, I imagine myself in the country as my forebears were—exposed, vulnerable, and unprotected—a target of cruelty and hate.

> *T*he river bed is a story—
> and I'm immediately aware that I don't know how to read it. There are tracks and trails and tales; spoor, in bush lingo, large and small. I round a curve and have the first chest-tightening experience of feeling alone in Africa. I can hardly breathe. There is a short, silent debate about irresponsibility, stupidity, and courage. Africa wins and I walk on.
>
> ◆
>
> —Wendy Blakeley,
> "Elephant Wells"

I'm certain that the terror I felt in my Oregon cabin is directly linked to my memories of September 15, 1963. On that day, Denise McNair, Addie Mae Collins, Cynthia Wesley, and Carol Robertson were sitting in their Sunday school class at the Sixteenth Street Church in Birmingham, Alabama. Before the bright-eyed black girls could deliver the speeches they'd prepared for the church's annual Youth Day program, a bomb planted by racists flattened the building, killing them all. In black households throughout the nation, families grieved for the martyred children and expressed their outrage at whites who seemed to have no limits on the depths they would sink in their ultimately futile effort to curtail the Civil Rights movement.

To protest the Birmingham bombing and to show solidarity with the struggles in the South, my mother bought a spool of black cotton ribbon which she fashioned into armbands for me and my siblings to wear to school the next day. Nine years old at the time, I remember standing in my house in Gary, Indiana, and watching in horror as my mother ironed the black fabric that, in my mind, would align me with the bloody dresses, limbless bodies, and dust-covered patent leather shoes that had been entombed in the blast.

The next morning, I put on my favorite school dress—a V-necked cranberry jumper with a matching cranberry-and-white pin-striped shirt. Motionless, I stared stoically straight ahead, as my mother leaned down and pinned the black ribbon around my right sleeve shortly before I left the house.

As soon as I rounded the corner at the end of our street, I ripped the ribbon off my arm, looking nervously up into the sky for the "evil white people" I'd heard my parents talk about in the aftermath of the bombing. I feared that if I wore the armband, I'd be blown to bits like the black girls who were that moment rotting under the rubble. Thirty years later, I know that another part of my "defense strategy" that day was to wear the outfit that had always garnered me compliments from teachers and friends. "Don't drop a bomb on me," was the message I was desperately trying to convey through my cranberry jumper. "I'm a pretty black girl. Not like the ones at the church."

The sense of vulnerability and exposure that I felt in the wake of the Birmingham bombing was compounded by feelings that I already had about Emmett Till. Emmett was a rambunctious, fourteen-year-old black boy from Chicago, who in 1955 was sent to rural Mississippi to enjoy the pleasures of summer with relatives. Emmett was delivered home in a pine box long before season's end, bloated and battered beyond recognition. He had been lynched and dumped in the Tallahatchie River with the rope still dangling around his neck for allegedly whistling at a white woman at a country store.

Those summers in Oregon when I walked past the country store where thick-necked loggers drank beer while leaning on their big rig trucks, it seemed like Emmett's fate had been a part of my identity from birth. Averting my eyes from those of the loggers, I'd remember the ghoulish photos of Emmett I'd seen in *JET* magazine with my childhood friends Tyrone and Lynette Henry. The Henrys subscribed to *JET*, an inexpensive magazine for blacks, and kept each issue neatly filed on the top shelf of a bookcase in their living room. Among black parents, the *JET* with Emmett's story was always carefully handled and treated like one of the most valuable treasures on earth. For within its pages rested an important lesson they felt duty-bound to teach their children: how little white society valued our lives.

Mesmerized by Emmett's monstrous face, Lynette, Tyrone, and I would drag a flower-patterned vinyl chair from the kitchen, take the Emmett *JET* from the bookcase, and spirit it to a back bedroom where we played. Heads together, bellies on the floor as if we were shooting marbles or scribbling in our coloring books, we'd silently gaze at Emmett's photo for what seemed like hours before returning it to its sacred place. As with thousands of black children from that era, Emmett's murder cast a nightmarish pall over my youth. In his pummeled and contorted face, I saw a reflection of myself and the blood-chilling violence that would greet me if I ever dared to venture into the wilderness.

I grew up. I went to college. I traveled abroad. Still, thoughts of Emmett Till could leave me speechless and paralyzed with the heart-stopping fear that swept over me as when I crossed paths with loggers near the McKenzie River or whenever I visited the outdoors. His death seemed to be summed up in the prophetic warning of writer Alice Walker, herself a native of rural Georgia: "Never be the only one, except, possibly, in your own house."

For several Oregon summers, I concealed my pained feelings about the outdoors until I could no longer reconcile my silence with my mandate to my students to face their fears. They found the courage to write openly about incest, poverty, and other ills that had constricted their lives: How could I turn away from my fears about being in nature?

But the one time I'd attempted to be as bold as my students, I'd been faced with an unsettling incident. Legend had it that the source of the McKenzie was a tiny trickle of water that bubbled up from a pocket in a nearby lake. Intrigued by the local lore, two other Flight teachers and a staff person, all white women, invited me to join them on an excursion to the lake. The plan was to rent rowboats and paddle around the lake Sacajawea-style, until we, brave and undaunted women, "discovered the source" of the mighty river. As we approached the lake, we could see dozens of rowboats tied to the dock. We had barely begun our inquiry about renting one when the boathouse man interrupted and tersely announced: "No boats."

We stood shocked and surprised on a sun-drenched dock with a vista of rowboats before us. No matter how much we insisted that our eyes belied his words, the man held fast to his two-note response: "No boats."

Distressed but determined to complete our mission, we set out on foot. As we trampled along the trail that circled the lake we tried to make sense of our "Twilight Zone" encounter. We laughed and joked about the incident and it ultimately drifted out of our thoughts in our jubilation at finding the gurgling bubble that gave birth to the McKenzie. Yet I'd always felt that our triumph was undermined by a searing question that went unvoiced that day: Had we been denied the boat because our group included a black?

In an effort to contain my fears, I forced myself to revisit the encounter and to reexamine my childhood wounds from the Birmingham bombing and the lynching of Emmett Till. I touched the terror of my Ibo and Ashanti ancestors as they were dragged from Africa and enslaved on southern plantations. I conjured bloodhounds, burning crosses, and white-robed Klansmen hunting down people who looked just like me. I imagined myself being captured in a swampy backwater, my back ripped open and bloodied by the whip's lash. I cradled an ancestral mother, broken and keening as her baby was snatched from her arms and sold down the river.

Every year, the Flight of the Mind workshop offers a rafting trip on the McKenzie River. Each day we'd watch as flotillas of rafters, shrieking excitedly and with their oars held aloft, rumbled by the deck where students and teachers routinely gathered. While I always cheered their adventuresome spirit, I never joined the group of Flight women who took the trip. I was always mindful that I had never seen one black person in any of those boats.

Determined to reconnect myself to the comfort my African ancestors felt in the rift valleys of Kenya and on the shores of Sierra Leone, I eventually decided to go on a rafting trip. Familiar with my feeling about nature, Judith, a dear friend and workshop founder, offered to be one of my raftmates.

With her sturdy, gentle and wise body as my anchor, I lowered myself into a raft at the bank of the river. As we pushed off into the cur-

> *M*oss covered
>   Smooth
> Stable, unmovable
> A little shaky
> Stepping stones
> Some are behind you
> Many lie before you
> The bridge ended
> The stepping stones begin
>   right here
> No other way to cross this
>   water.
>
> ◆
>
> —Cheryl L. McCullers,
> "Beginning at the End"

rent, I felt myself make an unsure but authentic shift from my painful past.

At first the water was calm—nearly hypnotic in its pristine tranquillity. Then we met the rapids, sometimes swirling, other times jolting us forward like a runaway roller coaster. The guide roared out commands, "Highside! All forward! All back!" To my amazement, I responded. Periodically, my brown eyes would meet Judith's steady aquamarine gaze and we'd smile at each other as the cool water splashed in our faces and shimmered like diamonds in our hair.

Charging over the river, orange life vest firmly secured, my breathing relaxed and I allowed myself to drink in the stately rocks, soaring birds, towering trees, and affirming anglers who waved their rods as we rushed by in our raft. About an hour into the trip, in a magnificently still moment, I looked up into the heavens and heard the voice of black poet Langston Hughes:

> "I've known rivers ancient as the world and older than the flow of human blood in human veins. I bathed in the Euphrates when dawns were young. I built my hut near the Congo and it lulled me to sleep. I looked upon the Nile and raised the pyramids above it. My soul has grown deep like the rivers."

Soaking wet and shivering with emotion, I felt tears welling in my eyes as I stepped out of the raft onto solid ground. Like my African forebears who survived the Middle Passage, I was stronger at journey's end.

Since that voyage, I've stayed at country farms, napped on secluded beaches, and taken wilderness treks all in an effort to find peace in the outdoors. No matter where I travel, I will always carry Emmett Till and the four black girls whose deaths affected me so. But comforted by our tribal ancestors—herders, gatherers, and fishers all—I am less fearful, ready to come home.

Evelyn C. White grew up as the eldest of five children in Gary, Indiana. She has been a reporter for the San Francisco Chronicle *and is the author of* Chain Chain Change: For Black Women Dealing with Physical and Emotional Abuse, *and the editor of* The Black Women's Health Book: Speaking for Ourselves.

★

"Come on in this house.
It's gonna rain!
Come on in this house.
It's gonna rain.
Door swing wide open
Just call his name
Come in the house
It's gonna rain...."

These words keep ringing in my ears as I travel to the Sea Islands, the home of my ancestors who were enslaved in America. The opportunity to feel their energy again and converse with their spirits draws me in, and I can hear them in the distance sending the "grapevine" message by the drum: "Come Home."

As I journey by Interstate Highway 95, I watch the American terrain change. The skyline shifts from skyscrapers to small houses and office buildings to trees. The more grass and trees, the less smog, the lighter my spirit becomes. Only to sink my fingers into rich soil...only to dance in the salt water....

The journey takes hours to cross the numerous state lines on the east coast, but finally we pass through the Carolinas from North into South. It's only a short time before we head across a large bridge over a major waterway. I roll down the window to take in the smell of the salt air and to feel the warmth of the spirit cleansing Sea Island breeze. I hear the ancestral call of the drum whisper "Welcome home." I don't vocalize my praise, but they hear, feel it, and respond by blowing a bit of warmth into the car which encircles and embraces me.

> —Marquetta L. Goodwine, "A House Built on Spiritual Soul:
> A Gullah Gal's Journey Home"

* * *

Survival at Sea

The will to live is strong indeed.

"COME ON! WE'RE GOING!"

Someone was screaming, jolting me out of a deep sleep. Was it time to go on watch again? I felt as if I'd just closed my eyes.

"We're going! Now!" It was Brad. He had me by the arm and was dragging me out of my bunk. When my feet hit the floor, I was almost up to my knees in water.

"Go!" Brad shouted and pushed me toward the galley.

What was going on? Why was he pushing me? Then I understood: the Coast Guard must have come, or one of the merchant ships. Staggering toward the main cabin, I heard a strange rushing noise, as if the ship were right on top of us. And then I saw water cascading into the cabin through the port-side windows. My God, had they hit us? Had they smashed the windows? I saw Mark splashing through the rising water, coughing, his eyes huge. Then Meg was in the doorway, rigid with shock. She opened her mouth to scream, but no sound came out.

"Come on, Meg!" Brad yelled. John came up behind her, glanced at the flooding cabin, and shoved Meg forward toward the companionway. Then he lunged for the radio as Brad pushed me toward the stairs.

"Mayday…mayday…we're sinking, we're sunk—" John was hollering. Why bother with the radio when the ship is already here? I wondered. We didn't have time to screw around; the water was nearly shoulder deep.

I crawled up the campionway behind Brad, fighting to keep my balance as the boat hurtled down the face of a wave. We both made it to the deck. But where was the ship? Where were the people who had come to rescue us? There was nothing, only the monster seas and the freight-train wind and the ugly sky. The Coast Guard wasn't here for us. No one was here—not off our port side, not off our starboard.

To stand there with the deck dropping out from under my feet and the water pouring down and seeing nothing! The blood rushed from my head, and my legs buckled. I was dizzy with the sickening truth. *Trashman* was sinking and we were alone. And then it all became a terrifying slow-motion dream.

I saw Mark dive for the compartment at the stern where the life raft filled with emergency supplies was stowed in a fiberglass canister the size of a giant suitcase. I saw Brad on top of the cabin, waves breaking over him, struggling to untie the rubber Zodiac, which was still lashed to the deck. I saw the muscles in his arms as he dug into the iron-hard knots—knots that were being pulled tighter by the force of the sinking boat. I heard the Zodiac burst free, and I saw Brad swimming after it. He pounced on it as it stalled in the leeward shoulder of a wave.

A dark tower of water hanging above the deck came crashing down on Meg and me, dragging us into the rigging of the mainmast. I was under water and then I was up, and I could hear Meg screaming before we were both sucked back toward the stern by another surge.

In the lull between waves I managed to swim away. Treading water and riding the enormous swells, I could see Mark with his arms wrapped around the life raft canister and Meg being lifted forward by another wave. She screamed again as she slammed into the rigging. When she washed back across the deck I saw blood on her arms. The sweatpants she had been wearing were floating free.

"Meg!" I shouted. "Swim away from the boat."

"I can't!"

"Swim away. Wait for a wave to come, then swim away."

I watched her get dragged back into the shrouds. I knew she didn't understand. She didn't know enough about waves to time them so she could get away. I swam back to the boat to try to help her. When I got close, she lunged at me.

I screamed and tried to pry her hands off my shoulders. "Damn it, Meg, you're going to drown us both!" Somehow I pulled her away from the rigging and we were both in the water, free of the boat. I saw Brad holding onto the Zodiac, and I began swimming madly for it.

I grabbed onto the side of the pitching, overturned rubber dinghy, and then Meg was there, then John appeared next to Brad. The four of us clung to the line threaded around the gunwale, stunned by the sight of the sinking boat and Mark, still at the stern, fighting with the life raft canister. It looked as if it was going to pull him under.

Then, in one instant, the canister exploded and the life raft filled with air. The wind caught the raft, and Mark held on, dragged behind it like a fallen water-skier who could not let go of the towline. I held my breath and watched him fight for the raft. If he gets into that boat we'll never see him again, I thought. He won't come back for us. A tremendous gust ripped the raft from Mark's grasp. It blew through the rigging, skimmed the top of a wave, and vanished. Mark swam hard for the Zodiac.

"I couldn't hold it!" he sputtered when he pulled himself up next to Brad. "I couldn't hold it."...

We dropped into a trough, then rose to the summit of another wave. Now we could see just the tips of *Trashman's* two masts as they went under. Finally, all that was left of her was the top of the mainmast. I watched in horror as that last bit vanished. The sinking had taken no more than two minutes. And now there was only the raging sea.

"We're all going to fuckin' die!" Mark screamed.

"Shut up, Mark," I shouted back. "Shut up."

I hung on. That was all I could do. Hang on while the dinghy rode the insane contours of the sea. Every wave threatened to yank me away from it. My palms burned. My God, my hands are on fire! I can't hold it. I can't hold it! We slid down into a trough, into a momentary calm.

Am I really here? I thought. I felt so small, so helpless, so exposed—and it had all happened in a heartbeat. Brad had dragged me from my bunk, and then what? Had the life raft really blown away? Had I really just watched *Trashman* be swallowed up by the sea?

I could still hear Mark screaming, but his voice seemed muffled and far off—as if his head was underwater and the words were bubbling up from below. Beneath the steady high roar of the wind I was conscious of the rapid-fire slamming of my heart against my chest. I pressed my forehead against the Zodiac as it climbed another moving hill. I could smell rubber and taste salt on my lips. I became keenly aware of the warmth of the water. Is the water supposed to feel this warm? Or is this what dying feels like?

I looked up again, and though I could still see Mark and John and Meg, they seemed featureless and vague, as though I was viewing them through fogged glass. An enormous wave dragged us up into the sky, and water hit me in the face, filling my mouth and nose. The salt stung my throat. I couldn't breathe. This is it, I thought. This is the end. I felt I was being drawn up into the furious, beating wings of some giant prehistoric bird, and I was powerless, limp, invisible. I was dead. No, I was still alive—but alive in the middle of the ocean with nothing to hold onto but an eleven-foot-long inflatable rubber boat—my God, my God, a boat of air!

Another wave broke over the dinghy, and I fought to keep my grip. I could see the others struggling in the turbulence. When we dropped into the quiet canyon between waves, I screamed again for Brad.

"Talk to me, Brad!" I hollered.

"What!"

I worked my way, hand over hand, to the other side of the dinghy to be next to him.

"What happened?" I asked.

"We fell," he said. He wouldn't look at me. "We fell off a wave. I saw it happen. We fell off and we landed on our side and the water came crashing through the windows."

I felt the gathering power of another wave, and the Zodiac started climbing again. Then there was an explosion of water, and the dinghy was torn out of my hands. I slammed backward into the water. When I was at last able to surface I could see the Zodiac stalled against the wall of the next huge swell. I stroked as hard as I could, but as I got close, the dinghy was picked up again and flung another twenty feet away. I didn't see any of the others. I screamed for Brad and got a mouthful of seawater. Fighting panic, coughing, praying, I swam again. The muscles in my arms and thighs started to cramp. I lunged for the dinghy and caught the line with the tips of my fingers. As another wave tried to peel me off, I closed my hand around the line and the Zodiac carried me with it on its wild ride. I screamed again for Brad, then for Meg and John and Mark.

I heard Meg calling my name. She was swimming for the dinghy. Then John, Mark, and Brad came up and grabbed onto the side. We had all made it.

"Let's turn it over," Mark said, straining to be heard. "We've got to get in."

Brad and I lifted the windward side while the other three held the line and let the wind carry the Zodiac over. It slapped down onto the water with a ringing thud. We helped Meg climb in. Her legs looked as if they had been slashed by a razor-clawed tiger. Startled, Brad looked at me—I mouthed, "The rigging." The rest of us scrambled aboard. The air was much colder than the water, and I started to shake violently.

We rose up and then, just as we crested, the Zodiac flipped and again I was tumbling, being held underwater, fighting for air. When I surfaced my head hit the floor of the dinghy and I went down and came up, hitting the floor again. I was trapped! I clawed at the rubber, my lungs tightening. Then I felt the surging sea building under me and I was carried up and thrown forward. When I surfaced, my head was free.

Meg shouted my name, and I turned and saw the dinghy. I swam over and grabbed the line, then closed my eyes and prayed as I had never prayed before. We were on the wind-lashed summits and then we were in the still canyons. I would be torn from the dinghy and then swimming again, swimming for my life, swimming and praying, until I found the hard rubber and reached up and closed my hand around the lifeline.

Minutes went by, maybe forty-five. I was trembling uncontrollably. I wanted to stop—I wanted everything to stop. I could feel the heat being drawn from my body and the strength being drained from my legs.

"I'm so fucking cold," Mark said through chattering teeth when the dinghy settled into a trough.

"Me, too," Meg whispered.

"We have to get warm somehow. We can't stay like this," I said.

"We're better off in the water," Brad said.

"Yeah, the air's cold as shit," Mark said. "We have to stay in the water."

"The dinghy won't stay upright anyway," Brad said as we were carried back up into the tumult. When the Zodiac dropped back down, John said, "I want to turn the dinghy over. I want to get in."

"I'm not getting in the dinghy," Mark said.

"It's too cold, John," Brad said. "And we can't keep it upright."

"I want to get in," John insisted.

When I was fifteen, my mother had sent me to a girls' boarding school in Colorado that taught Outward Bound survival skills. Why hadn't I paid more attention? What the hell had they said about hypothermia? I knew one thing; the wind was our biggest enemy right now—whatever body heat we had would be stolen by the wind. We had to shelter ourselves somehow.

"Maybe we could go under the dinghy," I said, thinking out loud.

"You mean hang on under there?" Brad said.

"I don't know. Maybe," I said.

"We'd be out of the wind," Brad said.

"Under?" Meg asked.

"We have to try something," I said as we rose to the top of a wave and the wind blasted us once more. When we were able to talk, Brad said he thought we should try getting under the boat. Everyone agreed to try it. Brad went under, then resurfaced and said, "I think it will work. Come on."

We all ducked and came up under the Zodiac. I grabbed the line and treaded water to keep myself up. The odd reddish light made our strained faces look like ghoulish masks. I could just make out the features of the rubber boat: the aluminum floorboards, a black rubber spray cover stretched across the bow, a wire meant to secure the motor when it was being used. I could hear the waters slapping against the boat; it was strange—the waves sounded no bigger than those left in the wake of a speedboat. It was deceptively peaceful under there, like being in the clear eye of a hurricane....

Each time we lifted the dinghy, we saw a little less light in the sky. Finally it was totally dark. When night overtook us, the fear and loneliness escalated. We knew it would be almost impossible for the rescue ships to find us in the dark.

Instead of concentrating on making it through the next few minutes, I had to think about living to see the sun come up again. Only with dawn could we hope that a ship would spot us. Maybe they'd send a plane again, maybe the same plane that had checked on us, when, this morning? or yesterday?—I didn't know anymore. All that mattered was that I was in this cold, dark hell with no chance of getting out until dawn. If we could hold it together, if we could keep from going crazy, if Mark could just be quiet, if Meg would just come back under here and do what we told her to do...

Poor Meg. Brad, John, Mark, and I had seen the wrath of the ocean before; we knew what it was capable of and we had chosen to come out in it. But Meg didn't have a clue. To her, sailing had been dockside parties, a way to get a tan, have some laughs. She never should have come out here, and John damn well knew it. I could hear the guilt in his voice when he talked to her. He had to deal with that guilt and with the fact that this was ultimately his failure. He would never get another boat to sail; nobody would turn over the helm of their vessel to a skipper who had sunk.

Meg was shouting something—something about a ship. We all ducked out from under the Zodiac. When I surfaced in the darkness, she was saying. "Over there, over there. There's a light!"

When the dinghy rose to the top of a wave, we could see a white light rising and falling with the sea.

"Do you think it's the Coast Guard?" Brad said.

"It looks like a spotlight," I said, straining to keep sight of it as we sank down into a trough.

"Where is it?" Meg asked.

"There," John said. "I see it over there."

"Yes!" I shouted.

Was it the Coast Guard? Or the *Exxon Huntington* or the *Gypsum King*? A fishing boat riding out the storm? It didn't matter—it was a boat.

"They're looking for us!" Brad said.

"Well, they're not going to see us," Mark snarled.

"They'll see us," Meg said weakly.

Again we slid down into a black canyon.

"Damn it," John said.

"Wait," Brad said.

When we rose, the light was there again. The others cheered, but my momentary euphoria was already going cold. The reality of our situation came back into focus. If it was a Coast Guard ship, it was probably using a grid system to search for us. In the darkness they would pass right by us—they might even run us over. And once they had gone by, they would probably eliminate this area from their search territory.

We watched in silence as the light appeared, then disappeared, with each roll of the sea. It grew fainter and fainter, and finally it

---

> ———— ☽ ————
>
> *T*he phrase "angry sea" seemed to sum up the raging water. Angry is a word usually attached to people. But when we describe the sea, we always ascribe it qualities— angry, calm, cruel—as if it had human moods.
>
> ◆
>
> —Dea Birkett,
> *Jella: A Woman at Sea*

was gone. With it went our brief joy. The night seemed blacker, the air colder, the sea fiercer....

"Where does it hurt, John?" I asked.

"I want to turn the boat over and get in," he said slowly. "I can't tread water anymore. It hurts too much."

"But, John—"

"Look, the man wants to get in the dinghy," Mark said.

Meg was in tears. "We've got to do something. He can't die."

"He's not going to die, Meg," Mark said. "You'll be fine, John. We'll turn the boat over and you'll get in and you'll feel a lot better."

"What do you think, Brad? Do you think we can keep it upright?" I said.

Brad shrugged.

"Yeah, come on. John wants to do it," Mark said.

"It's still so rough," I said. "I don't know if we can."

"We're going to do it," Mark said.

Brad and I said we'd try it. We all helped flip the Zodiac, and Brad climbed in first. Then Mark, Meg, and I lifted John up, while Brad pulled. Eventually we got him onto the floor. Then Mark and I boosted Meg on board, while Brad balanced the boat. We all grimaced when we saw her legs. Her gaping wounds were puffy and inflamed.

Mark boosted himself into the dinghy, leaving me alone in the water. I was reluctant to climb in—the air was so much colder than the ocean. And I felt as if I had somehow become a part of the sea. It felt safe, almost amniotic. I let my legs go limp and allowed my thoughts to drift. Maybe the sun would break through the low clouds this morning...maybe we would feel its warmth on our puckered skin...maybe the sea would quiet and the Coast Guard would see us...maybe by tonight I'd be in a warm bed...after a hot shower...

"It's cold as shit out here," Mark said. "Let's turn it back over."

His words were drowned out by the roar of a tremendous wave overtaking the dinghy. I shouted, and Brad jumped to the windward side as it broke over us. I gripped the line and was still hanging on when the dinghy was released from the force of the wave. It had filled with water but, amazingly, it was still upright. Brad had used his strength and bulk to keep the boat from flipping over.

"Come on, let's turn it back over," Mark said. "It was better that way. We'll freeze to death out here."

"Look, man, if you like it better in the water, then help yourself," John said. "There's a whole ocean out there."

Mark jumped into the water and held on to the dinghy directly across from me. I was getting ready to climb aboard, preparing myself for the shock of cold that I knew was coming.

"Don't kick me," Mark said.

"I'm not touching you," I said.

"You did it again," Mark said. "Cut it out."

"What are you talking about? I'm not kicking you."

"Cut it out."

I popped my head underwater to see where his feet were. I didn't think I had been kicking him, but the last thing I wanted to do was make him more agitated. I was afraid of what he might do.

I opened my eyes and felt the sting of salt water. I waited for my vision to clear. When it did, my stomach contracted. A cold sword of fear stabbed through me. I didn't believe what I was seeing. I didn't want to believe it. Now I knew what had been bumping Mark's legs. Sharks. There were sharks everywhere. Dozens, no, hundreds of them—as far as I could see. Some were so close I could see the membrane hooding their lifeless, clouded eyes. Others were just slow-moving angular shadows spiraling into the depths.

I yelled, "Sharks!" and launched myself into the dinghy, landing on top of John. A half-second later, Mark landed on top of me.

"Jesus fucking Christ!" he was screaming. "There are sharks everywhere!"

Fins broke the water all around us. For every shark that dove, two more seemed to surface. I couldn't believe I had just been in that water, spent maybe eighteen hours in that water with my legs hanging down and with Meg's open cuts…If the sharks had been there all along, why hadn't they attacked? And if they hadn't been there, why had they suddenly appeared—and in such huge numbers? What drew them to us now?

We watched them circle while the Zodiac shuddered with the motion of our trembling bodies. A wave picked us up, and we listed precariously to one side before righting ourselves. It was vital that we keep the dinghy balanced. The idea of turning turtle was unbearable.

"We have to find a way to stabilize this thing," I said.

"If we had some kind of sea anchor…" Brad said. But what did we have to use? Five bodies and the clothes on our backs and an open boat.

"What if we could get one of these floorboards out…" I studied the three aluminum boards that covered the bottom of the dinghy. There was also a small wooden board in the bow covering a storage space. I reached into the bow and was able to pop the wooden board right out.

"All right!" Brad said.

Brad and I talked it over. If we could run the wire through the hole in the board and drag it behind us, maybe it would make the dinghy more stable—and keep us closer to the area where the Coast Guard expected to find us. Brad rigged the wire to the board and tossed it over the side. I waited for the next wave to come, eager to see how it worked. And then, wham!—the dinghy was yanked backward and we all went sprawling. We saw the dorsal fin of a big shark streaking away from us, dragging the Zodiac with it. The shark had gone after the board like a bluefish striking a lure. Before I could scream, the dinghy had stalled as the fin kept moving, and I knew he had spit the board out and swum away.

We all lunged for the line at the same time, almost flipping the dinghy in our panic. Mark got hold of the wire and pulled it in. The big shark surfaced again just off our port side, rising from the blue-black depths like an enemy sub. He was a monster, longer than the Zodiac.

"Get out of here, you fucker!" Mark shouted, raising the board over his head like a sledgehammer and bringing it down on the shark's back.

"Stop!" Meg and I both screamed.

"Are you crazy?" Brad said as he ripped the board from Mark's hands.

"You idiot!" I said.

"Leave it alone," John said.

"If we leave them alone, maybe they'll leave us alone. Like bees, you know?"

Oh sure, Meg, just like bees, I wanted to say. Bees and sharks. God, we were losing it. I looked from one blue-lipped, pale, drawn face to the next. I was sure I looked as bad as they did. I closed my eyes, trying to get away from their death masks, from the sharks, from everything.

I knew a few sailors who had had to be rescued at sea. But somehow I had never imagined myself in that position. Bad things happened to other people—people who didn't know what they were doing, people who were unlucky. The boats I had been on in the past had seemed charmed somehow. I had always felt that no matter what happened, no matter how dicey things got, I would make it through.

But not this boat. I played back the chain of events in my mind. From the moment John and I left Southwest Harbor I had had misgivings. Why hadn't I just listened to my instincts? There were plenty of signs of trouble—Meg showing up and the unreliable engine and the whole thing with Mark. But I had, I had tried to get off! My God, if only I had stood my ground with Newberger. I could have just packed up and walked away. And now here we were—our legs entangled, our lives entangled…Brad and I at the bow, John and Meg in the stern, Mark in the middle, in a heaving rubber boat.

Deborah Scaling Kiley was born on a ranch in west Texas and graduated from Colorado Springs School, where she participated in an Outward Bound program that later helped her survive the wreck of Trashman. *She now lives on a farm in Massachusetts with her husband and two children.*

Meg Noonan has written for numerous magazines, including Esquire, Sports Illustrated, *and* Outside. *She lives in New Hampshire with her*

husband and two children. This story was excerpted from their book
Albatross: The True Story of a Woman's Survival at Sea.

✳

The roar increases. I imagine crawling out of the tent and getting swept away to sea. Then I worry that my little boat, my life line, will get swept away. *Did I tie the line high enough on the beach? Are my knots strong enough to hold?...*

For months now I've felt as if I'm in a wave, caught up in it, unable to control even its direction, much less its force. I can only hope to ride it rather than drown in it. I can only hope it will not dash me against a rock cliff or throw me, gasping, onto a beach.

—Marybeth Holleman, "The Wind on My Face," *Solo: On Her Own Adventure* edited by Susan Fox Rogers

PART FIVE

THE LAST WORD

✷

Undressing the Bear

...And embracing the wilds within.

HE CAME HOME FROM THE WAR AND SHOT A BEAR. HE HAD BEEN part of the Tenth Mountain Division that fought on Mount Belvedere in Italy during World War II. When he returned home to Wyoming, he could hardly wait to get back to the wilderness. It was fall, the hunting season. He would enact the ritual of man against animal once again. A black bear crossed the meadow. The man fixed his scope on the bear and pulled the trigger. The bear screamed. He brought down his rifle and found himself shaking. This had never happened before. He walked over to the warm beast, now dead, and placed his hand on its shoulder. Setting his gun down, he pulled out his buck knife and began skinning the bear that he would pack out on his horse. As he pulled the fur coat away from the muscle, down the breasts and over the swell of the hips, he suddenly stopped. This was not a bear. It was a woman.

Another bear story: There is a woman who travels by sled dogs in Alaska. On one of her journeys through the interior, she stopped to visit an old friend, a Koyukon man. They spoke for some time about the old ways of his people. She listened until it was time for her to go. As she was harnessing her dogs, he offered one piece of advice.

"If you should run into Bear, lift up your parka and show him you are a woman."

And another: I have a friend who manages a bookstore. A regular customer dropped by to browse. They began sharing stories, which led to a discussion of dreams. My friend shared hers.

"I dreamt I was in Yellowstone. A grizzly, upright, was walking toward me. Frightened at first, I began to pull away, when suddenly a mantle of calm came over me. I walked toward the bear and we embraced."

The man across the counter listened, and then said matter-of-factly, "Get over it."

Why? Why should we give up the dream of embracing the bear? For me, it has everything to do with undressing, exposing, and embracing the Feminine.

I see the Feminine defined as a reconnection to the Self, a commitment to the wildness within—our instincts, our capacity to create and destroy; our hunger for connection as well as sovereignty, interdependence and independence, at once. We are taught not to trust our own experience.

The Feminine teaches us experience is our way back home, the psychic bridge that spans rational and intuitive waters. To embrace the Feminine is to embrace paradox. Paradox preserves mystery, and mystery inspires belief.

I believe in the power of Bear.

The Feminine has long been linked to the bear through mythology. The Greek goddess Artemis, whose name means "bear," embodies the wisdom of the wild. Christine Downing, in her book *The Goddess: Mythological Images of the Feminine*, describes her as "the one who knows each tree by its bark or leaf or fruit, each beast by its footprint or spoor, each bird by its plumage or call or nest."

It is Artemis, perhaps originally a Cretan goddess of fertility, who denounces the world of patriarchy, demanding chastity from her female attendants. Callisto, having violated her virginity and become pregnant, is transformed into the She-Bear of the night sky by Artemis. Other mythical accounts credit Artemis herself as Ursa Major, ruler of the heavens and protectress of the Pole Star or *axis mundi.*

I saw Ursa Major presiding over Dark Canyon in the remote corner of southeastern Utah. She climbed the desert sky as a jeweled bear following her tracks around the North Star, as she does year after year, honoring the power of seasonal renewal.

At dawn, the sky bear disappeared and I found myself walking down-canyon. Three years ago, the pilgrimage had been aborted. I fell. Head to stone, I rolled down the steep talus slope stopped only by the grace of an old juniper tree precariously perched at a forty-five-degree angle. When I stood up, it was a bloody red landscape. Placing my hand on my forehead, I felt along the three-inch tear of skin down to the bony plate of my skull. I had opened my third eye. Unknowingly, this was what I had come for. It had been only a few months since the death of my mother. I had been unable to cry. On this day, I did.

Now scarred by experience, I returned to Dark Canyon determined to complete my descent into the heart of the desert. Although I had fears of falling again, a different woman inhabited by body. There had been a deepening of self through time. My mother's death had become part of me. She had always worn a small silver bear fetish around her neck to keep her safe. Before she died, she took off the bear and placed it in my hand. I wore it on this trip.

In canyon country, you pick your own path. Walking in wilderness becomes a meditation. I followed a small drainage up one of the benches. Lithic scatter was everywhere, evidence of Anasazi culture, a thousand years past. I believed the flakes of chert and obsidian would lead me to ruins. I walked intuitively. A smell of cut wood seized me. I looked up. Before me stood a lightning-struck tree blown apart by the force of the bolt. A fallout of wood

chips littered the land in a hundred-foot radius. The piñon pine
was still smoldering.

My companion, who came to the burning tree by way of
another route, picked up a piece of the charred wood, sacred to
the Hopi, and began carving a bull-roarer. As he whirled it
above our heads on twisted cordage, it wailed in low, deep tones.
Rain began—female rain falling gently, softly, as a fine mist over
the desert.

Hours later, we made camp. All at once, we heard a roar up-
canyon. Thunder? Too sustained. Jets overheard? A clear sky
above. A peculiar organic smell reached us on the wind. We got
the message. Flushed with fear, we ran to higher ground. Suddenly,
a ten-foot wall of water came storming down the canyon, filling
the empty streambed. If the flood struck earlier, when we were
hiking in the narrows, we would have been swept away like the
cottonwood trees it was now carrying. We watched the muddy
river as though it were a parade, continually inching back as the
water eroded the earth beneath our feet.

That night, a lunar rainbow arched over Dark Canyon like a
pathway of souls. I had heard the Navajos speak of them for years,
never knowing if such magic could exist. It was a sweep of stardust
within pastel bands of light—pink, lavender, yellow, and blue. And
I felt the presence of angels, even my mother, her wings spread
above me like a hovering dove.

In these moments, I felt innocent and wild, privy to secrets and
gifts exchanged only in nature. I was the tree, split open by
change. I was the flood, bursting through grief. I was the rainbow
at night, dancing in darkness. Hands on the earth, I closed my
eyes and remembered where the source of my power lies. My
connection to the natural world is my connection to self—erotic,
mysterious, and whole.

The next morning, I walked to the edge of the wash, shed my
clothes, and bathed in pumpkin-colored water. It was to be one
of the last warm days of autumn. Standing naked in the sand, I noticed bear tracks. Bending down, I gently placed my right hand
inside the fresh paw print.

Women and bears.

Marian Engel, in her novel *Bear*, portrays a woman and a bear in an erotics of place. It doesn't matter whether the bear is seen as male or female. The relationship between the two is sensual, wild.

The woman says, "Bear, take me to the bottom of the ocean with you, Bear, swim with me, Bear, put your arms around me, enclose me, swim, down, down, down, with me."

"Bear," she says suddenly, "come dance with me."

They make love. Afterward, "She felt pain, but it was a dear sweet pain that belonged not to mental suffering, but to the earth."

I have felt the pain that arises from a recognition of beauty, pain we hold when we remember what we are connected to and the delicacy of our relations. It is this tenderness born out of a connection to place that fuels my writing. Writing becomes an act of compassion toward life, the life we so often refuse to see because if we look too closely or feel too deeply, there may be no end to our suffering. But words empower us, move us beyond our suffering, and set us free. This is the sorcery of literature. We are healed by our stories.

By undressing, exposing, and embracing the bear, we undress, expose, and embrace our authentic selves. Stripped free from society's oughts and shoulds, we emerge as emancipated beings. The bear is free to roam.

If we choose to follow the bear, we will be saved from a distractive and domesticated life. The bear becomes our mentor. We must journey out, so that we might journey in. The bear mother enters the earth before snowfall and dreams herself through winter, emerging in spring with young by her side. She not only survives the barren months, she gives birth. She is the caretaker of the unseen world. As a writer and a woman with obligations to both family and community, I have tried to adopt this ritual in the balancing of a public and private life. We are at home in the deserts and mountains, as well as in our dens. Above ground in the abundance of spring and summer, I am available. Below ground in the deepening of autumn and winter, I am not. I need hibernation in order to create.

We are creatures of paradox, women and bears, two animals that are enormously unpredictable, hence our mystery. Perhaps the fear of bears and the fear of women lies in our refusal to be tamed, the impulses we arouse and the forces we represent.

Last spring, our family was in Yellowstone. We were hiking along Pelican Creek, which separated us from an island of lodge-pole pines. All at once, a dark form stood in front of the forest on a patch of snow. It was a grizzly, and behind her, two cubs. Suddenly, the sow turned and bolted through the trees. A female elk crashed through the timber to the other side of the clearing, stopped, and swung back toward the bear. Within seconds, the grizzly emerged with an elk calf secure in the grip of her jaws. The sow shook the yearling violently by the nape of its neck, threw it down, clamped her claws on its shoulders, and began tearing the flesh back from the bones with her teeth. The cow elk, only a few feet away, watched the sow devour her calf. She pawed the earth desperately with her front hooves, but the bear was oblivious. Blood dripped from the sow's muzzle. The cubs stood by their mother, who eventually turned the carcass over to them. Two hours passed. The sow buried the calf for a later meal, she slept on top of the mound with a paw on each cub. It was not until then that the elk crossed the river in retreat.

We are capable of harboring both these responses to life in the relentless power of our love. As women connected to the earth, we are nurturing and we are fierce, we are wicked and we are sublime. The full range is ours. We hold the moon in our bellies and fire in our hearts. We bleed. We give milk. We are the mothers of first words. These words grow. They are our children. They are our stories and our poems.

By allowing ourselves to undress, expose, and embrace the Feminine, we commit our vulnerabilities not to fear but to courage—the courage that allows us to write on behalf of the earth, on behalf of ourselves.

With her first book, Refuge: An Unnatural History of Family and Place, *Terry Tempest Williams won an immediate reputation as an eloquent and impassioned naturalist-writer in the traditions of John Muir, Rachel Carson, and Wallace Stegner. Her books since then have included* Red: Passion and Patience in the Desert, Leap, Pieces of White Shell: A Journey to Navajoland, Coyote's Canyon, *and* An Unspoken Hunger: Stories from the Field, *from which this story was excerpted. She lives in Salt Lake City with her husband, Brooke.*

Recommended Reading

We hope *Women in the Wild* has inspired you to read on. A good place to start is the books from which we've made selections, and these are listed below, along with other books that we have found to be valuable. Some of these may be out of print but are well worth hunting down.

Ackerman, Diane. *A Natural History of the Senses.* New York: Vintage Books, 1990.

Allison, Stacy with Peter Carlin. *Beyond the Limits: A Woman's Triumph on Everest.* Boston: Little, Brown and Company, 1993. New York: Delta Trade Books, 1996.

Birkett, Dea. *Jella: A Woman at Sea.* London: Victor Gollancz, 1992.

Campbell, SueEllen. *Bringing the Mountain Home.* Tuscon, Arizona: The University of Arizona Press, 1996.

Chisholm, Margo and Ray Bruce. *To the Summit: A Woman's Journey into the Mountains to Find Her Soul.* New York: Avon Books, 1997.

Cox, Lynne. *Swimming to Antarctica: Tales of a Long Distance Swimmer.* New York: Alfred A. Knopf, 2004.

Davidson, Robyn. *Desert Places.* New York: Viking, 1996.

Davidson, Robyn. *Tracks.* New York: Pantheon Books, 1980.

Deming, Alison Hawthorne. *Temporary Homelands: Essays on Nature, Spirit and Place.* San Francisco: Picador, 1994.

Dew, Josie. *The Wind in My Wheels: Travel Tales from the Saddle.* London: Little, Brown & Co., 1992.

Dillard, Annie. *Teaching a Stone to Talk: Expeditions and Encounters.* New York: HarperPerennial, 1982.

Donner, Florinda. *Being-in-Dreaming.* San Francisco: Harper San Francisco, 1991.

Ehrlich, Gretel. *A Match to the Heart.* New York: Penguin Books, 1994.

Ehrlich, Gretel. *Islands, The Universe, Home.* New York: Penguin Books, 1991.

Ehrlich, Gretel. *The Solace of Open Spaces.* New York: Viking Penguin, 1985.

Ehrlich, Gretel. *This Cold Heaven: Seven Seasons in Greenland.* New York: Random House, 2001.

Erdman, Sarah. *Nine Hills to Nambonkaha: Two Years in the Heart of an African Village.* New York: Henry Holt & Co., 2003.

Erdrich, Louise. *The Blue Jay's Dance: A Birth Year.* New York: HarperCollins, 1995.

Estes, Clarissa Pinkola. *Women Who Run with the Wolves: Myths and Stories of the Wild Woman Archetype.* New York: Ballantine, 1992.

Frawley-Holler, Janis. *Island Wise.* New York: Broadway Books, 2003.

Friedman, Sally. *Swimming the Channel: A Memoir of Love, Loss and Healing.* New York: Farrar, Straus and Giroux, 1996.

Gelman, Rita Goldman. *Tales of a Female Nomad.* New York: Three Rivers Press, 2001.

Goldberg, Natalie. *Chicken and In Love.* Duluth, Minnesota: Holy Cow! Press, 1980.

Goldberg, Natalie. *Long Quiet Highway: Waking Up in America.* New York: Bantam Books, 1993.

Goodall, Jane. *Through a Window: My Thirty Years with the Chimpanzees of Gombe.* New York: Houghton Mifflin, 1990.

Govier, Katherine (ed.). *Without a Guide: Contemporary Women's Travel Adventures.* St. Paul, Minnesota: Hungry Mind Press, 1994.

Griffin, Susan. *Woman and Nature: The Roaring Inside Her.* New York: Harper and Row, 1978.

Hiestand, Emily. *The Very Rich Hours: Travels in Orkney, Belize, the Everglades, and Greece.* Boston: Beacon Press, 1992.

Johnston, Tracy. *Shooting the Boh: A Woman's Voyage Down the Wildest River in Borneo.* New York: Vintage Departures, 1992.

Jordan, Teresa and James Hepworth (eds.). *The Stories That Shape Us.* New York: W.W. Norton, 1995.

Kaza, Stephanie. *The Attentive Heart: Conversations with Trees.* New York: Fawcett Columbine, 1993.

Kiley, Deborah Scaling and Meg Noonan. *Albatross: The True Story of a Woman's Survival at Sea.* New York: Houghton Mifflin, 1994.

Kingsolver, Barbara. *Hide Tide in Tucson: Essays From Now or Never.* New York: HarperPerennial, 1995.

Leden, Judy. *Flying with Condors.* London: Orion Books, 1996.

Leeson, Ted (ed.). *The Gift of Trout.* New York: Lyons and Burford, 1996.

Lindbergh, Anne Morrow. *Gift from the Sea.* New York: Pantheon, 1955.

Logan, Pamela. *Among Warriors: A Martial Artist in Tibet.* Woodstock, New York: Overlook Press, 1996.

Markham, Beryl. *West with the Night.* New York: Farrar, Straus & Giroux Publishers, Inc., 1942.

Montgomery, Sy. *Walking with the Great Apes: Jane Goodall, Dian Fossey, Birute Galdikas.* New York: A Peter Davidson Book, 1991.

Morris, Holly (ed.) *Uncommon Waters: Women Write About Fishing.* Seattle: Seal Press, 1991.

Morris, Mary. *Nothing to Declare.* Boston: Houghton Mifflin Co., 1988.

Nickerson, Sheila. *Disappearance: A Map.* New York: Doubleday, 1996.

Nyala, Hannah. *Point Last Seen: A Woman Tracker's Story.* Boston: Beacon Press, 1997.

Orion: People and Nature (magazine). New York: The Orion Society.

Page, Margot. *Little Rivers: Tales of a Woman Angler.* New York: Lyons and Burford, 1995.

Rogers, Susan Fox (ed.). *Another Wilderness: New Outdoor Writing by Women.* Seattle: Seal Press, 1994.

Rogers, Susan Fox (ed.). *Solo: On Her Own Adventure.* Seattle: Seal Press, 1996.

Savage, Barbara. *Miles from Nowhere: A Round-the-World Bicycle Adventure.* Seattle: The Mountaineers, 1983.

Stange, Mary. *Woman the Hunter.* Boston: Beacon Press, 1997.

Teal, Louise. *Breaking into the Current: Boatwomen of the Grand Canyon.* Tucson, Arizona: University of Arizona Press, 1994.

Walker, Alice. *Living By the Word: Selected Writings 1973-1987.* Orlando, Florida: Harcourt Brace & Company, 1988.

Williams, Terry Tempest. *An Unspoken Hunger: Stories from the Field.* New York: Vintage, 1994.

Index of Contributors

Acknowledgments

Editing a travel collection, one could say, is a kind of journey into the wild, and I feel fortunate to have had the very best of companions along for the adventure. My sincerest thanks to the series editors, Larry Habegger and James O'Reilly, for their guidance and work in shaping this book. Many thanks to Tim O'Reilly, Sean O'Reilly, Wenda O'Reilly, the still-amazing Raj Khadka, and to others who blessed this project with their talent and input: Cynthia Lamb, Deborah Greco, Trisha Schwartz, Kathryn Heflin, Susan Bailey, and Leili Eghbal. And as with all Travelers' Tales books, this one would not have been possible without the superb abilities and patience of production chief Susan Brady.

I have been blessed with family and a circle of friends who have supported and inspired me with their humor, faith, and love. I appreciate you more than you can know. This book is for each of you, and for Charles Bambach, with love.

"Looking for Lovedu" by Ann Jones published by permission of the author. Copyright © 1998 by Ann Jones.

"To Jump or Not to Jump?" by Hannelore Hahn published by permission of the author. Copyright © 1998 by Hannelore Hahn.

"Climbing Mt. Everest" by Margo Chisholm and Ray Bruce excerpted from *To the Summit: A Woman's Journey into the Mountains to Find Her Soul* by Margo Chisholm and Ray Bruce. Copyright © 1997 Margo J. Chisholm and Raymond C. Bruce. Reprinted by permission of Avon Books, Inc. and Curtis Brown Ltd.

"Bread upon the Waters" by Brenda Peterson originally appeared in the January/February 1993 issue of *Sierra* magazine. Copyright © 1993 by Brenda Peterson. Reprinted with permission from *Sierra* and the author.

"The Deer at Providencia" by Annie Dillard excerpted from *Teaching a Stone to Talk: Expeditions and Encounters* by Annie Dillard. Copyright © 1982 by Annie Dillard. Reprinted by permission of HarperCollins Publishers, Inc.

"Rocks in My Head" by Terry Strother published by permission of the author. Copyright © 1998 by Terry Strother.

"Alone with the Rabari" by Robyn Davidson excerpted from *Desert Places* by Robyn Davidson. Copyright © 1996 by Robyn Davidson. Reprinted by permission of Penguin USA and International Creative Management.

"Lightning Strike" by Gretel Ehrlich excerpted from *A Match to the Heart* by Gretel Ehrlich. Copyright © 1994 by Gretel Ehrlich. Used by permission of Viking Penguin, a division of Penguin Putnam, Inc. and Darhansoff and Verrill.

"Hyena" by Joanna Greenfield reprinted from the November 11, 1996 issue of *The New Yorker*. Copyright © 1996 by Joanna Greenfield. Reprinted by permission of International Creative Management.

"Looking for Footprints" by Susan Fox Rogers published by permission of the author. Copyright © 1998 by Susan Fox Rogers.

"Beyond the Ruins" by Joy Nicholson published by permission of the author. Copyright © 1998 by Joy Nicholson.

"Nature, Fear, and Race" by Evelyn C. White originally titled "Black Women and the Wilderness," excerpted from *The Stories That Shape Us* edited by Teresa Jordan and James Hepworth. Reprinted by permission of the author. Copyright © 1995 by Evelyn C. White

"Survival at Sea" by Deborah Scaling Kiley and Meg Noonan abridged from *Albatross: The True Story of a Woman's Survival at Sea* by Deborah Scaling Kiley and Meg Noonan. Copyright © 1994 by Deborah Scaling Kiley. Reprinted by permission of Houghton Mifflin Company and Little, Brown & Company UK. All rights reserved.

"Undressing the Bear" by Terry Tempest Williams excerpted from *An Unspoken Hunger: Stories from the Field* by Terry Tempest Williams. Copyright © 1994 by Terry Tempest Williams. Reprinted by permission of Pantheon Books, a division of Random House, Inc. and Brandt & Brandt.

Additional Credits (Arranged alphabetically by title)

Selection from "Animals and People: The Human Heart in Conflict With Itself," reprinted from the Winter 1997 edition of *Orion*. Copyright © 1997 by *Orion*. Reprinted by permission of *Orion*.

Selection from *The Attentive Heart: Conversations with Trees* by Stephanie Kaza copyright © 1993 by Stephanie Kaza. Reprinted by permission of Random House, Inc.

Selection from "The Bear in the Woods, the Bear in Us," by Pam Houston reprinted from the June 22, 1996 issue of *The New York Times*. Copyright © 1996 by The New York Times Co. Reprinted by permission.

Selection entitled "Beginning at the End" by Cheryl L. McCullers copyright © 1995 by Cheryl L. McCullers. Published by permission of the author.

Selection from *Being-in-Dreaming* by Florinda Donner copyright © 1991 by Florinda Donner.

Selection from "Between the Volcanos" by Lea Aschkenas published by permission of the author. Copyright © 1998 by Lea Aschkenas.

Selection from *Beyond the Limits: A Woman's Triumph on Everest* by Stacy Allison with Peter Carlin copyright © 1993 by Stacy Allison. Reprinted by permission of Little, Brown and Company.

Selection from *How Deep the High Journey* by Margaret P. Stark published by permission of the author. Copyright © 1997 by Margaret P. Stark.

Selection from "Immersed" by Daisy Scott published by permission of the author. Copyright © 1998 by Daisy Scott.

Selection from "In Africa" by Thalassa Wild Skinner published by permission of the author. Copyright © 1998 by Thalassa Wild Skinner.

Selection from "Irish Horses" by Archer T. Gilliam. Copyright © 1998 by Archer T. Gilliam. Published by permission of the author.

Selections from *Islands, The Universe, Home* by Gretel Ehrlich copyright ©1991 by Gretel Ehrlich. Used by permission of Penguin Books USA and Darhansoff and Verrill.

Selection from *Jella: A Woman at Sea* by Dea Birkett copyright © 1992 by Dea Birkett. Reproduced by permission of Curtis Brown Ltd., London and Victor Gallancz Ltd.

Selection from "*Kituo* (Stopping Place)" by Bird Cupps published by permission of the author. Copyright © 1998 by Sarah Cupps.

Selection from "Lights Out" by Leila Dunbar published by permission of the author. Copyright © 1998 by Leila Dunbar.

Selection from "Meltemi" by Lynn Shirey published by permission of the author. Copyright © 1998 by Lynn Shirey.

Selection from "The Middle Aged Woman and the Sea" by Judith M. Huge published by permission of the author. Copyright © 1998 by Judith M. Huge.

Selection from "A Modest Adventure" by Catherine Olofson published by permission of the author. Copyright © 1998 by Catherine Olofson.

Selection from *A Natural History of the Senses* by Diane Ackerman copyright © 1990 by Diane Ackerman. Reprinted by permission of Random House, Inc.

Selection from "Ndume: A Moment in Time" by Rosalind Aveling published by permission of the author. Copyright © 1998 by Rosalind Aveling.

Selection from "The Old Mill" by Irene-Marie Spencer published by permission of the author. Copyright © 1998 by Irene-Marie Spencer.

Selection from "Primates 101, On an Island in the Sun" by Jo Broyles Yohay originally appeared in the April 1993 issue of *Travel & Leisure*. Copyright © 1993 by Jo Broyles Yohay. Published by permission of the author.

Selection from "Romantic Journey" by Anna Kenning published by permission of the author. Copyright © 1998 by Anna Kenning.

Selection from "Saturday Night in Nauru" by Cleo Paskal published by permission of the author. Copyright © 1998 by Cleo Paskal.

Selection from "Saturday Night on the Mohave" by Candace Dempsey published by permission of the author. Copyright © 1998 by Candace Dempsey.

Selection from "Something Told Me" by Amy Meltzer published by permission of the author. Copyright © 1998 by Amy Meltzer.

Selection from "The Stronghold" by Marcia Fairbanks published by permission of the author. Copyright © 1998 by Marcia Fairbanks.

Selection from *Swimming the Channel: A Memoir of Love, Loss and Healing* by Sally Friedman copyright © 1996 by Sally Friedman. Reprinted by permission of Farrar, Straus, and Giroux, Inc. and Martin, Secker & Warburg (a division of Random House UK).

About the Editor

Lucy McCauley is the editor of *A Woman's Path* and *Travelers Tales: Spain*. Her writing has appeared in such publications as *The Atlantic Monthly*, the *Los Angeles Times*, *Harvard Review*, and several Travelers' Tales books. A freelance writer and editor based in Texas, she is a member of the International Women's Writing Guild.

TRAVELERS' TALES

THE POWER OF A GOOD STORY

New Releases

THE BEST $16.95
TRAVELERS' TALES 2004
True Stories from Around the World
Edited by James O'Reilly, Larry Habegger & Sean O'Reilly
The launch of a new annual collection presenting fresh, lively storytelling and compelling narrative to make the reader laugh, weep, and buy a plane ticket.

INDIA $18.95
True Stories
Edited by James O'Reilly & Larry Habegger
"*Travelers' Tales India* is ravishing in the texture and variety of tales."
—*Foreign Service Journal*

A WOMAN'S EUROPE $17.95
True Stories
Edited by Marybeth Bond
An exhilarating collection of inspirational, adventurous, and entertaining stories by women exploring the romantic continent of Europe. From the bestselling author Marybeth Bond.

WOMEN IN THE WILD $17.95
True Stories of Adventure and Connection
Edited by Lucy McCauley
"A spiritual, moving, and totally female book to take you around the world and back." —*Mademoiselle*

CHINA $18.95
True Stories
Edited by James O'Reilly, Larry Habegger & Sean O'Reilly
A must for any traveler to China, for anyone wanting to learn more about the Middle Kingdom, offering a breadth and depth of experience from both new and well-known authors; helps make the China experience unforgettable and transforming.

BRAZIL $17.95
True Stories
Edited by Annette Haddad & Scott Doggett
Introduction by Alex Shoumatoff
"Only the lowest wattage dim bulb would visit Brazil without reading this book." —Tim Cahill, author of *Pass the Butterworms*

THE PENNY PINCHER'S PASSPORT TO $14.95
LUXURY TRAVEL (2ND EDITION)
The Art of Cultivating Preferred Customer Status
By Joel L. Widzer
Completely updated and revised, this 2nd edition of the popular guide to traveling like the rich and famous without being either describes, both philosophically and in practical terms, how to obtain luxurious travel benefits by building relationships with airlines and other travel companies.

Women's Travel

A WOMAN'S EUROPE $17.95
True Stories
Edited by Marybeth Bond
An exhilarating collection of inspirational, adventurous, and entertaining stories by women exploring the romantic continent of Europe. From the bestselling author Marybeth Bond.

WOMEN IN THE WILD $17.95
True Stories of Adventure and Connection
Edited by Lucy McCauley
"A spiritual, moving, and totally female book to take you around the world and back."
— *Mademoiselle*

A WOMAN'S WORLD $18.95
True Stories of Life on the Road
Edited by Marybeth Bond
Introduction by Dervla Murphy

—— ★ ★ ★ ——

Lowell Thomas Award
—Best Travel Book

A MOTHER'S WORLD $14.95
Journeys of the Heart
Edited by Marybeth Bond & Pamela Michael
"These stories remind us that motherhood is one of the great unifying forces in the world"
— *San Francisco Examiner*

A WOMAN'S PASSION FOR TRAVEL $17.95
More True Stories from A Woman's World
Edited by Marybeth Bond & Pamela Michael
"A diverse and gripping series of stories!"
— Arlene Blum, author of
Annapurna: A Woman's Place

Food

ADVENTURES IN WINE $17.95
True Stories of Vineyards and Vintages around the World
Edited by Thom Elkjer
Humanity, community, and brotherhood comprise the marvelous virtues of the wine world. This collection toasts the warmth and wonders of this large extended family in stories by travelers who are wine novices and experts alike.

FOOD $18.95
A Taste of the Road
Edited by Richard Sterling
Introduction by Margo True

—— ★ ★ ★ ——

Silver Medal Winner of the
Lowell Thomas Award
—Best Travel Book

HER FORK IN THE ROAD $16.95
Women Celebrate Food and Travel
Edited by Lisa Bach
A savory sampling of stories by the best writers in and out of the food and travel fields.

THE ADVENTURE OF FOOD $17.95
True Stories of Eating Everything
Edited by Richard Sterling
"Bound to whet appetites for more than food."
— *Publishers Weekly*

THE FEARLESS DINER $7.95
Travel Tips and Wisdom for Eating around the World
By Richard Sterling
Combines practical advice on foodstuffs, habits, and etiquette, with hilarious accounts of others' eating adventures.

Travel Humor

SAND IN MY BRA AND OTHER MISADVENTURES $14.95
Funny Women Write from the Road
Edited by Jennifer L. Leo
"A collection of ridiculous and sublime travel experiences."
— *San Francisco Chronicle*

HYENAS LAUGHED AT ME AND NOW I KNOW WHY $14.95
The Best of Travel Humor and Misadventure
Edited by Sean O'Reilly, Larry Habegger, and James O'Reilly
Hilarious, outrageous and reluctant voyagers indulge us with the best misadventures around the world.

LAST TROUT IN VENICE $14.95
The Far-Flung Escapades of an Accidental Adventurer
By Doug Lansky
"Traveling with Doug Lansky might result in a considerably shortened life expectancy…but what a way to go."
— Tony Wheeler, Lonely Planet Publications

NOT SO FUNNY WHEN IT HAPPENED $12.95
The Best of Travel Humor and Misadventure
Edited by Tim Cahill
Laugh with Bill Bryson, Dave Barry, Anne Lamott, Adair Lara, and many more.

THERE'S NO TOILET PAPER…ON THE ROAD LESS TRAVELED $12.95
The Best of Travel Humor and Misadventure
Edited by Doug Lansky

Humor Book of the Year
— Independent Publisher's Book Award

ForeWord Gold Medal Winner — Humor Book of the Year

Travelers' Tales Classics

COAST TO COAST $16.95
A Journey Across 1950s America
By Jan Morris
After reporting on the first Everest ascent in 1953, Morris spent a year journeying across the United States. In brilliant prose, Morris records with exuberance and curiosity a time of innocence in the U.S.

TRADER HORN $16.95
A Young Man's Astounding Adventures in 19th Century Equatorial Africa
By Alfred Aloysius Horn
Here is the stuff of legends—thrills and danger, wild beasts, serpents, and savages. An unforgettable and vivid portrait of a vanished Africa.

THE ROYAL ROAD TO ROMANCE $14.95
By Richard Halliburton
"Laughing at hardships, dreaming of beauty, ardent for adventure, Halliburton has managed to sing into the pages of this glorious book his own exultant spirit of youth and freedom."
— *Chicago Post*

UNBEATEN TRACKS IN JAPAN $14.95
By Isabella L. Bird
Isabella Bird was one of the most adventurous women travelers of the 19th century with journeys to Tibet, Canada, Korea, Turkey, Hawaii, and Japan. A fascinating read.

THE RIVERS RAN EAST $16.95
By Leonard Clark
Clark is the original Indiana Jones, telling the breathtaking story of his search for the legendary El Dorado gold in the Amazon.

Spiritual Travel

THE SPIRITUAL GIFTS $16.95
OF TRAVEL
The Best of Travelers' Tales
Edited by James O'Reilly and Sean O'Reilly
Favorite stories of transformation on the road
that shows the myriad ways travel indelibly
alters our inner landscapes.

PILGRIMAGE $16.95
Adventures of the Spirit
Edited by Sean O'Reilly & James O'Reilly
Introduction by Phil Cousineau

ForeWord Silver Medal Winner
—Travel Book of the Year

THE ROAD WITHIN $18.95
True Stories of Transformation
and the Soul
Edited by Sean O'Reilly, James O'Reilly &
Tim O'Reilly

Independent Publisher's Book Award
—Best Travel Book

THE WAY OF $14.95
THE WANDERER
Discover Your True Self Through Travel
By David Yeadon
Experience transformation through travel
with this delightful, illustrated collection by
award-winning author David Yeadon.

A WOMAN'S PATH $16.95
Women's Best Spiritual Travel Writing
Edited by Lucy McCauley, Amy G. Carlson &
Jennifer Leo
"A sensitive exploration of women's lives that
have been unexpectedly and spiritually
touched by travel experiences.... Highly
recommended."
         —Library Journal

THE ULTIMATE JOURNEY $17.95
Inspiring Stories of Living and Dying
James O'Reilly, Sean O'Reilly & Richard
Sterling
"A glorious collection of writings about the
ultimate adventure. A book to keep by one's
bedside—and close to one's heart."
         —Philip Zaleski, editor,
      The Best Spiritual Writing series

Special Interest

THE BEST $16.95
TRAVELERS' TALES 2004
True Stories from Around the World
Edited by James O'Reilly, Larry Habegger &
Sean O'Reilly
The launch of a new annual collection pre-
senting fresh, lively storytelling and com-
pelling narrative to make the reader laugh,
weep, and buy a plane ticket.

TESTOSTERONE PLANET $17.95
True Stories from a Man's World
Edited by Sean O'Reilly, Larry Habegger &
James O'Reilly
Thrills and laughter with some of today's best
writers: Sebastian Junger, Tim Cahill, Bill
Bryson, and Jon Krakauer.

THE GIFT OF TRAVEL $14.95
The Best of Travelers' Tales
Edited by Larry Habegger, James O'Reilly
& Sean O'Reilly
"Like gourmet chefs in a French market, the
editors of Travelers' Tales pick, sift, and prod
their way through the weighty shelves of con-
temporary travel writing, creaming off the
very best."
   —William Dalrymple, author of City of Djinns

DANGER! $17.95
True Stories of Trouble and Survival
Edited by James O'Reilly, Larry Habegger &
Sean O'Reilly
"Exciting...for those who enjoy living on the
edge or prefer to read the survival stories of
others, this is a good pick."
         —Library Journal

365 TRAVEL $14.95
A Daily Book of Journeys, Meditations, and Adventures
Edited by Lisa Bach
An illuminating collection of travel wisdom and adventures that reminds us all of the lessons we learn while on the road.

THE GIFT OF RIVERS $14.95
True Stories of Life on the Water
Edited by Pamela Michael
Introduction by Robert Hass
"...a soulful compendium of wonderful stories that illuminate, educate, inspire, and delight."
—David Brower,
Chairman of Earth Island Institute

FAMILY TRAVEL $17.95
The Farther You Go, the Closer You Get
Edited by Laura Manske
"This is family travel at its finest."
—*Working Mother*

LOVE & ROMANCE $17.95
True Stories of Passion on the Road
Edited by Judith Babcock Wylie
"A wonderful book to read by a crackling fire."
—*Romantic Traveling*

THE GIFT OF BIRDS $17.95
True Encounters with Avian Spirits
Edited by Larry Habegger & Amy G. Carlson
"These are all wonderful, entertaining stories offering a *bird's-eye view!* of our avian friends."
—*Booklist*

A DOG'S WORLD $12.95
True Stories of Man's Best Friend on the Road
Edited by Christine Hunsicker
Introduction by Maria Goodavage

Travel Advice

THE PENNY PINCHER'S PASSPORT TO LUXURY TRAVEL (2ND EDITION) $14.95
The Art of Cultivating Preferred Customer Status
By Joel L. Widzer
Completely updated and revised, this 2nd edition of the popular guide to traveling like the rich and famous without being either describes, both philosophically and in practical terms, how to obtain luxurious travel benefits by building relationships with airlines and other travel companies.

SAFETY AND SECURITY FOR WOMEN WHO TRAVEL $12.95
By Sheila Swan & Peter Laufer
"An engaging book, with plenty of first-person stories about strategies women have used while traveling to feel safe but still find their way into a culture."
—*Chicago Herald*

THE FEARLESS SHOPPER $14.95
How to Get the Best Deals on the Planet
By Kathy Borrus
"Anyone who reads *The Fearless Shopper* will come away a smarter, more responsible shopper and a more curious, culturally attuned traveler."
—Jo Mancuso, *The Shopologist*

SHITTING PRETTY $12.95
How to Stay Clean and Healthy While Traveling
By Dr. Jane Wilson-Howarth
A light-hearted book about a serious subject for millions of travelers—staying healthy on the road—written by international health expert, Dr. Jane Wilson-Howarth.

GUTSY WOMEN $12.95
More Travel Tips and Wisdom for the Road
By Marybeth Bond
Second Edition
Packed with funny, instructive, and inspiring advice for women heading out to see the world.

GUTSY MAMAS $7.95
Travel Tips and Wisdom for Mothers on the Road
By Marybeth Bond
A delightful guide for mothers traveling with their children—or without them!